The Politics of Poverty

Thank you for choosing a SAGE product! If you have any comment, observation or feedback, I would like to personally hear from you. Please write to me at <u>contactceo@sagepub.in</u>

—Vivek Mehra, Managing Director and CEO,
SAGE Publications India Pvt Ltd, New Delhi

Bulk Sales

SAGE India offers special discounts for purchase of books in bulk. We also make available special imprints and excerpts from our books on demand.

For orders and enquiries, write to us at

Marketing Department
SAGE Publications India Pvt Ltd
B1/I-1, Mohan Cooperative Industrial Area
Mathura Road, Post Bag 7
New Delhi 110044, India
E-mail us at <u>marketing@sagepub.in</u>

Get to know more about SAGE, be invited to SAGE events, get on our mailing list. Write today to <u>marketing@sagepub.in</u>

This book is also available as an e-book.

The Politics of Poverty

Planning India's Development

D. K. Rangnekar

www.sagepublications.com

Los Angeles • London • New Delhi • Singapore • Washington DC

First published in 2012 by

SAGE Publications India Pvt Ltd
B1/I-1 Mohan Cooperative Industrial Area
Mathura Road, New Delhi 110 044, India
www.sagepub.in

SAGE Publications Inc
2455 Teller Road
Thousand Oaks, California 91320, USA

SAGE Publications Ltd
1 Oliver's Yard, 55 City Road
London EC1Y 1SP, United Kingdom

SAGE Publications Asia-Pacific Pte Ltd
33 Pekin Street
#02-01 Far East Square
Singapore 048763

Published by Vivek Mehra for SAGE Publications India Pvt Ltd, typeset in 10/12 Palatino Linotype by Tantla Composition Services Private Limited, Chandigarh, and printed at Saurabh Printers Pvt Ltd.

Library of Congress Cataloging-in-Publication Data Available

Rangnekar, D. K.
    The politics of poverty : planning India's development / D. K. Rangnekar.
        p. cm.
    Includes index.
    1. Poverty—Government policy—India.   2. India—Economic policy.
3. India—Social conditions—21st century.   I. Title.

| HC440.P6R35 | 339.4'60954—dc23 | 2012 | 2012025642 |

ISBN: 978-81-321-0902-0 (HB)

The SAGE Team: Sharel Simon, Aniruddha De, Rajib Chatterjee and Dally Verghese

CONTENTS

FOREWORD

Dinanath Kashinath Rangnekar made an impression at your first meeting. Short, with frizzy hair that flared out like Einstein's, and eyes that scanned your face quizzically for signs of disagreement, and always well dressed, Dr Rangnekar cut an unusual figure in a 1970s newspaper office populated mostly by down-at-heel journalists, some of them still recovering from the previous night's drinking bouts. *Time* magazine, considered a minor oracle in those days, had picked him out as one of 50 people of the future. He was a Tata scholar and an economist, with gravitas and a reputation that he brought with him to journalism: his doctoral thesis on poverty, capital development and planning (published by Chatham House) was talked about, as in later years was his membership of the Wanchoo Committee on direct taxes (which estimated for the first time the size of India's black economy, at a seventh of GDP). Interestingly, Dr Rangnekar wrote a note of dissent on the role of auditors, anticipating with amazing accuracy the issues raised in the wake of the Satyam and other (e.g. Enron) scams, and making some recommendations that might have come from an expert committee today! So Dr Rangnekar (as everyone in the office called him) was an egghead, an intellectual activist in the public sphere, with a flair for the sharp phrase; no one could mistake him for your average hack.

Still, journalistic blood seeped into his veins quite early. He talked once of walking down Dadabhai Naoroji Road, opposite what was then known as VT Station in what was Bombay, and peering into the Times of India building where huge printing machines rolled out copies of the next day's newspaper. In the telling, you knew that the newspaper bug had bitten him when still a boy.

So when he finished with his studies in London, he didn't head for an academic perch or a slot in Bombay House where some other Tata Scholars went, but headed for a newspaper chain in what was then Ceylon. An academic stint followed, at the Australian National University in Canberra, before he returned to India and the birth of economic newspapers: the *Economic Times* was starting up in 1961, Dr Rangnekar (then barely 30) became its first Delhi bureau chief and quickly built a reputation with a sharply angled, well-informed weekly column for the paper's Bombay readers. Three years later, he moved to Bombay as the editor, a job that he held for more than 14 years before moving to the *Business Standard* in what was Calcutta for the last five years of his life, cut short by a heart attack when he was only 54.

I met him when a common acquaintance telephoned to say that he was looking for people to work with him at *Business Standard,* which he was about to join. We met twice, he commented back in Calcutta that I was 'okay', and soon I was an assistant editor, which in those days meant a leader writer, one of three who attended his 10.30 editorial conference. It was light work—if you wrote four editorials in a week, you were considered very productive, and he didn't make many changes to the drafts I gave him, which meant I was usually free to go home at 5 pm; even better, Saturdays were half-days for the leader-writers (which meant you did no work)! After more than a year of this leisurely schedule, I felt I was not doing enough with myself, and Calcutta felt like a backwater. The new magazines that were making waves in Delhi seemed to offer a more interesting life, but Dr Rangnekar was reluctant to have me switch to a group magazine. Eventually, he was persuaded and, when the magazine that I joined folded up in six months, he was gracious enough to take me back as a special correspondent in the Delhi bureau—where, at a still restless age, I worked for a year before moving on. I didn't know then that I would be his successor, a couple of steps removed, at both the *Economic Times* and the *Business Standard.*

The morning editorial 'conferences' are engaging because, in almost all Indian newspaper offices, discussion of the subjects for the next day's leaders is laced liberally with gossip about matters public and private. Dr Rangnekar knew the newsmakers in Delhi as well as the businessmen whom the paper wrote about in

Bombay, and he was a good storyteller. We listened while drinking his coffee and, when it came to work, it was obvious that he had forgotten more economics than any of his three assistant editors had ever learnt. He defined his mission as shifting the paper's thrust away from what he had done till then (macroeconomics, poverty, development, planning) and introducing some corporate attention to its reporting and analysis.

But there was little by way of a corporate database to guide corporate understanding. Dr Rangnekar tried to fill the gaps. He set up the Business Standard Research Bureau, and produced an annual review of the economy as well as a banking annual— building on a tradition of special annual numbers that he had started at the *Economic Times*. Watching him from the under-employed corner of a leader writer, I suspected that as a long-time Bombayite he felt out of place in Calcutta. But he was always cheerful, and gentle. I never heard him raise his voice at anyone, but he had a plastic face and you knew when he was not pleased.

Those were socialist days, and Dr Rangnekar held on to his socialist ideals while questioning the way they were put into practice. Like most others of the time, he was an export pessimist who would rather focus on creating domestic demand. So when he was made a member of the Prakash Tandon committee on exports, he found himself in a hopeless minority in the committee's meetings. One morning he read in *Business Standard* that the committee had submitted its report to the government. Shocked out of his wits because he had been kept in the dark by his colleagues on the committee, he turned to me and asked if I would quickly draft for him a dissent note. Much of that draft surfaced in the dissent note that he subsequently sent jointly with Amit Bhaduri, and which initially got an airing in the left-of-centre *Mainstream* magazine. I was proud of my draft at the time. Looking back on what has happened since then, I think we were wrong, but that is another matter.

In a fundamental sense, Dr Rangnekar belonged to the India of the 1950s–70s—Nehru, planning, socialist ideals, the focus on tackling poverty.... By the time the 1980s came, the currents of economic thinking and policy had begun to shift in directions with which he was fundamentally uncomfortable.

In an article in mid-1982, by which time Indira Gandhi had begun her hesitant deregulation of the economy and liberalisation of policy, and the middle class had begun to assert itself, thereby changing the political debate as well, Dr Rangnekar noted that no one in the Congress mentioned '*garibi hatao*' (the 1971 election slogan that helped Mrs Gandhi sweep back to power after the Congress had split) any more, and asked whether pragmatism and the belief in the death of ideology wasn't itself an ideology. So when it came to poverty, he wrote:

> In Indian conditions, poverty cannot be banished merely by high growth rates. High growth rates are known to have coincided with gross inequalities of income and wealth in the West. In Indian conditions, the development policy has got to aim at equitable redistribution of income, consumption and wealth without which the percentage of population below the poverty line cannot be significantly diminished…. Dire malnutrition and massive poverty will continue to dog Indian development even if relatively high growth rates are achieved.

Many would endorse that even today, for what after all is the cry of 'inclusive growth' about?

Reading his articles today, what comes through is a clean writing style, and a forceful, direct way of putting across his arguments. He was not writing for the policy wonk or the specialist, but for the lay reader who wanted to be educated. And his lifelong concerns remained in laser focus: the poor and the common man, and a distrust of various vested interests, including organised labour. Some of the debates and arguments seem at a disconnect with today's world. Much of what was written was on effective planning, development and anti-poverty schemes, and there was very little of what is the focus today: infrastructure, markets, competitiveness, trade, investment (including foreign). There were annual numbers that focused on Big Business and the North-South divide, but approached from a strictly 1970s mindset.

When he did write on monetary policy and fiscal excess, the arguments were different from what a reader would run into today. As he wrote,

> Even if the growth of money supply and government deficit were intended to signify excess demand, there is no

conclusive evidence of a stable relationship between the two. Fluctuations in the stock of money are also not the only factor that affects or influences the general level of prices, particularly in Indian conditions.

Inflation, he said, must be viewed in the larger context of development strategy. And he brought into the debate on the issue the government's lack of direction, the pattern of investment, the structure of production, and economic management. He pointed out that fixed income groups suffered on account of inflation, while those getting rents, profits, fees and commissions had a field day. He argued further that if the government had mobilised resources (presumably for productive investment in the public sector), it would have helped control money in the market and thereby fought inflation. At one point he argued that a 'more than restrictive' monetary policy, combined with an exchange rate policy and distribution of consumer goods through the public distribution system, would have combated inflation. He regretted that black money and company deposits negated the Reserve Bank's credit curbs. 'Black money,' he declared, 'has taken full command of the market mechanism'; and, 'the black-income elite dominates the Indian scene'.

A lot of this reflected the dark forebodings of a decade when GDP growth had slipped to 3.5 per cent after the heady optimism of the Nehru years, and when negative social and political trends mirrored the poor economic performance and undermined the system's legitimacy—the milieu that gave birth to Amitabh Bachchan's angry young man in the film world. Dr Rangnekar related slow economic growth to the inability to push up the rates of savings and investment. Then, looking at the increase in these rates in the 1970s, he asked why that was not accompanied by faster growth. It was a valid and indeed prescient question that would be answered in the 1980s, when GDP growth experienced a step jump, to just under 6 per cent.

It was to be expected that the pattern of investment—what the system's surpluses went into—would be a matter of concern for him, since it affected the evolving pattern of demand. And so he regretted that the money with the new rich class was going into hotels, cinema, theatres and houses, not into 'productive' investment.

xi

He could spot the contradictions that pointed to nascent trends. For instance, he noted a rising share of GDP being in the government sector, but saw that the government's share of investment was falling—an early sign that the private sector would soon become the lead sector. He also noted the endemic project delays, but did not take the next step of saying that it did not matter whether the cat was black or white so long as it caught mice, the position that Deng Xiaoping had articulated by then in China. So he did not advocate turning more to market-based solutions, because of an intrinsic suspicion of the players in the marketpace the repeated references to hoarders, black-marketers, rentiers, unproductive beasts that fed on others.

Instead, Dr Rangnekar was faithful to the Nehruvian frame-work, with his emphasis on controlling the propensity to consume, and increasing savings and investment. Today's loan-driven spending culture, which is driving investment in areas like housing and the auto industry, would probably have made him ask questions. Certainly, he argued against spending crores of rupees on expanding the TV network, and allowing the produc-tion of luxury and non-essential goods. And he wanted to control inflation by extending taxation to farming, dairying, forestry…a proposition that is fraught with all manner of risks, including the likelihood that little tax revenue and much harassment of farmers will be the results.

In April 1966, he writes with a sense of foreboding (Today's controversies–I), presaging the rupee devaluation of June that year, which had disastrous consequences. The dependence on US aid that was not forthcoming, the dangers to the 4th five-year Plan (which was called off and a Plan holiday declared), the sense of a country gripped by crisis and not sure where to turn. Dr Rangnekar wrote with a sure sense of the pulse in New Delhi, and with lively suspicions of American intentions (on which he was to prove right in the post-devaluation context).

Still, he was not your doctrinaire leftist. In 'Today's controver-sies–II', he wrote:

There is reason to believe that some of the ineffective controls are harming growth and social change. This is something some of the professional Leftists cannot perhaps comprehend.

They measure the degree of socialist progression by the intensity of governmental control merely on paper. And they tend to equate any sign of decontrol with a right-wing swing.

The piece is instructive in many ways. At one level, it reminds us about how controlled and regulated the economy was. The government could commandeer 30 per cent of all fertiliser production, and private industry was not allowed to invest by using borrowed funds (it had to bring in equity—but the government was at the same time guaranteeing foreign loans given to foreign companies!). Some of the questions debated were whether fertiliser manufacturers could make profits at the cost of the farmer, whether free marketing rights should be given to foreign fertiliser firms when these were denied to private Indian firms, and whether policy changes were being made under pressure from USAID and the World Bank (a leaked letter from USAID to the finance ministry being the provocation). There followed a long debate on the role of foreign capital in industry, with extended quotes from the Industrial Policy Resolution of 1956, Nehru's statements in Parliament from 1948, and the finance minister's statement to Parliament in 1961, and on the question of whether the fertiliser policy had worked (demand had increased, not supply).

Dr Rangnekar asked: Why not switch to freer investment to increase supply? But then followed the larger question: if policy changed for fertiliser, would it change in other sectors too? You can see all the contradictions that flow from having a multiplicity of objectives (increase fertiliser supply, but don't show favours to foreign capital, staying faithful to declared policy and past statements of intent, giving in to external advice/pressure, whether socialism was being advanced, allegations of policy change by stealth). This is at a time of drought and famine, when increasing farm and fertiliser output are paramount. Dr Rangnekar finally decided that there was nothing wrong with change *per se*. He carefully couched his own socialist instincts in specific contexts, and was pragmatic enough to say that if a policy was not working, it should be changed.

On occasion, he seemed to be advocating a more radical kind of politics. Writing at a time of widespread rural unrest, farmer agitations and calls for debt relief, he said: 'The fact remains that the possibility of united action for better conditions for the poor rests…mainly on party cadres…. The need to establish a new society with restructured economic relations has receded into background.' It is almost as though farmer suicides in Vidarbha, land agitations in Nandigram and Singur, and the Maoist challenge in Lalgarh were happening then.

Dr Rangnekar died a quarter of a century ago. It is futile to try and second-guess what he might have written in today's context. The socialist in him would have been critical of many currents. The pragmatist would have welcomed policies that worked and made a difference to the poor. But it is interesting that, although editing a business newspaper, Dr Rangnekar's personal attention was rarely on the stock market and on how policy issues would play out there. At all times, he was focused on public policy and how it affected the poor, and how the productive capacity of the economy could be increased. Indeed, he was even an advocate of the peak income tax rate being 97.75 per cent. When I raised the issue with him once, he said it didn't matter since no one paid that rate. He was not persuaded that, for that very reason, the rate should be lowered. It was a funny mix—hot-button corporate reporting on the front page, and socialist arguments on the editorial page— as though covering business was important, but businessmen themselves were rapacious and their concerns not very relevant.

He wasn't happy when I wrote to him from Delhi in 1982, that I was leaving the paper. But he was typically gracious about the way he expressed his disappointment. Like many others in Delhi, I continued to wait for the paper to reach in the afternoons to see what saucy corporate story the paper had broken each day. But it seemed as though Dr Rangnekar was writing less than before. Then one morning came the telephone call, to say that he had passed away after a heart attack. Death is always a bigger tragedy when a life is cut short too early, and it was terrible news. His lasting memory with me is of a gentle human being. In the summer of 1984, it also felt like the last Nehruite had just passed on.

T. N. Ninan
Chairman and Editorial Director
Business Standard Ltd

PREFACE AND ACKNOWLEDGEMENTS

The publication of this collection marks an incredibly long and deeply personal project. At each turn and twist, we have benefitted from the generous and encouraging support of a vast array of individuals and institutions. There have been colleagues and friends of my father who have eased our burden and weighed in with ideas and there have been family members who have instilled hope. The publication of this volume, the first of several we hope, is testimony to this constellation of support and encouragement.

I still remember the days in late 1984, a few months after my father's demise, when we had just moved to Delhi, where in a 'temporary' room resided a mix of tea chests and other storage containers with his papers and books. This included newsprints of his articles from the papers he edited at different times, *The Economic Times* and *Business Standard*, and those published in other outlets. A discovery for us was copies of his articles from *Ceylon Daily News* that covered his period in Sri Lanka. Then we found copies of *New Delhi Diary*, his column in *The Economic Times*, that he penned during the tumultuous mid-1960s, which in later months was the topic of animated discussion and remains on the anvil as a subsequent volume. As our sifting through the papers progressed, we also came upon a mix of handwritten notes, collections of articles and personal papers—all of which were indicative of unfinished projects on some of his pet themes, such as black money, the planning process, and uneven development, among others, that are now housed in a collection at *Nehru Memorial Library*.

Our first endeavour was to collect his writings from these papers and catalogue them, which included the tiring job of hand-counting the number of words for each article. Friends from my student days at Jawaharlal Nehru University, in particular, Nandini, Nattu, Pranab, Shobhit, Sukti, Sushil and Vaishali will remember these moments, possibly with a fondness for the home-cooked food that accompanied these day-long endeavours. More challenging was transferring the newsprint into a typed manuscript—and this in a pre-digital age! Here, we remain ever so grateful to Mary Samuels for generously spending time in Delhi to type the 'first' manuscript.

Many a times we returned to his colleagues at the newspaper to assure us of the details and the completeness of this information. And in this respect, Mary Samuels, T. Bhanu and A. Kuruvilla were generous with their time and indispensable to the task. At the time, as a fledgling masters student of political economy, sifting through and reading this material was itself a route at discovering my father as an intellectual. Thus, the tentative steps at organising the list of articles depended on the numerous interventions of colleagues and collaborators of my father. Initial discussions of the project benefited from the wisdom of Boudhayan Chattopadhyay, M. V. Desai, D. N. Panigrahi, Inder Jit, Anil Nauriya, A. C. Ananthraman, G. M. Telang, T. N. Ninan and collaborators like Amit Bhaduri, who co-authored with him the 'Note of Dissent' to the Tandon Committee critiquing its formulation for an export led growth strategy.

The idea of publishing a collection of articles was always going to be complicated: would it be one or several volumes, how to constitute a volume or even the several volumes, and then, should the integrity of *New Delhi Diary* be disturbed or maintained? Our efforts in attending to these questions benefitted from the inputs of Paranjoy Guha Thakurta and M. K. Venu. Personally, I must also acknowledge my friends from my JNU days who have been steadfast in assisting with this project. As the form of a single (ideally, first) volume took shape and the focus moved towards taking the project to a publisher, the constellation of help that came forward also changed. These efforts were guided by a mix of colleagues, friends and admirers that included Sushil Aaron, Sanjaya Baru, Upendra Baxi and Ramachandra Guha. I still remember the initial discussions on the book with Sugata Ghosh of SAGE: over a couple of rounds of coffee at Green Park, he shared a vision of the volume. This did prompt us to return to the selection of articles and the thematic categorisation—it also sharpened our ideas of having a commentary to speak to the volume. In terms of the latter, it is a great privilege to have the contributions of Sanjaya Baru, Pratap Bhanu Mehta and T. N. Ninan in the volume. Not only have they given freely their time and attention; but, their contributions have crucially situated the collection.

Among the many memories of the process is the unwavering support we have received from the two newspapers, *The Economic Times* and *Business Standard*, and their publishing houses. The support has been manifold—and in getting swift clearance for the use of the articles that make this volume, a particular acknowledgement is made of Arindam Sengupta and Jaideep Bose at *Times of India* and Aveek Sarkar at *Ananda Bazaar Patrika*. Also acknowledged is the support from Haena Kim, at *Time* magazine, for the clearance for one of the articles included here.

Dwijen Rangnekar (Son of Late Dr D. K. Rangnekar)
Associate Professor (Law)
University of Warwick
Gibbet Hill Road
Coventry CV4 7AL, United Kingdom

INTRODUCTION AND OVERVIEW

Humanist Economics as Public Reason

I t is often said that there is a dearth of writing on contemporary history in India. At one level this observation is profoundly true. But at another level, it overlooks one possible source for the reconstruction of contemporary history: the work of our most analytical columnists and public writers. D. K. Rangnekar represents the best amongst them. Although he was primarily an economics columnist, the range of his interests was breathtaking. He could weave insights into the technical aspects of policy, with deep historical insight; he could reflect upon the political economy constraints in operation and combine them with an analysis of institutional logic; he could deal in equations and accessible prose. The essays on offer in this volume, drawn from his published columns, are an invaluable resource at multiple levels. Read together they offer a cogent account of an important episode in Indian economic history during the 1960s and 1970s. They shed enormous light on how we thought on a range of subjects, from the sources of growth to the appropriate form of subsidies. In many ways, with the exception of a couple of interventions, the 1970s are often considered the lost decade of Indian growth and equity. And this collection of essays helps us deeply understand why. He demonstrates, with considerable vigour and verve, how the state was incapacitated by a combination of faulty intellectual thinking and timid political imagination. Second, these essays will restore a great deal of complexity to our understanding of the ideological roots of Indian policy making. It places Indian policy making both in the context of international ideological currents and domestic political concerns. One of the striking things that emerges from his discussion is that Indian policy making, even during the 1970s, was less ideological than we suppose. For example, he argues that there was no first principles based hostility to either foreign investment or trade. Rather our reluctance to push in these areas stemmed from contingent political circumstances. Third, these essays are unusually fascinating in the light they shed on institutions and the policy process. There is a searing critique of the planning process, where we consistently confused a statement of objectives with actual planning.

These essays are extraordinary examples of the first virtue in a democracy: a commitment to public reason. They are complex without being inaccessible, they do not insult the intelligence of the reader, they are mostly fair minded without giving up on judgement. With the benefit of hindsight readers will find things to disagree with. For example, his emphasis on self reliance seems a little dated. But even here a sharp reader will come away with a deeper understanding of why that policy made sense in its time and context. But what is most impressive about these essays is how they have stood the test of time. In many respects, the biggest surprise on reading these essays is that they feel so contemporary. In some ways the fact that so many of the issues Rangnekar wrote about are still with us, is an extraordinary testament to his insights, particularly about the path-dependent characteristics of institutions. Every single one of the challenges he catalogues— lack of leadership, the self-serving character of India's elites, corruption, the fallacies of the planning process, the lack of state capacity, the absence of intellectual integrity—are still with us. But what is remarkable is that Rangnekar was able to analytically dissect these problems, without ever falling prey to a self defeating cynicism.

These essays are rich and diverse. But I will signal three themes of particular interest. The first theme is the failure of the Indian state to undertake bold and creative initiatives. In writing about Mrs Gandhi's visit to the United States, for instance, Rangnekar reflected upon the controversy that had arisen by her alleged plea for aid. The government had been reluctant to concede that aid had been sought for two reasons. The first related to the fact that, despite the publicity surrounding the incident, there had been no indication of a change in America's policy. The second reason was a reaction to the criticism that the government had faced. Not only had it received criticism from the left; it had also, unexpectedly, invited flak from the right. It therefore sought to downplay the incident. This reluctance, Rangnekar suggested, illustrated the government's timid nature. India's negative attitude towards its economic situation could, Rangnekar feared, indicate to other countries that she could be easily moulded. India's defeatist attitude had led to, Rangnekar argued, aid becoming a central feature of her development strategy. A bold and courageous government would have informed the nation of the seriousness of India's economic crises, and obviated the need to make false claims.

The timidity that concerned Rangnekar was also revealed in his essay on the government's fertiliser policy. Instead of announcing a new dynamic policy, the government had been denying any change in central controls on fertilisers. The new policy did not result in complete decontrol, and led to misgivings about its origins. Many had suggested that the policy has been changed due to the pressure of USAID and the World Bank. Exhibiting greater respect for the criticism that the previous policies had received in India could have allowed the government, Rangnekar argued, to avoid such misgivings. At any rate, Rangnekar emphasized, it was clear that there was a definite change in the government's policy. Sadly, however, the present form of the debate on India's fertiliser policy had ignored vital aspects of the change and focused instead on other issues. For instance, it concentrated on the problems with foreign capital when in fact there had been many deviations in the past from the proposed principle that the state must set a certain pattern of industrial development to determine the course of social change. Further, Rangnekar highlighted, the Indian state had never held that no foreign capital will be allowed in the country. Rangnekar drew on a range of historical sources to highlight how the policy of the Indian government had always been to recognise the important role that foreign capital can play in India's development. The entire incident relating to India's fertiliser policy brought to light several important issues. First, those in support of foreign capital did not question fertiliser targets or the role of the public sector in India. Enough attention was not devoted to the fact that foreign majority participation was sought in the private sector. Second, the fertiliser deal could become a precedent and consequently be used as an argument, in due course, for alternating national plans in other sectors. Since such changes were taking place close to a general election, a long-term debate was required on how the government had performed and the principles by which it was operating. Finally, because of India's very delicate balance of payments position, it was vital to pay attention to the remittance liabilities while framing the desired policy.

The second theme that emerges from Rangnekar's writings is the emphasis placed upon addressing long-term institutional questions and creating an Indian state that can be self-reliant. For example, in an essay in the *Economic and Political Weekly* in 1967, Rangnekar focused on Indian planning. It was necessary, he wrote, to ask some inescapable questions: (1) Has India embarked upon planning without being prepared for it? (2) Has India devoted enough attention to the process of planning? (3) Is planning for political and social change in line with the parliamentary framework of government that India adopted from the British? Unhelpful debates and the failure to approach planning in any serious way were sad realities of the time and they must, Rangnekar argued, be addressed. Intellectuals had a special role to play, and it was essential for them to take a far more active interest in the manner in which social and economic planning was being conducted. It was essential, for instance, to focus not merely on a plan's size but also on its priorities and content. A historical survey indicated, Rangnekar argued, that India was never really, as a nation, prepared for planning. Planning in India had always been focused on statistical projections and target setting, and ignored ground realities. The targets set revealed no relationship to the social problems that India faced and the political climate under which it operated. There was insufficient attention to how policies would be impactful over the long-run. Most analyses were conducted in financial terms, and while priorities were often set out they were hardly ever enforced. Importantly, Rangnekar argued, a major portion of the economy had been removed from the scope of planning. The planned sector was only the public sector, and the private sector remained unplanned. There was no discussion on its priorities and role, and yet there has been an elaborate structure of controls and regulations over this sector. Planners had failed, most fundamentally, to direct resources to priorities. Rather than asking how planning may have inspired some degree of industrial development, we should ask how much more we may have achieved if we had developed a comprehensive approach towards planning and brought the private sector within its purview. The government had shifted, Rangnekar observed, from the role of an underwriter to that of an undertaker, taking over losing concerns from the private sector and entering those areas in which nobody else was willing to enter. Rather than the state being a catalyst and a focal point for developmental activity, this had become its new role. Without a comprehensive approach to planning, Rangnekar feared, our political institutions will not survive and we will have no answer to our poverty.

Rangnekar's emphasis on creating a self-reliant Indian state was also evident from his writings on the international economic system. In reflecting upon the North–South divide, Rangnekar discussed the growing imbalance in the world economy, with rich countries becoming richer and poor countries becoming poorer. Although the international system was built on the hope that development would spread, several trade imbalances had soon appeared. There existed, Rangnekar argued, fundamental inequalities in the structure of economic relations; this was especially true of trade. The problem of liquidity led to exchange rate management and manipulation becoming a new way through which the Third World could be attacked. While efforts had been undertaken to remedy the international economic order and make it more just, the negotiations had emerged largely unsuccessful. On important trade issues like the stabilization of commodity prices or development aid, there had been little agreement or progress. There was a need, Rangnekar argued, to develop a coherent economic system at the international level that takes care of several issues, ranging from the need for stable systems of exchange rates to opportunities for greater participation from developing countries. Greater cooperation was also needed amongst the Southern countries. However, until this change took place at the global level, countries like India should concentrate on being self-reliant.

This belief of Rangnekar's also emerges from his reflections on India's trade prospects. Writing in 1977, he discussed how, while trade was an essential path to development, it was being curbed by Western nations. In India, there had been a major effort to reduce dependence on foreign aid and engage in import substitution. This policy, Rangnekar pointed out, had resulted in many successes; but nonetheless, India was very much dependent on imports. The Third Plan focused on making the Indian economy self-reliant. Although important substitution was undertaken in several vital sectors like capital goods industries, its process was interrupted by the oil crises. Consequently, exports became the path to self-reliance. Rangnekar provided a detailed overview of how India's policy on trade had developed. He elaborated upon how India's export earnings had steadily increased over time. The central question we must confront, Rangnekar argued, was whether the rise in exports would be sufficient enough to meet the import bill. This question was linked to a deeper normative question upon which Rangnekar reflected: could a developing country like Indian treat exports as the leading factor in the growth process? Rangnekar felt that global experiences could not inform this answer for India, but it would be wise to continually remember that export planning must share a definite relationship to production planning. Over the years, developing countries had faced a serious debt crises, and many solutions including a division of labour between developed and developing countries were being proposed. However, Rangnekar urged us to remember that the reason why India's trade and payments problems remained unsolved was the loaded value system of international trade. A new pattern of international division of labour would only serve to adversely impact India's domestic growth. We should focus on the core problem at hand: the restrictions imposed by the global institutional framework governing trade. Many changes were necessary. For instance, the compensatory finance scheme needs liberalisation. Ultimately, India should stay focused on self-reliance and self-sustained growth.

Rangnekar also discussed the government's plan to borrow money from the IMF. The key issue, Rangnekar suggested, was whether the government had considered all possible options before proposing to borrow money from the IMF. Would this be the only way to respond to the balance of payments crises? What India should focus on, Rangnekar argued, was adjusting its economy to the changes in world trade. There should be a serious programme of import substitution, focus on curbing consumption, tackling black money, enlargement of the public distribution system, and so forth.

The third theme that is evident from Rangnekar's work is a focus on specific issues of domestic policy. For instance, Rangnekar focused on taxes and the crucial importance of the budget in a country like India, where there is major state intervention in investment, production and distribution. The First Plan was, Rangnekar argued, a bit of a sham. Most projects had been undertaken before partition, and the government had failed to put forth development-oriented budgets. Things could not be subsequently improved by the time of the Second and Third Plans; further, food and foreign exchange difficulties were making the situation worse. Although the Centre's budget had grown almost ten times by 1971, this figure was, Rangnekar argued, misleading for two reasons. First, Plan investments in recent years had been stable. Second, defence and non-development expenditure weighed heavily on the budgetary scheme. The government's lopsided approach to budgeting reflected its inability to make the tax base more equitable while simultaneously prevent leakage of income on domestic and foreign accounts. For the future, the government needed to remedy the present situation where the incidence of taxation falls too heavily on fixed income earners. Further, Rangnekar suggested, agricultural income should be taxed in the same way as any other current income.

On domestic policy, Rangnekar also turned to India's food policy. India, unlike several other nations, had failed to capitalise on surpluses in the world food grain markets, and over time the domestic shortages increased significantly along with the cost of imports. Rangnekar commented on how India was facing a crisis in the food sector; a crisis caused by erratic purchases of food abroad and poorly planned procurement and distribution policies at home. Further, this had caused a drain on India's foreign exchange reserves and impacted the delicate domestic supply-demand balance. A major problem had been the tendency to hoard stocks. This tendency made the government's procurement policy ineffective, and, as Rangnekar observed, the lags would have to be remedied through imports, which would in turn come at the cost of other important imports. Despite all the hype surrounding the green revolution, Rangnekar observed that India's deep food crises revealed how the revolution had failed, and how our food policy lacked direction. The green revolution has resulted in increasing the wealth of already rich farmers and consequent income polarisation and increased inequality. Rangnekar also investigated specific aspects of the government's policy. Inter-state restrictions had, for instance, created artificial shortages. It was essential, Rangnekar felt, for the government to build a minimum stock.

The final theme from Rangnekar's writings is a disenchantment with the Indian state. In *The Deepening Social Crises*, and a companion piece *A Quiet Burial for Ideology*, Rangnekar reflected upon the paradoxical nature of India's growth and the problems of planning that its mixed economy posed. Vast number of individuals were, as a result of poverty, excluded from the development processes; large sections of the population were without basic essentials. This was a direct consequence of India's national income being too small relative to its large population, and the uneven distribution of this income. Rangnekar also explored the correspondence between poverty and income, and the growth of income inequality. A major factor for India's social crises was, Rangnekar argued, the indifference of politicians and their incapacity to initiative necessary changes in the economy. India's economy was a strange muddle of various Western economic theories. There was no land reform, laws like minimum wage guarantees were routinely violated, and ultimately dominant social groups used the system to exploit the landless peasantry. The problem for the poor was that the system had made it impossible for them to organise themselves. The poor, Rangnekar observed, were of little relevance to the political class, and the battle for social justice had been abandoned. The only way forward, Rangnekar argued, would be major institutional changes; it was an open question as to whether they would come into being.

Rangnekar's disappointment with India's political elite in the early 1980s was also evident from his piece on Mahatma Gandhi. He observed how remembering Gandhi on 2nd October had become a mere ritual, and that his and Nehru's principles were no longer visible in public life. Today's politicians, Rangnekar commented, had characteristics that contrasted sharply with those of Gandhi. The end of Nehru marked the end of a certain kind of politics that Gandhi believed in, a politics infused with values and integrity. It would do us well, Rangnekar felt, to remember Gandhi's democratic values and observe the extent to which we had departed from them.

Rangnekar's disenchantment was also evident through other writings. For instance, he wrote about the Nasik agitation in Maharashtra, in which farmers had protested their plight. The agitation signalled, Rangnekar felt, the emergence of the poor as a social force, and could be an indication of things to come. Rangnekar also spoke extensively about the role of black money in the economic and political system, and how the government's approach on several issues had been one of 'non-policy making'. Reliance upon foreign aid had become a strategic component of India's economic planning. The ultimate tragedy was, Rangnekar argued, that the present system favoured landlords, traders and so forth, and that political leaders had little incentive to reform the system. Whether reform would ultimately take place was, Rangnekar felt, an open question.

Rangnekar's analysis is a testament to his clarity, commitment to public reason and his broad sympathies. He was a model of what a broadly left-of-centre economic vision of India should look like. Even though our circumstances and historical opportunities are different, Rangnekar's essays provide an important starting point for understanding how we go where we are. They will unfailingly provoke readers to think harder.

Pratap Bhanu Mehta
President and Chief Executive
Center for Policy Research

Part One

The Politics of Poverty—
The Social Crisis of Development in India

1

Crisis Today

*The Dimming of Hope**

A climate of violence appears to have gripped the country today. Whether it is Punjab, Delhi or Bengal, violence and cynicism appear to predominate. The government does not seem to have got full measure of the crisis situation. Almost everywhere there are signs of anguish and dismay at the way the situation is allowed to drift and violence allowed to spread. The Punjab policy, for example, is marked by dithering and dilly-dallying. There appears to be no firm hold on the social tension. Consequently, the mood in the country is one of disenchantment. This is only an outward manifestation of the seething discontent among India's articulate classes who are dissatisfied with the pace of progress, frustrated with their own lot, and bored with the endless hypocrisy of politicians, who thrive on empty slogans.

Indian politics is perhaps a field where the choice lies between two blunders. On the Punjab issue, for example, the government has been bungling from the start.

Even in Punjab, at the root of the crisis is the social inequities and quest for identity. If today the country is passing through a traumatic experience it is because the social crisis has deepened, inequalities have increased, and unemployment has become chronic. The gains of years of sacrifice borne in the name of development

* Article first published in *Business Standard* on 3 April 1984.

have been cornered by ill-deserving, power-hungry groups, people who have no integrity and no sense of social responsibility.

Behind the intellectual crisis lies a total collapse of values. One cannot but hark back to our great leaders of the past who not only had certain perception and values, but concern for the weak and deprived. This was indeed the spur for the plan for a well-ordered and just society. The collapse of values represents the collapse of a system, of a style, the erosion of principles and norms with the emergence of manipulative politics, opportunism, and downright chicanery. In the process, thinking people have got alienated from the mainstream of economic and political activity.

What was once the cradle of an unique civilization now has several question marks hanging over it. Nehru did not exactly solve all problems, but he did not let the flame of hope die out. It is the hope phenomenon that remains a constant feature of human volition and activity, and it is hope that inspires people and beckons them to new, if distant, vistas of life.

There was then a sense of security and a sense of direction. There was what we may call a rational approach to economic and social issues, and evaluation of concepts, consideration of choices, not in the context of political opportunism, but from the point of view of conscious and well reasoned decision-making in the larger interest of the masses.

Today who knows which way we are going? What is in store for us? Have we, for example, drifted from the accepted, scientific approach and declared goals? Most politicians are obsessed with success even though most of them have a genuine flair for the exact opposite.

Today we no longer know what our objectives are and how we propose to get there. We set out to industrialise India and industrialisation and technology are known to be the greatest unifier equaliser one can think of. But this truism has been disproved in India. Have we then got lost in the jungle of our own creation? Democracy appears a cant word because opportunists pursue self-centered purposes. With the rise of unreason, superstition and tantrics in high-places it is astrologers who decide our fate. Mendicants chant mantras, while crooks employ Rs. 4500 crores in black money deals in sugar, cement, paper, edible oil and other items of essential consumption.

4

Do we have to submit to this age of unreason and a thoroughly unscientific approach to life and society? Do we have to let the entire system stay under stress? The crisis today is predominantly economic and social in character. But there are also other dimensions to the crisis which go deeper. They concern the direction of national policy, political integrity, quality of leadership and intellectual honesty. There is a strange intellectual ambivalence in New Delhi today. There are frequently attempts to ride two horses at the same time. In the case of Punjab, for example, the authorities have been hobnobbing with two rival groups, deluding themselves into believing that the balance of the two will result in the emergence of the moderates who can be persuaded to see sense. As the situation has developed, it is clear enough that there is no such thing as a moderate element among the Sikhs in Punjab today.

In the economic field the impact of intellectual ambivalence has been a near disaster. Starting with immense demonstrative faith in 'pragmatism', New Delhi was soon "persuaded" to hug the IMF and the World Bank, to let them be the guiding star of policies and fortunes. Step by step, the process of dismantling the economic framework laboriously built over decades began. Trade priorities were thrown out of the window and there was a free-for-all in the investment field. The next stage was the dangerous and thoroughly unwarranted negotiation for a massive loan of $5000 million from the IMF which carried irksome conditionalities and which eventually aggravated the balance of payments problem, upset the tonal quality of investment and development and compelled the government forgo $1.1 billion of the loan.

In the case of NRI investment also, the government has been running with the hares and hunting with the hounds. So also with industrial policy. For example, assurances were publicly given that companies with good management and a track record would not be destabilised. Even when the convertibility clause was introduced in loan agreements signed by public sector financial institutions with companies, the understanding was that the institutions would be sleeping partners. Yet today the LIC issues a notice to Escorts to drop its directors and the matter goes to court!

The manifestation of all this confusion is to be seen in the structural crisis, continued inflation, growing army of landless labourers and urban discontent. There has been very little structural change in this country in spite of three decades of planning. All that has happened is that the share of agriculture in national output has fallen from over 50 per cent to around 43 per cent at constant prices. But the increase in the share of the industrial sector has been very small.

Unlike so many other countries which have forged ahead, the momentum of the Indian economy appears to have slowed down. In 1983–84 the GNP growth rate is expected to be around 6 per cent, mainly because of a bumper agricultural crop. But this rate of growth has to be seen against the lower base of 1982–83 when the GNP had dropped to 1.8 per cent. Per capita income is still growing at a trend rate of 1.3 per cent, which in conditions of mass poverty provides no margin for comfort.

The industrial performance is particularly disappointing. The average index of industrial production in the first eight months of 1983–84 showed an increase of a mere 4.2 per cent as against the rate of growth of 8 to 10 per cent originally envisaged. Perhaps this rate of growth of 4.2 per cent or 4.5 per cent may be considered a marginal improvement on the growth rate of 3.9 per cent in 1982–83.

The experience of the last three odd decades reveals the dilemma of planning which keeps a major proportion of the economy out of the scope of planning. In a mixed economy the government has very little influence on the overall level of investment in the economy as a whole. What the so-called five year plans could do is to regulate, to some extent, the level of public investment. But gross fixed investment in the public sector, after increasing in the heyday of planning, has sharply declined over several years, though in money terms plan expenditure may have risen or even exceeded provisional targets. The experience of public planning has also shown that there is no inbuilt mechanism to protect resources and investment from the ravages of inflation.

Inevitably, the impact of public investment on the overall pace of expansion is profound. The development of public enterprises does give the impression that the government competes with the private sector in the mobilisation of savings; this could have the effect of reducing the savings available for private investment. In actual practice, however, the modalities of funding investments

6

of our leaders practise the opposite, Gandhiji preached tolerance, but our politics is dominated by intrigue and intolerance. He eulogized the Harijan and Daridranarayan, but today everybody is breathlessly in quest of opulence, caste prestige and vested interests though clever politicians swear by Gandhiji whenever they are caught on the wrong foot. Gandhiji was a flexible phenomenon. The pretenders are rigid.

If Gandhiji believed in something, he not merely said so but strived to realise the truth of it by his profound reverence of the precept in the actual life. The great man had roots in the philosophy identified with him. His hold over his people during his time lay not in the magic and charm, in forsaking offers and in remaining rooted in his mission which was, in simple words, a passionate search for truth, sacrifice, simplicity tolerance and a perpetual quest for truth. His dominant emotion was not one of sorrow but of pride in the privilege of having lived in his era and done something to spread social consciousness among the illiterate million and set out a philosophy which might have provided a guideline for Indian transformation had it not been interpreted narrowly or rather misinterpreted by those who battled with Nehru in the earlier evolution of India's aims, goals and instruments.

Gandhiji was a man out of time, and perhaps out of proportion to the country which happened to give him birth. He was able by his own genius to earn for India a place in the world which even before India became independent had ceased to correspond with its resources and political maturity. This is a lesson which our leaders have still to learn.

If today we are not able to adjust ourselves to the new conditions of science and technology it is mainly because we did not really understand Gandhi's principles of nonviolence, truth and understanding, and also because the obstinacy of some political leaders tended to put fear into our hearts, thereby creating a wide gap between the leaders and the people. The gap has widened to such an extent that we must painfully confess that the Gandhian era is over. So also is the Nehru era.

In a sense the end of Nehru marked the end of Gandhi's style of politics—faith in the people, understanding of the people's support, consent and consensus, and seeking the guidance of the people. Today decisions are made at the top according to the whims and moods of individuals and foisted on the people by what Gandhi also used to call 'exercise of the brute majority'. I have no doubt in my mind that this type of functioning of democracy would never have got the blessings of the Mahatma or of Nehru. When I say this I also realise that such statements will be angrily disputed by the lingering relics of the conscience-keepers. The extent to which India's politics and philosophy have drifted from the Gandhian way of life can be best illustrated by contrasting these with a few of Gandhiji's utterances.

Mahatma Gandhi gave this country a set of values, norms of public conduct, a certain sense of personal humility and dedication. He spread social consciousness far and wide in an attempt to convey the message of universal brotherhood, plant a sense of dynamism in the ever stagnating village, and seek to inculcate secularism with a concern for weaker and backward sections of society. Nehru sought to build on these traditions, drawing extensively on more modern concepts of industrial development and social change based on an adaptation of science and technology and pursue a strategy to change the economic and social structure, achieve faster rate of growh and redistribute income and wealth in order to usher in a quiet and peaceful economic and social revolution. The combination of the two leaders and their ideas baffled western observers and often invited ridicule.

'After I am gone' Gandhiji said once, 'no single person will be able completely to represent me. But a little bit of me will live in many...if each puts the cause first and himself last, the vacuum will, to a large extent, be filled'. But as we find today the void has grown even much bigger after the death of Nehru. When we look at the growing religious intolerance around us and the increasing tendency to 'parochialism' and 'casteism' one recalls what Gandhiji said: 'Religion does not mean sectarianism. It means a belief in ordered moral government of the universe...Religions are different roads converging at the same point. What does it matter that we take different roads so long as we reach the same goal? In reality there are as many religions as there are individuals.'

On the question of political practice, humility and truth, this is what Gandhiji had to say: 'All that I can in true humility present to you is that Truth is not to be found by anybody who has not got

24

an abundant sense of humility. If you would swim on the bosom of the ocean of Truth, you must reduce yourself to a zero.'

As regards social and economic transformation there was hardly any difference between Gandhi's ideas and those of Nehru. Gandhiji said: 'No one under it should suffer from want of food and clothing. In other words, everybody should be able to get sufficient work to enable him to make the two ends meet. And this ideal can be universally realized only if the means of production of life remain in the control of the masses. These should be freely available to all as God's air and water are or ought to be; they should not be made a vehicle of other.' '...My ideal is equal distribution, but so far as I can see, it is not to be realized. I therefore work for equitable distribution.' '...Economic equality is the master key to non-violent independence. Working for economic equality means abolishing the eternal conflict between capital and labour. It means the leveling down of the few rich in whose hands is concentrated the bulk of the nation's wealth on the one hand, and a leveling up of the semi-starved naked millions on the other. A non-violent system of government is clearly an impossibility so long as the wide gulf between the rich and the hungry millions persists'.

As one who lived among the poor and preferred to live as poor he was horrified at the sharp contrast between the palatial extravagance of New Delhi and the hunger of the downtrodden. Our present-day leaders are copying the feudal traditions of the Moghuls and the social stratification left by the British. They rejoice in the paraphernalia and pomp as soon as they enter the palatial homes exclusively reserved for the higher-ups. This is an important factor in the transformation of politics after Gandhiji. And it is this transformation that has separated the rulers of today from the masses.

Mahatma Gandhi said that the contrast between the palaces of New Delhi and the miserable houses of the poor labouring class cannot last one day in a free India in which the poor will enjoy the same power as the rich. This hope of Gandhiji has been falsified by our leaders. Gandhiji foresaw the possibilities and warned 'a violent and bloody revolution is a certainty one day unless there is a voluntary abdication of riches and the power that riches give and sharing them for the common good. I adhere to my doctrine of trusteeship in spite of the ridicule that has been poured upon it. It is true that it is difficult to reach. So is non-violence difficult to attain...I hate privilege and monopoly. Whatever cannot be me...Every man has an equal right to the necessaries of life even as birds and beasts have. And since every right carries with it a corresponding duty and the corresponding remedy for resisting any attack upon it, it is merely a matter of finding our corresponding duties and remedies to vindicate the elementary fundamental equality.'

Even Gandhiji's concept of democracy and the relationship of government and people were widely different from what we know of the system today. Today might is right. But Gandhi's notion of democracy is that the weakest should have the same opportunity as the strongest. He said: I am not interested in freeing India merely from the English yoke. I am bent upon freeing India from any yoke whatsoever. I have no desire to exchange 'King Log for King stork'.

Mahatma Gandhi was frequently criticized. In fact, at various times he was the most hated political leader in India from the point of view of the British and even from the point of view of some Indian leaders of the time. He was more passionately and widely disliked not as a man but as a man of certain strong views by those who believed in a philosophy contrary to his own. But to all those who criticized him he was a friend. He welcomed criticism in the true sense of the term, unlike our politicians who say they welcome criticism but intensely hate it and frequently bear a grudge against the critics.

To Gandhiji, difference of opinion never meant hostility. 'If they did' he said, 'my wife and I should be sworn enemies of one another.' It is clear from this that Gandhiji did not envisage a system of government where the majority would exercise the steamroller and throw out every good suggestion from the opposition merely for the sake of black sports or in order to hide some black sports or to push through legislation or a measure which might not be regarded by many as a desirable one.

He rejected the philosophy of the 'greatest good of the greatest number' because it meant that in order to achieve the supposed good of 51 per cent the interests of 49 per cent, were to be sacrificed. This he characterized as a heartless doctrine'...'The rule of the majority has narrow application i.e. one should yield to the majority in matters of details. But it is slavery to be amenable to the majority, no matter what its decisions are. To Mahatma Gandhi, 'democracy is not a state in which people act like sheep. Under democracy individual liberty of opinion and action is jealously guarded.'

Looking at the inequalities around one might recall Gandhiji's observations that the rich cannot accumulate wealth without the cooperation of the poor in society. If this knowledge were to penetrate to and spread amongst the poor they would become strong and would learn how to free themselves by means of non-violence from the crushing inequalities which have brought them to the verge of starvation.

A born democrat, Gandhiji was also a very disciplined and tolerant person. Democracy came very naturally to him. He said 'man must think not in terms of self or party but only of democracy...I do not believe that honest difference of opinion will injure our cause. But opportunism, camouflage, or patched up compromises certainly will'.

It would be an enlightening exercise for each politician of the day to recall that to Mahatma Gandhi democracy was not a state in which people act like sheep. Under democracy the individual liberty of opinion and action is jealously guarded.

Note

The complete bibliographic information for this article is as follows:
D. K. Rangnekar, 'The Ritual of Remembering Gandhiji', *Business Standard*, 7 October 1982.

5

Farmers' Stir–I

Writing on the Nasik Wall*

The two-week old farmer's agitation in Nasik-Dhulia district of Maharashtra could normally have been dismissed as a politically motivated stir, a stunt best left for politicians to deal with. It is easy enough to identify elements of partisan strategy and tactics in certain demonstrations, strikes or campaigns. But there are two aspects of the current movement which must cause widespread concern.

First, the Nasik stir appears to be the outward manifestation of a deep-seated crisis in the agrarian structure which, if unresolved, can pose a serious political problem. What is today a localised stir in certain parts of the country could become the signpost of a major upheaval, the full magnitude and impact of which could pose a major challenge to policy makers and politicians alike.

We are probably witnessing for the first time the consolidation of forces of poverty at a time when much of the Government's attention has been focussed on the problems of inflation and energy shortage. The farmer's stir is, in this sense, a reminder of the core problem of land and man, one which calls for an effort based on the realisation that human society is indeed confronted with one of the most crucial problems that has ever occurred in India's long history.

* First published in *Business Standard* on 25 November 1980.

For much too long the poor peasants of India have waited patiently for the dawn of a better day. Politicians have tended to feed them on promises of plenty, of reform, but usually peasants are regarded as little more than a vote bank to be tapped at the time of election and forgotten thereafter. The mobilisation of poverty as a political force will change that and much else.

The second important factor is the change in the inter-sectoral price parity against agriculture. This has been imperceptible, but significant in more recent years, and has put the small labourers and cultivators under intense pressure. In a sense the inter-sectoral price disparity appears to have drained the agricultural economy.

Though the Nasik stir is probably the first well-organised demonstration of peasant power, we heard rumblings of peasant revolt last year in Bhojpur, Bihar, in Telengana in Andhra Pradesh. We cannot also forget the powerful no tax campaign of Naidu in Tamil Nadu, where the agriculturists' association demanded, among other things, the write off of rural debts and remunerative prices for farm products. It is expedient for Delhi leaders to dismiss the Nasik agitation with a shrug and argue that the interests of millions of urban consumers would be affected if the farmer's demands were met. This is a predictable elitist approach which overlooks the fact that India is a predominantly agricultural country, the dominant feature still being the semi-feudal character of agrarian relations and structure, modified by the penetration of modern capitalist farming in what is in certain areas called the green revolution belt. The capitalisation may have developed in certain pockets, but the bulk of the producers still remain tied down and doomed to remain petty producers, sweating in conditions of semi-feudal exploitation and oppression.

The crisis in agriculture which hinders the growth of the economy as a whole is essentially the crisis of petty production in semi-feudal conditions. If Nasik brings out anything at all it is that the poor peasants may be emerging as a social force, waking up from deep slumber and seeking to emerge as an agent of social change. We have had politics of poverty in terms of slogans, but seldom has it come forth as an issue of power struggle with the direct involvement of the poor. The concern for the poor has always been a platform of political campaigns, but the distance from the poor has been no less startling. In this sense poverty was not at issue so long as there was an evocative approach to the poor and a blind block vote by them.

This inbuilt contradiction is now showing up, though not with full force yet, in the sense that the poor peasants are still not on the centre of the political stage but are approaching it. History shows that the transformation of the poor from passive beings, automatic voters and a sullen, sulky group into a socially conscious, politically aware, struggling class has much to do with the accentuation of poverty in striking contrast with affluence and ostentation in and around the poor people. It also has to do with the emergence of radical intellectuals as leaders or creators of a new outlook on poverty seeking directly to link poverty with the exploitation of those directly involved in producing by those who maximise gains on the produce.

In our country all these elements are to be found in spite, or perhaps because of, the green revolution. The so-called green revolution brought the development of capitalist social economic relations to the rural areas. The development of agrarian capitalism took one of two forms; either the ancient class of feudal landed property owners became transformed into a class of great capitalist landed property owners who employed free or wage workers with much more power invested to improve output and essentially produce for the market or else the feudal property got divided in the process of change and the competition gradually led to concentration, the peasant system slowly giving way to agrarian capitalism of large or middle size farmers. This change is visible in the wheat growing areas of Punjab, Haryana, U.P. and in the commercial crop areas of Gujarat and Maharashtra. The change has been anything but smooth. Most of these areas are tense and clashes are frequent, though unreported. Who can forget the upheaval in the Tarai region of U.P. and the increasing peasant unrest in Punjab and Haryana?

In fact, the most striking feature of the green revolution and agrarian change in recent times is the continuous growth of rural wage labour in its working population. This represents eviction, dispossession and deprivation of what was one time a class of small property cultivators. Between 1961–71 the total number of agricultural workers increased by 11 per cent from 118.29 to

129.16 million. But during the same period the number of workers under agricultural labour households soared by 70 per cent. This reflected (a) a dispossession of land held by tenants; (b) distress sales of land by poor farmers and (c) peasants with concealed tenancy. The Agricultural Labour Enquiry which submitted its report in 1978 showed that the proportion of farm labour households with and without land had increased sharply, probably reflecting the pressure of inflation and living costs compelling small and marginal peasant farmers to supplement their incomes by working on other people's land to the extent where wage displaces farm income.

However, as a factor responsible for the pauperisation of small peasants, inflation which has benefited the rich farmers and businessmen may be relatively more than important. The Agricultural Enquiry also revealed that wage employment trends for peasants and agriculture labour households have been declining. Average daily earnings of agriculture labour workers if deflated with the consumer price index applicable to agriculture labour workers levels showed a decline of 12 to 14 per cent since 1964–65. Numerous studies have highlighted the peculiar phenomenon of unequal sharing of benefits from agricultural developments. Even money wage rates are low (Table I). The average daily real earnings appear to have slumped from Rs. 1.43 in 1964–65 to Rs. 1.26 in 1975. The Labour Enquiries throw no light on dispossession of small and marginal farmers of their land, but differences certainly bring out the fact that the increasing proportion of small and marginal farmers are now swelling the ranks of agriculture labour households.

Thus the proportion of agriculture labour households had gone up in less than 10 years by as much as 49.2 per cent. That was not all. According to the Agricultural Census of 1970–71, 70 per cent of the rural households had operational holdings of 5 acres or less, and 51 per cent had 2.5 acres or less. Since the number of holdings reported were 70.49 million the ratios implied that about 49 million holdings belong to the category of small farmers of which 36 million were marginal. The draft plan for 1978–83 had estimated that the number of landless labourers was in the region of 50.4 million at the time of the census. Whereas 70 per cent of the operational holdings were small or marginal, they accounted for nearly 21 per cent of the operated area.

EXHIBIT 1

States	AWI estimates		Rs. per day NSS estimates		
	1956-57	1970-71	1956-57	1964-65	1970-71
	1	2	3	4	5
Andhara Pradesh	1.14	2.97		1.21	2.22
Assam	2.20	3.92	1.54	2.21	3.78
Bihar	1.19	n.a.	0.91	1.39	2.29
Gujarat	1.44	3.06	n.a.	1.47	2.45
Karnataka	1.24	2.33	0.84	1.21	1.91
Kerala	1.45	4.89	1.28	2.11	3.25
Madhya Pradesh	1.07	2.08	0.76	1.11	1.68
Maharashtra	1.31	2.78	n.a.	1.47	2.28
Orissa	1.00	2.12	0.80	1.33	1.90
Punjab/Haryana	2.27	6.89	1.98	2.13	4.60
Rajasthan	n.a.	n.a.	0.98	1.76	3.03
Tamil Nadu	1.32	2.56	0.84	1.39	2.42
Uttar Pradesh	0.80	2.52	0.92	1.10	2.47
West Bengal	1.63	2.98	1.43	1.81	n.a.

Sources: Columns 3 and 4, Table 4.4, in Rural Labour Enquiry, 1963–65, Final Report. Column five gives wage rates of working men (13–44 years) in rural non-cultivating wage earner households, taken from Kalpana Bardhan, 'Rural Employment, Wages and Labour Markets in India, A Survey of Research' Part II, EPW, Volume XII, No. 27 July 2, 1977; 'Real Wages, Employment and Income of Agricultural Labourers' by A.V. Jose, Economic and Political Weekly, Vol XIII, No. 12, March 25, 1978.

The proportion of farm labour households which had gone into deep debt was as high as 66.4 per cent in 1974–75. The incidence of indebtedness was more than 70 per cent in 7 States. What is significant is that the increase in indebtedness among rural labour households was the heaviest in Haryana (80 per cent) and Punjab (75 per cent), two star performers of the green revolution. The average debt per indebted rural household went up from Rs. 244 to 584 during 1964–75. In some States the debt was as high as Rs. 1434–1648. Hereditary debt accounted for only 5 to 6 per cent of the loans, though the absolute amount had doubled. Significantly, the hereditary indebtedness was about the highest (9.6 per cent) in Maharashtra and Gujarat.

32

It is important to bear in mind that many people described as cultivators in the census are in fact part-time or marginal operators, mainly labourers. It is significant that in terms of the NSS, the percentage of people below the minimum level in rural India went up by 40 per cent in the 1960s. This percentage nearly trebled in West Bengal and more than doubled in Punjab and Haryana. It also went up by much more than 40 per cent in Assam, Bihar, Madhya Pradesh. Households belonging to size groups with relatively high proportion of owned land accounted for an almost correspondingly high proportion of leased-in land, except in the case of those at the two extremities of the size-distribution. Though households with relatively small operational holdings (less than $2^1/_2$ acres in size) were more than half the number reporting leased-in land, they had in all less than $7^1/_2$ per cent of the total area leased in; on the other hand, households with relatively large operational holdings (more than 10 acres in size) were about one-sixth of the total number of households reporting leased-in area, but they accounted for more than 60 per cent of such area.

It is clear enough, therefore, that the social situation in our country has been undergoing a qualitative change with the emergence of a new type of poverty, a poverty due not entirely to economic stagnation but to the economic system in which millions get alienated from the property structure and the mode of production and are consequently denied the benefits of production and distribution. This endures in spite of economic growth because the core lies in the economic system itself. This new social situation provides an objective basis for a sharp crystallization of the power of the poor as a class deprived for generations. Greater impact can develop if frustrations and desires and aspirations can be articulated. This is what Mr. Sharad Joshi has done in Nasik and this is how resurgence can be dramatised.

In fact, Mr. Joshi has made it amply clear that what he is seeking is not an ad hoc solution to the prices of onions and sugarcane, but the evolution of a system whereby prices get rationally adjusted to the changing economic and social situation. On the face of it, the Nasik farmers' demand for a mark-up in the price of sugarcane at Rs. 300 per tonne and onions by Rs. 100 per quintal seems to be rather on the high side. But when viewed in the context of the black marketeering and profiteering of, say, sugar, the perspective changes. The Government has given special incentive to sugar mills for early crushing and pegged the minimum sugar prices at Rs. 13 per quintal for the season which began in October 1980. But this is meaningless when sugar has been marketed for the last seven months for as much as Rs. 20 per kg. The Nasik farmer's demand for sugarcane from Rs. 13 to Rs. 29 does bear some consideration when the ruling sugar prices have been Rs. 15–20 per kg. Indeed the main thrust of the farmer's movement is that consumers are already being exploited and paying through their nose for their sugar. They can offer sugar on a sustained basis at reasonable rates if cane prices were made remunerative relating to the prevailing costs. For example, khandsari manufacturers are already willing to pay cane growers more than Rs. 25 per quintal. It is strange, therefore, that the Nasik farmer's demand should be considered unrealistic and injurious to consumer interests.

What impact the Nasik agitation will ultimately have on the present system is not clear. But indications are that this would be utilised by the sugar industry to push up sugar prices again. According to an industry spokesman, sugar prices were to tumble in November, but consumers are still to see the slide down. Sugar is available almost everywhere but at a premium. If cane crushing is delayed, or cane gets diverted to khandsari or gur producers to a larger extent, we can rest assured that sugar prices will shoot up, that there will be an artificial cutback in sugar releases, and once again we will be at the mercy of imports and black marketeers. In the case of the Nasik farmers much would depend on the holding capacity of the sugarcane growers.

True, the leadership of the Nasik farmer's movement has Kulak links. The architect, Mr. Sharad Joshi, now in jail, comes from an affluent family, has an economics degree of Bombay University, was a member of the IAS, and had spent several years in Europe, where he is believed to have, among other things, worked for University Postal Union in Switzerland. His team-mate is a sugar co-operative leader. But the majority of the farmers following the leadership are small, marginal farmers, one and two acre holders.

Their holding capacity cannot be sustained for long and in a month or two they will be compelled to sell the cane at falling prices unless of course khandsari and gur producers lap up available supplies at higher prices. The organised sugar industry operates a cartel and has ample holding capacity in contrast. Confrontation of the type that is on is ill-advised. While inflationary pressures continue there will be a natural tendency to seek to contain price increases, but not all prices can be held back. And the Government itself has pushed up the administrative prices of a range of manufactured products, in some cases by as much as 80 per cent. In the present case the question is whether sugarcane prices can be raised and whether there can be a system of procurement. The Government has sanctioned higher prices than those recommended by the Agricultural Prices Commission in the case of food grains. Those critical of the procurement prices would probably suggest that the higher prices will carry no benefit to small or marginal farmers who in any case have negligible or no surpluses. But then, procurement prices are intended to provide satisfactory remuneration to those producers who have surpluses. If there is a procurement system in the case of foodgrains and other crops why should not there be a similar system in the case of sugarcane and onions? The pricing and procurement system is not a charitable operation; there are other ways of providing relief to the afflicted. The objective is to provide incentives for better productivity and higher growth rates. In the case of sugarcane and onions incentives would be intended to speed up the rate of growth of commercial crops at the same level as food crops. The thrust of the policy then would be to remove the deterrents to generating surpluses to enable farmers to pay higher wages and make possible changes in the agrarian structure.

Lack of a proper procurement and pricing system has affected not only the growth of pulses, which is serious enough, but also of sugarcane. The price support operations in foodgrains, especially wheat, and the technological changes have created imbalances in the structure of production. It has had the effect of diverting acreage away from core cereals and pulses and also key cash crops like sugarcane. Consequently, expansion of crops like wheat or even rice have been partly at the expense of significantly important crops like cotton, groundnut and sugarcane.

The long-term trend must cause concern. The all Indian compound rate of growth of cane production shows a fall from 5.91 per cent in 1952–65 to 3.80 per cent in 1967–79. The compound rate of growth of area is down from 4.03 during the same period and yield from 1.82 per cent to 0.78 per cent. If returns are satisfactory and there is a proper pricing and procurement system the trend will be reversed.

Note

The complete bibliographic information for this article is as follows:
D. K. Rangnekar, 'Farmer's Stir–I: Writing on the Nasik Wall', *Business Standard*, 25 November 1980.

6

Farmers' Stir–II

Changes in Inter-sectoral Price Parity*

In an economy, the inter-sectoral flows of funds are determined by changes in their price parities. Historically, every society develops an economic structure with a determined parity system in the process of economic growth, and it is inevitable that the price parities in between the sectors (at a macro level) get changed, resulting in inter-sectoral flows of funds.

Thus, determining and maintaining inter-sectoral price parity is very important and significant in a planned economy. If the price parities are so disturbed (with or without motivation) that huge funds are diverted to a sector of the economy where there is little chance of these funds being ploughed back for further growth, the acceleration or the propelling momentum which is the necessary ingredient of a growing economy is affected. Moreover, despite the unwanted results of wrong policies, if the policy of favouring one sector over another in the economy is stretched to illogical limits, there is the danger of economic growth stagnating.

According to the accepted system of national accounts, the entire Gross Domestic Product (GDP) originates in broadly classified sectors. There are two main sectors, the production sector consisting of primary (agriculture and allied activities) and secondary (manufacturing, industries, construction and power and

* First published in *Business Standard* on 28 November 1980.

37

water supply) sectors, and the tertiary sector, comprising services and the administrative infrastructure. In the underdeveloped stage of an economy, there is greater reliance on the primary sector as it constitutes a larger percentage of the GDP. Over the years the structure of the Indian economy has changed somewhat. The contribution of agriculture (excluding allied activities like forestry, hunting and fishing) which was about 48 per cent (at current prices) in 1960–61 came down to less than 42 per cent in 1975–76. The contribution of the manufacturing sector (that is, registered and unregistered industries and excluding construction, water and power), on the other hand, increased from around 14 per cent to 16 per cent during the same period. However, these percentages fail to reveal whether the increase in GDP in a particular sector was more due to a rise in production or a rise in prices.

We now turn to inter-sectoral flows of funds during the period 1961–62 to 1977–78. For this purpose, final as well as provisional data of GDP at current and constant (i.e., 1960–61) prices have been used. For subsequent years, estimates have been prepared. The entire GDP has been classified as originating from four broad sectors, namely, (1) agriculture (2) manufacturing (3) other industrial sectors (mining and quarrying, construction, power and water supply) and (4) other sectors. The aim is to measure the impact of the changes in inter-sectoral price parity with the parity in 1960–61 as the base. The exercise is meant to quantify the changes in inter-sectoral transfers of funds caused by changes in inter-sectoral price parity during the years.

The basic equation giving the GDP (which is equal to the sum of products originating in the four sectors at current prices) in the year 't' would be

$$Pt = At + Mt + It + Rt \qquad (1)$$

There would be two more equations to estimate the inter-sectoral flows at constant parity prices in the sectors classified above;

$$P^I_t = A^I_t + M^I_t + I^I_t + R^I_t \qquad (2)$$

$$P^{II}_t = A^{II}_t + M^{II}_t + I^{II}_t + R^{II}_t \qquad (3)$$

Equation (2) gives us the sector-wise actual GDP at constant prices, while equation (3) denotes the share of a sector in the GDP in a year, assuming the inter-sectoral price parity the same as at the 1960–61 level. Since P^I_t and Pt denote GDP at constant and current prices, respectively, their ratio $\lambda t = Pt/P^I_t$ would be an inflator indicating the share of a sector at a constant price parity level. Obviously, prices in all the four sectors must not have moved uniformly; hence λt would help knowing the gains or losses of the individual sectors due to changes in the inter-sectoral price parity from what it was in 1960–61.

Thus, equation (3) gives us sectoral distribution in year 't' under the assumption of constant price parity level. Subtracting the product in equation (3) from that in equation (2) in year 't' we get an idea of inter-sectoral transfer of funds due to the disturbance or changes in a given price parity. The final result of the entire exercise for the year 't' would be as shown in Exhibit I.

EXHIBIT I
Year = t

Sectors	GDP at current prices	GDP at constant prices	GDP at constant parity price level	Inter sectoral transfer
Agriculture	At	A^It	$A^{11}t = At^I\lambda t$	$At-A^{11}t$
Manufacturing	Mt	M^It	$M^{11}t = Mt^I\lambda t$	$Mt-M^{11}t$
Other Industry	It	I^It	$I^{11}t = I't\lambda t$	$It-I^{11}t$
Other Sectors	Rt	R^It	$R^{11}t = R't^I.\lambda t$	$Rt-R^{11}t$
GDP	Pt	P^It	$P^{11}t + P^It \lambda t$	

$$\lambda t = Pt/P^It$$

Year = t.

P = GDP at current prices

P^I = GDP at constant prices

P^{11} = GDP that would have been if the 1960–61 inter sectoral price parity would have been maintained.

t = the year.

The signs over A, M, I and R denote the same as over P.

Now the picture as it emerges using the above methodology is shown in Exhibit II.

EXHIBIT II

Inter-sectoral Flow of Funds on the Assumption of Constant Price Parity Level (1961–62 to 1975–76).

A-Agriculture

M-Manufacturing

I-Other Industries

R-Other Sectors

P-Total GDP

(Rs. crores)

Sector	GDP at current prices	GDP at constant prices (1960–61 prices)	GDP as would be at constant price-parity level	Inter-sectoral transfer of funds (+) or (−)
(1)	(2)	(3)	(4)	(5)
1961–62				
1.A	6967	6808	6964	+ 3
2.M	2206	2191	2241	− 35
3.I	929	908	929	−
4.R	4856	4716	4824	+ 32
5.P	14958	14623	14958	−
1961–62				
1.A	7113	6640	7025	+ 88
2.M	2470	2405	2544	− 74
3.I	1030	983	1040	− 10
4.R	5298	5012	5302	− 4
5.P	15911	15040	15911	−
1963–64				
1.A	8237	6817	7818	+ 419
2.M	2850	2601	2983	− 133
3.I	1180	1092	1252	− 78
4.R	5935	5361	6149	− 214
5.P	18202	15871	18202	−
1964–65				
1.A	10093	7477	9354	+ 739
2.M	3160	2815	3522	− 362
3.I	1314	1118	1399	− 85
4.R	6757	5634	7049	− 292
5.P	21324	17044	21324	−
1965–66				
1.A	9795	6367	8662	+ 1133
2.M	3387	2836	3858	− 471

Sector	GDP at current prices	GDP at constant prices (1960–61 prices)	GDP as would be at constant price-parity level	Inter-sectoral transfer of funds (+) or (–)
(1)	(2)	(3)	(4)	(5)
3.I	1417	1127	1533	– 116
4.R	7405	5845	7951	– 546
5.P	22004	16175	22004	–
1966–67				
1.A	11785	6320	9800	+ 1985
2.M	3698	2906	4506	– 808
3.I	1615	1176	1824	– 209
4.R	8420	6054	9388	– 968
5.P	25518	16456	25518	–
1967–68				
1.A	15887	7429	12471	+ 2416
2.M	3920	2970	4986	– 1066
3.I	1895	1281	2150	–255
4.R	9446	6279	10541	– 1095
5.P	30148	17959	30148	–
1968–69				
1.A	14207	7415	12322	+ 1885
2.M	4199	3096	5145	– 946
3.I	2003	1287	2139	– 136
4.R	10178	6608	10981	– 803
5.P	30587	18406	30587	–
1969–70				
1.A	15298	7799	13410	+ 1888
2.M	4685	3252	5592	– 907
3.I	2263	1379	2371	– 108
4.R	11031	6920	11898	– 867
5.P	33277	19350	33271	–
1970–71				
1.A	16690	8248	14789	+ 1901
2.M	4959	3364	6032	– 1073
3.I	2371	1578	2830	– 459
4.R	12297	7064	12666	–369
5.P	36317	20254	38317	–

In the first phase of 1960–61 to 1971–72 changes in the inter-sectoral price parity levels conferred certain benefits on agriculture. Exhibit II in particular, column IV, reveals progressively increasing transfers to the agricultural sector. It would be rash to conclude from this transfer that the sector as a whole benefited at the expense of the other sectors of the economy. There are two qualifications to be entered at this stage.

First, one must bear in mind that agricultural prices have remained depressed for several decades and the changes that came about as a result of the Government's conscious decision were in the nature of a corrective to the depredation of the past. Secondly, with the kulak lobby pretty powerful in Delhi, the bulk of the benefit of the rising agriculture prices went to the rich farmers of superior crops, especially rice and wheat, in the so-called green belt. Officially released prices were in the nature of support prices and the actual market prices tended to be higher than the support prices. The complexity of agricultural marketing which this dualism represented had the effect of traders cornering a large part of the grain supplies, pushing up market prices ever higher, and the Government being unable to procure enough to feed the then existing public distribution system. Here again the beneficiaries of higher market prices were the rich farmers and traders, particularly those who were directly and indirectly involved in the so-called green revolution. Owing to the extremely unequal structure of land holdings they represented a new class of cultivator-cum-trader enjoying the full benefits of the changes in the price parity. After all the big and medium land holders constituting only 25 per cent of the total commanded nearly two-thirds of the cultivated area. This is what gave them leverage and capacity to corner the economic and social benefits of the parity shifts. The majority of the small cultivators, the landless labourers and others, were left out in the cold.

The general wholesale price index (1961–62 as base) was 254.2 (average) for 1973–74. It has been relentlessly increasing, the main contributory factor for the increase in the price index being the sharp rise in the prices of foodgrains and agricultural raw materials. The foodgrains price index stood at 296 and that of industrial raw materials at 299.1 in 1973–74 against 219.8 in the case of manufactures. The rise was even greater in favour of agriculture in later years when in 1974–75 and 1975–76 the food articles price index stood, respectively, at 364.0 and 347.7 against those of 254.5 and 252.9.

While the wholesale price index for cotton has been successively increasing and stood at 277.3 in 1973–74, that for cotton manufactures had only a gradual rise standing at 183.5 in

1973–74. The situation was slightly different in the case of sugar as the prices of sugarcane and the distribution pattern of the finished product (i.e., sugar) were both controlled. At an overall economic level the general price level in the Indian economy depends upon the level of prices of foodgrains which constitute about 60 per cent of the consumer expenditure of an average Indian.

Owing to the dual nature of the Indian taxation system, agricultural incomes are exempt from direct taxation unlike non-agricultural incomes. These huge funds in the hands of big landlords have not been invested voluntarily by them in any industrial or developmental activities because of their natural disinclination to transfer funds to a tax sector from a completely tax-free sector. Indications are that the use of these funds for improvement in agricultural technology for increasing farm produce has also been tapering off. Until recently inputs like fertilisers, improved seeds, tractorisation, etc. were all being heavily subsidised by the Government.

There has, however, been a qualitative change in more recent years. For our purposes the final data of GDP at current and constant prices (1970–71) have been considered in order to determine the volume of inter-sectoral flows or transfer. The picture as it emerges on the basis of the earlier methodology is presented in Exhibit III. It reveals that during the period 1971–72 and 1977–78, though they had been favourable years for agriculture on a net basis the sector has suffered from inter-sectoral price disparity. The beneficiary has been mainly the manufacturing sector.

TABLE A

SECTORS	INTER-SECTORAL TRANSFERS (In Crores Rs.)
Agriculture	−691
Manufacturing	+1491
Other industries	−244
Other sectors	−556

The manufacturing sector received inter-sectoral transfer of Rs. 1491 crores during 1970–71 to 1977–78, reversing the earlier trend during the entire period. Sectoral classification might

EXHIBIT III

Inter-sectoral Flow of Funds on the Assumption of Constant Price Parity Level (1971–72 to 1977–78).

A-Agriculture

M-Manufacturing

I-Other Industries

R-Other Sectors

P-Total GDP

(Rs. crores)

Sector	GDP at current prices	GDP at constant (1970–71 = 100 prices)	GDP as would be at constant price-parity level	Inter-sectoral transfer of funds (+) or (−)
(1)	(2)	(3)	(4)	(5)
1971–72				
1.A	17380	16661	17532	− 152
2.M	5749	5367	5647	+ 102
3.I	2598	2425	2552	+ 46
4.R	13536	12860	13532	+ 4
5.P	39263	37313	39263	−
1972–73				
1.A	19169	15601	18277	+ 892
2.M	6375	5590	6549	− 174
3.I	2807	2477	2902	− 95
4.R	14890	13242	15513	−623
5.P	43241	36910	43241	−
1973–74				
1.A	25879	16805	23382	+ 2497
2.M	7572	5861	8155	− 583
3.I	2930	2324	3234	−304
4.R	17391	13656	19001	− 1610
5.P	53772	38646	53772	−
1974–75				
1.A	27998	16445	26609	+ 1389
2.M	9867	6004	9715	+ 152
3.I	3366	2319	3752	− 386
4.R	21738	14148	22893	− 1155
5.P	62969	38916	62696	−
1975–76				
1.A	26700	18517	28663	− 1963
2.M	10396	6150	9520	+ 876
3.I	4276	2698	4176	+ 100

44

Sector	GDP at current prices	GDP at constant (1970–71 = 100 prices)	GDP as would be at constant price-parity level	Inter-sectoral transfer of funds (+) or (–)
(1)	(2)	(3)	(4)	(5)
4.R	24621	15268	23634	+ 987
5.P	65993	42633	65993	–
1976–77				
1.A	27575	17468	28926	– 1351
2.M	11602	6731	11146	+ 456
3.I	5182	3021	5003	+ 179
4.R	27257	16028	26541	+ 716
5.P	71616	43243	71616	–
1977–78				
1.A	31326	19467	33329	– 2003
2.M	12933	7167	12271	+ 662
3.I	5710	3209	5494	+ 216
4.R	30071	16907	28946	+ 1125
5.P	30040	46750	30040	–
Total 1971–72 to 1977–78				
1.A	176027	120964	176718	–691
2.M	64494	42870	63003	+ 1491
3.I	26869	18473	27113	– 244
4.R	149504	102109	150060	–556
5.P	416894	284416	416894	–

have some influence in the performance pattern, but this shows a brighter outlook for the manufacturing sector. The wholesale price index (base 1970–71) for the manufacturing sector stood at 175 in 1976–77 against that of 167 of the primary sector (including agriculture). The wholesale price index changed again in favour of the primary sector in 1977–78 when it stood at 184 against that of the manufacturing sector's 179. The agricultural sector contributed inter-sectoral transfer of Rs 691 crores during 1971–72 to 1977–78. The negative result reflected diversion of resources from agriculture, though it is very difficult for want of statistics to quantify the funds which have been syphoned out. It is likely that huge funds were simply locked up or engaged in speculative activities or squandered away in conspicuous consumption. We can only infer this from the fact that productive investment has been lagging despite the fact that the industrial sector has been the beneficiary of inter-sectoral parity changes. This is particularly reflected in the low growth rate of the economy and the lopsided development.

To give a general idea of the more recent situation in regard to inter-sectoral flow of funds certain estimates have been compiled and presented in Exhibit IV. This covers the period 1975–76 to 1980–81. For limited purposes the data of GDP at current and constant prices (1970–71) have been compiled from the quick

EXHIBIT IV

Inter-sectoral Flow of Funds on the Assumption of Constant Price Parity Level (1975–76 to 1980–81).

A-Agriculture   I-Other Industries

M-Manufacturing   R-Other Sectors

P-Total GDP

Sector	GDP at current prices	GDP at constant (1970-71 = 100 prices)	GDP as would be at constant price-parity level	Inter-sectoral transfer of funds (+) or (–)
(1)	(2)	(3)	(4)	(5)
1975–76				
1.A	26700	18517	28663	–1963
2.M	10396	6150	9520	+ 876
3.I	4276	2698	4176	+ 100
4.R	24621	15268	23634	+ 987
5.P	65993	42633	65993	–
1976–77				
1.A	27575	17458	28926	–1351
2.M	11602	6731	11146	+ 456
3.I	5182	3021	5003	+ 179
4.R	27257	16028	26541	+ 716
5.P	71616	43248	71616	–
1977–78				
1.A	31326	19467	33329	–2003
2.M	12933	7167	12271	+ 662
3.I	5710	3209	5494	+ 216
4.R	30071	16907	28946	+1125
5.P	80040	46750	80040	–

Sector	GDP at current prices	GDP at constant (1970-71 = 100 prices)	GDP as would be at constant price- parity level	Inter-sectoral transfer of funds (+) or (−)
(1)	(2)	(3)	(4)	(5)
1978–79 (E)				
1.A	35634	20372	37851	−2217
2.M	14518	7356	13668	+ 859
3.I	6291	3274	6083	+ 208
4.R	34068	17712	32909	+ 1159
5.P	90511	48714	90511	−
1979–80 (E)				
1.A	40333	19761	42842	−2509
2.M	16432	7135	15469	+ 963
3.I	7120	3175	6884	+ 236
4.R	38560	17182	37250	+ 1310
5.P	102445	47253	102445	−
1980–81 (E)				
1.A	48639	20749	51665	−3026
2.M	19816	7492	18655	+ 1161
3.I	8586	3334	8302	+ 284
4.R	46503	18041	44922	+ 1581
5.P	123544	49616	123544	−
Total 1975–76 to 1980–81				
1.A	210207	115334	223276	−13069
2.M	85697	42031	80729	+4968
3.I	37165	18711	35942	+1223
4.R	201080	101138	194202	+ 6878
5.P	534149	278214	534149	−

Note (E) = estimated.

estimates regarding the growth rates. Accordingly the GDP at constant prices is taken as having grown by 4.2 per cent for 1979–80 and having declined by 3 per cent and grown by 5 per cent in 1980–81. With the help of these growth rates, the GDP has been estimated at constant prices and inflated by the wholesale price index to get an idea of the GDP at current prices.

What is significant here is that the change in the inter-sectoral price parity has been heavily to the disadvantage of agriculture, particularly since 1975–76. Table B sets out the inter-sectoral

---

TABLE B

SECTORS	INTER-SECTORAL TRANSFERS (In Rs. Crores)
Agriculture	−13069
Manufacturing	+4968
Other industries	+1223
Other sectors	+6878

---

transfers. One can notice that the manufacturing sector has gained at the expense of the agricultural sector by almost Rs 5000 crores during the five year period. Sectoral classification does have some influence in the transformation pattern. But one can clearly notice that while the industrial sector has gained in terms of inter-sectoral flows the tangible benefit to the economy has been relatively negligible. The wholesale price index (base: 1970–71, April–March) for the manufacturing sector stood at 215 in 1979–80 against that of 206 of the primary sector (including agriculture). But in 1980–81, the wholesale price index changed again in favour of the manufacturing sector, when it stood at 253.3 against that of the primary sector's (including agriculture) 227.1. The total inter-sectoral transfer from agriculture was as much as Rs. 13069 crores during 1975–76 to 1980–81. One point that emerges is that the outlook for agricultural developments has clearly deteriorated in contrast to that for industry and other sectors which are gaining inter-sectoral flows at the expense of agriculture.

In 1979–80 the wholesale price index for manufactured products increased by as much as 25.7 per cent over 1975–76 while for food articles the price increase was only 13.4 per cent. In 1980–81 the index for manufactured products went up by 48.1 per cent, but for agricultural and other primary products the index increased by only 36.8 per cent.

The foregoing analysis suggests that the structural crisis and inter-sectoral disparity provide an objective situation for the farmer's stir. It would be idle to pretend that this ferment can be contained by a fine mixture of force and platitudes. Indeed if the situation is allowed to drift there is a real danger of a grave crisis adding yet another dimension to the acute social and economic distress. Farmers are the fulcrum of this economy and almost every major crisis in India can be traced to a crisis in the agricultural sector. The greatest challenge facing the sector, nay the economy, is the gigantic problem of rural poverty and landlessness. Even the urban poor are but an overflow of the rural poor.

Unfortunately, the problem of agrarian reform has never been viewed in this broader perspective. Empty rhetorics about lower land ceilings, tenancy protection, fair prices and wage protection have left the peasants much as before, poor, miserable and at the mercy of semi-feudal or more modern exploitive systems. Nasik is a warning. If peasants managed to organise and articulate their grievances and demands on a national scale, with Nasik as a model, the consequences can be frightening. The revolutionary potential of poverty and landlessness must be recognised as a major factor in planning and policy making today.

The demand for remunerative prices is real. It implies sharing gains in the current situation—if the uptrend in foodgrain prices of the Sixties was a corrective to earlier depression. A system has got to be evolved which seeks to maintain inter-sectoral price parity and this must be backed by procurement operations. An ideal balance may be difficult to strike in the present chaotic situation, but various price decisions must at least have some internal consistency, and diversion of acreage by price manipulation must end. We have perhaps reached a stage where crop planning under proper direction has got to be an integral part of development strategy. If this is so, it should not be difficult to evolve a system wherein procurement and pricing are rational and do not discriminate between major corps. Sugarcane and pulses would then be seen as equally important as cereals and as inter-related crops.

Note

The complete bibliographic information for this article is as follows:
D. K. Rangnekar, 'Farmer's Stir–II: Changes in Inter-sectoral Price Parity', *Business Standard*, 28 November 1980.

7

Will the Rains Fill Our Bowls?*

We had a record production of 108.42 million tonnes of food grains in 1970–71. But last year a severe drought blighted our hopes—we produced a mere 95.2 million tonnes. This is tragic because, in the last five years, we have added another 55 million mouths to our population.

What has gone wrong with our food policy?

Reminders of abject poverty and human misery keep popping up every time there is a major crop failure. When hunger and malnutrition stalk the land, the consequences of a crop failure and rising prices can be disastrous. Not surprisingly, millions of people reeling under the pressure of accumulated distress are now less forgiving than before. No fatalism for them either. They squarely blame the Government for their current plight. The monsoon did fail in 1972–73 over a wide area and so did the crops. But there was nothing unusual about bad monsoon; it happened every few years in some part of the country or the other. Even in the sixties, there was a famine in Bihar and a drought in UP, followed by the devaluation of the rupee and recession in the engineering of the rupee and recession in the engineering industry. Yet the season of human misery was neither so acute, nor so prolonged.

The present crisis is indeed a crisis of frustrated expectations, of patience wearing thin, where millions have waited for years for a better deal and better food.

In our country, where so many areas are as often parched as not and where crop failures are an unfortunate feature of a long

* Article first published in *The Illustrated Weekly of India*.

history, people justifiably expect national policy to build on experience, anticipate a setback and ensure efficient management of the food economy. Unfortunately, food management in India has been less than efficient. If a good monsoon breeds undue optimism, a crop failure leads to despair. Both display non-empiricism which characterizes much of what is called economic policy-making in the country.

If food procurement and import planning went haywire, it was largely because the Government was excessively jubilant about its own emergency food programme and overanxious to broadcast to the world non-existent food self-sufficiency. The small point that was missed was that the Indian economy was too vulnerable and far too easily tipped into a crisis.

One good agricultural season and we had the Food Minister and his Deputy tom-tomming to the world the dawn of an era of plenty. As stocks got eroded, they were mumbling something about the possibility of arranging for marginal imports. The concept of marginal imports had, however, an entirely different meaning in the Food Ministry. It was as vague a concept as the Ministry's own notions of the food crop, market supply, buffer stocks, etc. While the Minister and his Deputy were toying with food statistics and taking an unduly long time to do their sums, we saw how, in 1973 the Soviet Union, Japan China, Latin America and other African nations were clearing the world foodgrain markets of available surpluses.

Consequently, the magnitude of domestic shortages increased as time passed, and so did the cost of imports as work prices started rocketing under the pressure of massive advance purchases by shrewd nations working to a time-table and a well-calculated policy.

In this context, droughts or floods in some areas meant groaning bellies in most parts of the country because, even without such a calamity, 50 per cent of the population knows not the difference between starvation and malnutrition. This is what happened in 1972–73 and may happen again, because of the lingering illusions of the alleged "green revolution" and the reluctance to tap world food markets for fear of advertising an unsolved problem of a hoary past.

In 1972–73, famine did not exist on the Government's parched paper but, from Bombay to Ahmednagar and from Calicut to

51

Surendranagar, hungry peasants joined a slow march to death. Even today hundreds of thousands of peasants have willy-nilly to turn beggars because they have lost their land and their wages are too low and erratic to cope with rising prices and food shortages. Such grim facts are frightening and cast a gloom over the faces of the hopeful and the young.

Since food and agriculture constitute the pivot of Indian social and economic life, a setback in this sector spells danger to our industrial economy and political stability. With all the industrial and technological advances behind us, a little less than one-half of the national output still originates in this sector.

Snowball Effect

The "average" Indian household spends 65–70 percent of its income on food and farm-based manufactures (as compared to, say, 20 per cent in advanced societies like that of the US). A setback in the farm sector is thus radiated to urban industry and, with the snowball effect, supplies, prices and social cohesion all come under pressure.

Erratic purchases of food abroad and ill-conceived and haphazard procurement and distribution policies at home have caused a drain on India's foreign exchange reserves and also inflicted a heavy pressure on the very delicate domestic demand supply balance. Thus, for example, while the general index of prices increased by 13 per cent between July 1972 and June 1973, the largest increase was noticeable in the case of agricultural products-food articles by over 24 per cent and raw materials by 60 per cent. And within these categories, there have been phenomenal prices increases ranging from 23 per cent to 113 per cent in a period of 12 months in widely consumed food articles like jowar, bajra, pulses edible oils, etc. In the case of industrial products also, some of the major price increases originated in agriculture-based industries.

What has gone wrong with our food policy? First, let us look at the production trends. After a remarkable increase in foodgrain production from 95 million tonnes in 1967–68 and 99 million tonnes in 1968–69 to 108.42 million tonnes in 1970–71, foodgrain production slumped to 105.17 million tonnes in 1971–72 and back to 95.20 million tonnes in 1972–73.

Meanwhile, over the last five years, we have probably added between 55 and 60 million additional mouths to our population. This meant a slidedown in availability of food to a growing population. The crash programme costing Rs 250 crores (emergency agricultural production programmes), launched in order to make good the losses of 1972 and produce an extra 15 million tonnes of food grains, all but crashed: the results add up to less than 40 per cent of the expectation.

New Delhi was either unconcerned or undaunted. It pitched the target for 1973–74 at 115 million tonnes—a rise of more than 21 per cent over the dismal crop out-turn of 1972–73. At the time of writing this, we had only conflicting appraisals. Even so, like Alice, we appeared to be doing all the running to stay practically in the same place.

Failure of Procurement

As against the target of 115 million tonnes, The Economic Survey presented to Parliament earlier this year forecast an out-turn of 110 million tonnes, qualified by several "ifs" and "buts". The Agricultural Prices Commission, in its latest report, was hesitant and suggested that the production in 1973–74 might not be much more than the level touched in 1970–71 perhaps slightly less than 107 million tonnes. In the prevailing inflationary conditions and with shifts of income in favour of rich farmers, there has been an increasing tendency to hoard stocks.

This tendency and the bungling of the Food Corporation of India have combined to make Government's procurement policy ineffective in recent years. In spite of the fact that weather conditions for Rabi wheat sowing were good in 1973–74, food procurement, as at the end of July 1974, was a mere 1.7 million tonnes, as against the target of 6 million tonnes and an achievement of 4.3 million tonnes at the same time last year (when crop conditions were poor), 5 million tonnes in 1971–72 and 5.1 million tonnes in 1970–71. Failure here is bound to have a telling impact in 1974–75, unless lags in procurement are more than made good by imports.

Market arrivals have declined by over 50 percent in the last three years. The fall in arrivals is common to almost all varieties of cereals, though perhaps more pronounced in the case of rice and wheat.

Undeterred by poor market arrivals, widespread hoarding and other adverse factors, the Food Ministry is reportedly planning for a harvest target of 118 million tonnes–69 million tonnes of Kharif crop now underway and 49 million tonnes of Rabi season to come. Such targets have no relationship to the laws of probability. And recent experience shows that there is perhaps an in-built element of non-fulfilment in the ad hoc process of target fixation.

With the recent increases in India's petroleum bill—which is projected to reach $1.2 to $1.4 billion by the end of this year, according to the World Bank staff estimates—a proportionately large amount of export earnings will have to go to foot this oil bill.

Such an increase can come about only at the expense of other equally essential imports like fertilizers, for example. Reductions here can severely hit food production in the country. And the signs are already there.

In Punjab, farmers are joining together to protest against restrictions on the use of fuel for irrigation pumps and tractors and against irregular and meagre supply of fertilizers. Not so long ago, the same farmers were being induced—because of electricity shortages and poor harvests—to switch to fuel and fertilizers. These are some 2.5 to 3 million operating pumps in the State which are now facing an "oil squeeze".

Even without this "squeeze", the new Kharif season of 1974–75 has got off to an ominous start. If in June the monsoon god was playing hide and seek, by mid-July and August the rains were coming down with overpowering generosity. Thus, if earlier sowing and transplanting were delayed by a prolonged dry spell or insufficient precipitation and distribution of rainfall, in July–August floods were ravaging tender seedlings in many parts of the country and killing them altogether in other parts. The Kharif outlook was fair to good in Maharashtra, UP and Tamil Nadu and parts of West Bengal. Before the August floods, it was promising even in Bihar, Assam, Kerala, Karnataka, Orissa and Madhya Pradesh. In Punjab and Haryana, which are expected to produce and contribute 1.45 million tonnes of rice to the Centre's pool, the harvest outlook was affected partly by delayed rains but mainly by inadequacy of inputs.

At this early stage of the agricultural season of 1974–75, it would be hazardous to forecast the outlook for the food economy. But indications are not at all promising. The food situation is certainly more grim than the Food and Agriculture Minister would care to admit. For one thing, the Kharif crop 1974–75 is bedeviled by bad weather and an acute shortage of inputs. The supply of high-yielding varieties of seed is 50 per cent of the estimated demand. This means the anticipated production of 69 million tonnes may not materialise.

Adulteration of Seeds

As regards the Rabi crop, the original target was 39 million tonnes; but here too we come up against ill forebodings. On account of power shortage, irrigation is affected. To cope with the power cuts, farmers had purchased diesel sets but, because of the haphazard policy in the matter of supply of diesel, even these sets may remain idle for most of the time. Last season the supply of diesel oil to Punjab did not touch the promised figure of 2,500 kilolitres.

Punjab has been one of the pioneers in mechanized farming but shortage of power and diesel has crippled farming operations. Besides, the farmer has also to face another handicap in the erratic arrival of fertilizers. Punjab's total fertilizer requirement during the year is estimated at 9.23 lakh tonnes. Against this, only about 6 lakh tonnes were made available by the end of the February.

Considering that the foreign reserve position is pretty tight, it is unlikely that, in the Rabi season 1974–75, prospects of fertilizer supply will improve unless of course, at the wave of a magic wand the domestic fertilizer industry starts booming in the intervening months. Because of acute shortage, fertilizers are now freely adulterated with granulated mud. Even seed is now pushed into the market as ordinary grain and vice versa. Adulteration is more wide-spread in the case of hybrid seeds. The National Seed Corporation, which was the principal agency in charge of foundation seeds, particularly self-pollinated crops like wheat and paddy,

55

has failed to deliver the goods. And even today, areas under HYV programme are lagging behind targets.

All these have ominous portents of another food crisis in the making. The Food Ministry's expectation of 118 million tonnes for 1974–75 may have to be drastically marked down. At the time of writing, the forecast seemed nearer 108 million tonnes. In view of floods and drought and the acute shortage and high prices of basic inputs, we would be lucky if the total food crop for 1974–75 was eventually in the region of 100 million tonnes. The target for Rabi wheat has already been marked down from 39 million tonnes to 30 million tonnes. Because the agricultural outlook continues to change with the fleeting clouds, food management has to balance considerations of procurement with imperatives of maintaining an efficient public distribution system. Since demand for foodgrains is highly inelastic, even a minor shortfall in production can make prices extremely volatile.

Marketed surplus forms only a small proportion of the total output of foodgrains and so a small decline in food grain production could be disproportionately magnified in the market arrivals and prices.

A feature of agricultural production trends, which has not received sufficient attention is the decline in the trends rates in spite of the alleged (or is it because of the aborted?) "green revolution". Our agricultural production in the decade and half, 1949–50 to 1964–65, was growing at a compound rate of nearly 3.2 per cent per annum. If performance of the aggregate agricultural economy was somewhat better in certain years—like 1966–67 and 1968–69—there was nothing extraordinary about it. But we were mesmerized by itinerant advisers and lost no time to proclaim the success of our green revolution.

Premature Praise

Men like Wolf Ladejivsky went about telling the world in 1970 that "Indian political and economic problems are currently as numerous and grave as usual, but for once food shortages do not claim the headlines". Ladejivsky spoke in praise of the "green revolution" too soon. The average annual increase in agricultural production as a whole dropped to 1 per cent between 1969–70 and 1972–73, and in the case of foodgrains to 0.9 per cent.

Even taking a long term view one would realize that the average annual increase between 1951–52 and 1972–73 worked out at 3.1 per cent for foodgrains and 2.5 per cent for non-foodgrains. But between 1961–62 and 1972–73, the average rates were as low as 1.6 per cent for all crops, 1.9 per cent for food crops and 1.3 per cent for non-foodgrains. The dismal conclusion is that the rate of growth of output has dropped in the last ten years in spite of the "green" schemes to promote higher yields.

Though the rate of growth of output has risen since the mid-sixties recent trends are disquieting. In 1972–73, there was a decline of 5.6 per cent; even more disturbing is the steady and at times sharp decline in the production of rice, jowar, bajra, pulses and other coarse cereals and the difficulty in extending cropped area. Area under grain cultivation dwindled from 124 million hectares in 1969–71 to 122 million hectares in 1971–72.

Thus, while food grain harvests in general have been on the decline in recent years, population has been swelling. Consequently, net availability of food has declined. Net availability of foodgrains per head of population is only 418 grams per day as compared with 469 to 480 grams in the early sixties. Availability of pulses is as low as 39.6 grams as compared with 69–70 grams ten to fifteen years ago.

The Revolution That Failed

The sad plight of tens of millions of peasants hit by near-famine conditions in several parts of India were evidence enough of the fact (a) that the "green revolution" had turned grey even before it had matured and (b) that our food policy had no sense of direction and no clearly defined aims. The "green revolution" was sought to be superimposed on a traditional society in Aladdin style. It was doomed to fail clearly or indirectly by spreading social tension, conflict of interest etc. The capital intensive technology supplanted in a labour-surplus economy called for an integrated approach to planning which was absent. Such an approach would have ensured that industry and other developments absorbed surplus labour provided the required inputs mobilised rural resources and built an imaginative food organization to procure store and distribute grains in order to ensure that the benefits of plan policy and the pricing system were conferred on the peasants and consumers.

Land reform has been half-hearted and cultivators in many cases have been converted into crop-sharers or landless labourers, according to a report of the Planning Commission. In UP, for example "crop sharing" is equivalent to personal cultivation. Rack-renting is widespread. Tenants or crop-sharers remain hopelessly unprotected. The large-scale eviction of tenants in Punjab and Andhra Pradesh brings out the insecurity of (tenant) cultivators and the poor approach to tenancy rights and tenurial conditions in most States. In recent years, tenant insecurity has probably increased. In contrast in three or four states, tenants did extract some legislative benefits but the beneficiaries were rich farmers.

Rich farmers became more rich, the rich became rich and the poor remain poor or destitute, following the income prioritisation brought about by the so called "green revolution". Increased inequalities probably constituted one factor which made the new strategy of production counter-productive. These results are brought out clearly by studies coming out of Punjab.

The "green revolution" had also pressed too heavily on resources. There is an indiscriminate use of chemical fertilizers, for example—rising from 14–17 per cent year in the fifties to 24–27 per cent in the sixties. To meet this demand, India will have to import 3.2 million tonnes to cover the shortfall in domestic output. India simply cannot afford this order this order of import in the context of the current crisis. And our people are blissfully unaware also of the fact that, in some countries like the US, use of chemical fertilizers and pesticides is strictly restricted for environment and other reasons.

Though lower agricultural production in many States may be attributes to shortage of power (whish hit tube-wells), shortage of fertilizers and fuel oils, the failure to increase adequately irrigated area has also frustrated many production plans. Thus, against the target of 4.80 million hectares to be brought under major and medium irrigation schemes, achievement was only 3.3 million hectares. Agricultural development in the Fourth Plan was particularly dependent on increasing production through the high-yielding varieties programme for major cereals and the multiple-cropping programme. Expect in the case of wheat, the high-yielding varieties programme did not click due to non-development of proper technology. Also, the major Plan strategy involving the mass rural population in agricultural production did not make much headway.

In a Shambles

Today, the "green revolution" is in a shambles. Even the success of HYV wheat is to be questioned: yields are declining. This distressing phenomenon is being underplayed. With all the inputs, yields of wheat have declined by 15–25 per cent in various production centres.

What does one say of policy-making which announces takeover of the wheat trade in the midst of a bad crop year and after much tub-thumping and after speculators have cleared floating stocks and gone underground? Under political pressure, the policy was reversed and trade was freed. The new policy provides for a levy system (50 per cent) and implied dual pricing—Rs. 105 per quintal for Government levy and Rs. 150 per quintal for market sale. This policy has also failed. Levy purchases are a small fraction of what was expected.

Also, there is a widespread disparity in the prices realized by actual food producers and paid by consumers. The gap is indeed so wide that there is an incentive for surreptitious deals. The counter-inflationary measures adopted by Government smack of moth-eaten textbooks and ignore the fact that there are structural imbalances including a genuine shortage of food supply. Mrs Gandhi, who is obviously concerned at the grim situation has felt let down by the food trade which pressed for denationalization. However, we cannot ignore, nor can we forget, that the Government's own fiscal and credit policies have made it difficult for food-deficit states to lift their grains quotas from surplus states.

The Government has failed also to ensure the flow of domestic supplies on an uninterrupted basis. The dual pricing system, for example, has turned out to be an instrument for manipulation of prices and what was intended to be a ceiling on the sale price of wheat in the open market has today become the floor. Action against hoarders has been of token nature and has come too late. New Inter-State restrictions have created little islands of plenty and large areas of poverty and artificial shortages. Indeed the desultory trends mock at what remains of Government's food policy.

Unable to skimp further on oil and other inputs, now cut to the bone, the Government is looking for immediate and short term imports as a cushion against disruption of the public distribution system which could lead to grave political disorders. The public distribution system is intended to ensure immediate foodgrain requirements to low-income groups. It has been estimated that such a system ought to mobilise at least 20 per cent of the total consumption of foodgrain in the country. Yet food statistics show that, expect for one or two years, until 1965 public distribution did not have more than 3 to 5 million tonnes to distribute, which was just about 7 per cent or so of India's total output of foodgrains. Even recently, with the increases in flow of supply through the public distribution system, the Government commands barely a little more than 10 per cent of output and relies very largely on imports to reach this quantum.

It is difficult at this stage to estimate what would be the size of public distribution in 1974–75 because the full impact of the new situation and the season is still, to be felt. However, in view of the heavy depletion of buffer stocks in the last two drought years and the shortfall in output of foodgrains in the last three years, there is no doubt about the need to sustain large-scale imports of foodgrain to maintain the public distribution system. The Government needs to build a minimum stock as a safeguard against artificial scarcities or drought and severe crop failures in any part of the country.

The total quantity of food imported during 1972 and 1973 was of the order of 4.1 million tonnes on commercial basis over and above the 2 million tonnes loaned by the Soviet Union. The commercial purchases were made from Argentina, Canada and the United States. Plans for the current year indicate authorization of import of about 3 million tonnes. But the Government will certainly have to review this position in view of the disappointing reports from Kharif States and input shortages which are likely to mar Rabi expectations. Import of food grains on concessional terms has been discontinued after 1971. In view of the pressure on balance of payment, the Government may have to explore the possibility of getting food on long term credits. So far we have received a Canadian aid offer of food valued at 25 million dollars and a token aid of 30,000 tonnes from the UK.

Current indications are that the shortfall in 1974–75 may be about 7 to 9 million tonnes. And this may be the order of imports that Government may have to negotiate for on an annual basis for three to five years if we are to come to terms with the climate of scarcity and refashion the strategy of agricultural revolution.

Note

The complete bibliographic information for this article is as follows:
D. K. Rangnekar, 'Will the Rains Fill Our Bowls?', *The Illustrated Weekly of India* (8 August 1974): 8–15.

Part Two

Dependencies' Independence—
The International Context
to India's Experiment

8

Economic Co-operation*

When, in February 1955, the Nehru Government decided to accept the Soviet offer of aid for the construction of a steel mill at Bhilai, many people abroad reacted with a predictable sense of shock. Until then, the West had been the only source of technological and financial aid to this part of the world for historical and other reasons. The West had complacently presumed that India would be content to let the country's international relationships stay that way, but Nehru had different ideas. When the Soviet Union evolved its own aid programme, he took the first opportunity to lend a new dimension to Indian planning and development policies.

Nehru's intentions were misunderstood, so was his 'new fangled non-alignment.' The west, in fact, misinterpreted the link with the Soviet Union as a naïve promotion of the expansionist aims of international communism. Leading newspapers in London, New York and Bonn warned India of dire consequences. Some of them even said that the Bhilai deal was the beginning of the end of democracy, freedom, and all that went with the Indian way of life. Nehru was, however, undeterred. Indo-Soviet economic co-operation has come a long way since the Bhilai deal and the Indian way of life is none the worse for it.

Nehru actually took a pragmatic view of Soviet aid. He had no illusions about the ideological clash in the world, and the rival quest for political supremacy, but he did not regard the Soviet Union as the menace that it was held to be by western political

* Article first published in *Seminar*, issue no. 73, 1965.

strategists. To him the issue of the age was the end of imperialism and mass poverty, not the advance of communism. The Soviet Union was, therefore, regarded as a countervailing force in a world which was otherwise dominated by imperialists, ex-imperialists and neo-colonialists. The availability of a new source of trade, aid and technology provided a new and unforeseen balancing factor in the international economy.

The Question

Yet, the moot question is: has India made the most of its open opportunities? First, let us look at Indo-Soviet trade, which is supposed to be the backbone of our economic alliance with the Russians. The percentages are impressive, but how is the trade actually faring? Three factors in the trade developments are particularly important in this context. First, contrary to the general impression, Indo-Soviet trade has remained more or less stagnant in recent years. During the celebrations of the decade of Indo-Soviet co-operation recently, it was claimed that trade between the two countries had grown a hundred times between 1953 and 1963 to reach the total of Rs. 107 crores.

But this was only nominally true. The rate of growth of trade was highly exaggerated by the adoption of a base year with non-existent links. Before the first trade agreement was signed in December 1953, the flow of goods was really negligible. It was worth as little as Rs. 81 lakhs both ways during the whole of 1953. The volume of exchange increased only after the aid and trade agreements. But what is noteworthy is that, after the initial spurt (during 1956–58), the level of trade perceptibly declined. Only since 1964–65 were there signs of recovery and growth.

Secondly, the flow of trade has not kept pace with the growth in India's exports and, more particularly, with the phenomenal rise in the Soviet Union's foreign trade in the last five years. The Soviet Union is supposed to rank third or fourth in the list of India's trading partners, but the gap which separates this country from other prominent suppliers and buyers is far too large to make the glorified new position meaningful. For example, India's sales to the Soviet Union in 1963 formed about 6 per cent of India's total exports, but the sales to Britain formed 22 per cent and to the United States 16 per cent.

What is even more discouraging is that, in the Soviet Union's growing volume of foreign trade, India's share has been dwindling, something which is lost in the sea of wishful thinking in Delhi. The Soviet Union's exports shot up from an estimated 4,298 million dollars in 1958 to 7,272 million dollars in 1963, but India's share during the period fell from over 3 per cent to 1.6 per cent. Similarly, global imports into the Soviet Union soared from an estimated 4,350 million dollars to 7,059 million dollars during these years, but India's share languished at 1 percent in 1958 and 1.4 per cent in 1963.*

Adverse Balance

A third factor of importance is the failure to strike a balance in the exchange which has persistently been adverse to India. Bilateral balancing of trade is supposed to be a major element in the new commercial arrangement but, until 1958, India had to settle its trade deficits in convertible currency, and since then (under the second five-year pact signed in November 1958) in nonconvertible rupees. The large deficits reflected, in part, the accelerated supplies of Soviet aided equipment for industrial projects notably Bhilai: but they also brought out India's inability to cover its liabilities by releasing surpluses and stepping up its own exports. Last year (1964) was probably the first in the history of Indo-Soviet trade to yield a positive surplus based on a fairly high level of sales on both sides. The only other favourable balance struck was in 1960, but it had only negative significance being largely due to a sharp decline in Soviet deliveries.

In the case of aid also, the general impression seems to be one of a gushing flow of roubles year after year. Yet, the actual position is somewhat different. Offers of aid came streaming in after

---

* Soviet Trade figures from United Nations *Economic Bulletin for Europe*, September 1964.

the Bhilai deal, but the flow soon became a trickle: of the six aid agreements, five came between February 1955 and September 1959. Only one new aid agreement was signed in the following five years. Does this then mean that the Russians and the Indians have tired of finding deeper roots of collaboration? Or have they discovered, from experience, that there is no sound basis for such collaboration?

The Pause

Here, too, one is apt to be misled by the pace of formal agreements. It is true that, in the first flush of excitement sparked off by the Bhilai deal, both sides went all out to transform the thrill of a new link into a new pattern of mutually beneficial industrial relationship. It is also true that, once the initial enthusiasm wore off, there came a long period of pause. But it was only a pause, not a complete break. For, the Soviet Union came out with big offers of trade and aid in 1964–65, not the least spectacular of which was the credit of Rs. 100.5 crores for the construction of the Bokaro steel mill.

The pause was of no material consequence. We had not found it possible to make full use of the volume of assistance offered for the second and third plan periods. The bulk of Soviet aid was in the form of export credits and, under the six aid agreements mentioned, we had received credits totalling Rs. 384 crores for use during the second and third plans, (In addition there had been some outright grants also, totalling perhaps about Rs. 10 million or so). But of the third plan credits worth over Rs. 238 crores authorised before the commencement of the plan something like Rs. 212 crores had been lying unutilised even in the third year of the plan.*

By mid-1965, which marks the fag end of the third plan, total orders had been placed probably to the tune of about Rs. 300 crores.

---

* *External Assistance* 1963, Ministry of Finance, New Delhi, August 1964.

But this still left unused a fairly large part of the credits authorised during 1966–62, not to mention the new line of credit for Bokaro. The Russians did not consider even placement of orders as utilisation; to them what mattered was the actual drawing of the amounts which, of course, was related to fulfilment of orders.

Yet, the fact remains that the expectations of rapidly developing Indo-Soviet collaboration generated at the time of the Bhilai deal have not, so far, been realized. True, the aid levels have gone up, and so have exports and imports. Since aid and trade are inter-twined in the concept of economic collaboration between the two countries, the limits to the one are, in a sense, set by the other. What we get by way of aid is largely determined by our own evaluation of Soviet association, by our trading preferences, by the speed with which aid is utilised and trade expanded, and, above all, by our willingness to base some of our plans on the use of Soviet equipment and technology. At the Soviet end the limits are set by Soviet resources, but more particularly by the value attached to the Indian links. The problems involved here are, therefore, not merely of economic significance, but they also concern respective attitudes, evaluation, preferences and policies.

Exploding the Myth

What really is the significance of the Soviet economic link to us and to our development aspirations? In an article like this the full ramifications cannot be discussed. But three important points may be made. First, Indo-Soviet industrial collaboration exploded the myth that there could never be any effective cooperation between an advanced country and a poorer one in the field of competitive technology. The older industrial powers nursed ideas of their technological superiority and regarded with horror the spread of new ideas in the East. They saw international trade as the swapping of goods manufactured by clever European and rich Americans with food and materials produced by Asians and Africans.

In order to perpetuate this traditional concept of division of labour, which they thought was vital to their economic prosperity and political supremacy, they perpetuated the myth that there could never be any effective tie-up between advanced economies and the backward areas for parallel economic advancement. The Soviet Union rejected these ideas and made India a test case. Bhilai was, in fact, the first major industrial project which undermined the traditional concepts and demonstrated the immense possibilities of international collaboration based on new patterns of trade, aid and development; while helping us in our industrial plans, the Soviet Union has also been taking an increasing volume of our newer lines of export. (For example, 40 per cent of Soviet purchases in India in 1963–64 comprised semi-processed and manufactured goods.)

Encouraging Independence

Secondly, Russian support encouraged India to pursue independent policies generally. Whatever the political motivation, the Soviet aid policies suited Indian interest at a time when the climate of opinion outside did not favour India's quest for planned development with State participation in industry. Soviet aid policies carried no stipulation regarding the economic and social policies to be followed by India. This was in striking contrast with the pre-conditions and other restrictions involved in some other aid arrangements. Had the Soviet Union kept aloof, it is questionable whether India would have been able to push through the type of developments it did over the last few years.

Until this alternative support was available India was totally at the mercy of traditionalists, who persistently refused to help the country in basic technological development plans. No western country was, for example, prepared to provide financial and technological aid for the government's oil exploration and petroleum development programme, or for the steel projects, or for the heavy engineering projects. In fact, the Bhilai deal was preceded by a long, frustrating search for western aid. It was only after Bhilai that some of the western countries started displaying interest in our steel, oil and other projects. It is significant that, even now, the government is under constant pressure to alter its

70

economic policies. The collapse of the negotiations for American aid for Bokaro is an instance in point.

The third important point about Soviet aid and trade is that the economic relationship imparted strength and meaning to India's non-aligned posture. There can be no doubt that Soviet economic aid and trade offers were politically motivated by the desire to keep India independent. The 40 aid projects, the offer to buy Indian manufactured goods, the rescue operations in steel, oil, machinery and other fields, the acceptance of relief payments in rupees—all these formed part of the Soviet policy to get closer to India and to keep it far away from rival political influences and military groupings which seemingly promised larger aid.

But these offers suited India's interests also. Under Nehru's leadership, India had already made its political choice, and the Soviet assistance became a pragmatic source of strength to reinforce India's determination to steer clear of rival blocs and adopt a positive posture in defence of peaceful co-existence and balanced world development.

Inhibitions

If, in spite of the deeper significance of Indo-Soviet economic relationship, trade and aid have remained well below their real potential, it is largely because some of our policy makers were too obsessed with the political overtones of Soviet strategy. They could not readily grasp the meaning and potentialities of rupee payment trade: they only knew of trade involving dollars and sterling. Moreover, since the novel concept of bilateral balancing of payments in Indian rupees was initially associated with Soviet transactions, those who had been liberally fed on theories of communist subversion were doubly suspicious. The hue and cry over the Bhilai deal in the western press and political circles intensified their prejudices. Even after Nehru had demonstrated the strength and resilience of Indian nationalism and expatiated on the larger value of the Soviet link, inhibitions still lingered in important quarters.

There was, as a result, no such thing as a positive pursuit of economic co-operation with the Soviet Union. There was only negative tolerance of whatever emerged from Nehru's ideas and initiatives. There is reason to believe that the acute foreign exchange crisis in the latter half of the second plan, and some of our more recent difficulties in the matter of trade, equipment and military supplies, might have been mitigated to some extent if we had been more open-minded uninhibited and more purposeful in our economic relationship with the Soviet Union, particularly in the earlier phases.

At the Russian end, also, there were signs of inhibition and ignorance, India was successively regarded, as a by-lane of the capitalist world, as an idealistic irritant, as a misguided visionary. It took the Russian leaders a long time to appreciate the significance of Nehru's aims, ideas, and policies. They were slow to realise the relevance of friendship and economic ties with this country. In fact, the Russians were not very keen about trade and aid developments in this area until Khruschev came on the scene.

Positive Meaning

In his goal of peaceful co-existence, India's non-alignment acquired a positive meaning and he saw the potentialities of Indo-Soviet economic collaboration in its proper perspective. The powerful impact made by the Bhilai project and the emergence of India as a forward looking force balancing between the two major blocs, brought home the value of the association and the potentialities of a peaceful economic contest in the world. But the brash propaganda advantages sought to be derived from every aspect of Indo-Soviet economic relationship seemed, at times, jarring in a country so intensely nationalistic as India.

There have also been some genuine institutional and other difficulties. India, for example, was originally unfamiliar with the technique of trading at governmental level while the Russians were awkward in a mixed economy. Subsequently, Indian suspicions were aroused by the barrage of western propaganda about the so-called 'political pricing' of products by Russian export organisations and it took our policy-makers some time to comprehend the socialist theory and mechanism of pricing and to realise that Russian pricing was actually advantageous to us over a significant part of our trade.* Paradoxically, with experience the Russians also seemed aggrieved by the restrictions placed on their freedom to buy in the open competitive market, following our government's decision to channelise all trade with the Soviet Union through the specially created State Trading Corporation.*

'Last Resort'

Another factor which seems to have created some misunderstanding is the unfortunate tendency in certain quarters in Delhi to treat the Soviet Union as the 'rescuer of last resort'. The impression seems to have been created that we approach the Soviet Union only when our western friends rebuff us. Whenever there is a major project on hand, or any important development, or defence scheme, involving external assistance, the tendency seems to be to entreat and cajole the West first and, only when there is a certainty of failure, to draw on Russian goodwill.

In the case of Bokaro, for example, the Soviet Union was sounded, but for a long time (almost two years) there was no follow up, because some people were waiting for the U.S. Government to make up its mind. A formal approach was made to the Russians only after the Americans backed out. Similarly, in the case of military aid, which has added a new dimension to India's economic relations with the Soviet Union. India has given the impression of waiting for the Americans without losing touch with the Russians.

Exaggeration

At the Russian end the pro-West tendencies in India are at times exaggerated. Wild inferences are drawn about policy changes from what may be only a temporary tactical move to obtain larger aid or to push through some critically important project. After

* See Rangnekar D.K., 'Trade with Russia Should Be Open to Private Sector', *The Economic Times*, November 1961.

Nehru's death, and the removal of Khrushchev, the old ties were snapped, and the successors in both countries are still to build a comparable bridge.

When one considers the future prospects, the first important point which ought to be realised is that the Soviet Union today is a great and a highly respected world power. There is no longer any stigma attached to Soviet association. President Kennedy openly lauded Soviet effort in India in the larger context of world order and peaceful co-existence.

Secondly, the Soviet economy is growing rapidly. The current rate of growth of national income is about 7 per cent per annum. Because of this and the consequent pressure of demand for light engineering goods and other types of consumer goods in the Soviet Union, I think that that country can be regarded as a highly promising market for our manufacturers for at least another 10 years to come. We have the capacity for this type of production and our capacity is rapidly growing.

In the Soviet Union—and even in the eastern bloc—this is precisely the type of capacity which is inadequately developed. We have already got a foothold and, from January 1965, the Soviet Union has abolished tariff levies on the exports of developing nations like India. Now it is only a question of expanding the volume, range and type of sales. No other single market in the world can offer us similar opportunities today or in the next decade. If we fail to capitalise on these opportunities now (when competition is negligible) the western countries will break in and expose us to a type of struggle (and a prospect of loss) we have not encountered so far.

Speed

The third important point is that, because of its complete control of foreign trade activities, the Soviet Government is in a position to offer us quick orders and take up our supplies with great speed and freedom. We have only to sell the idea of buying our increasing range of manufactures. Once the Russian Government decides that we are going to be their suppliers of a particular

74

range of products, nobody else can cut in, although the infusion of the traits of a market economy may pose new problems of publicity and salesmanship to hold the attention of the Soviet people. Our prospects may improve if we can link up our sales drive with a conscious effort to increase our purchase of Soviet machinery and equipment wherever feasible.

Thus, for example, we can arrange to obtain from the Soviet Union an aluminium plant of a production level of say 100,000 tons on the understanding that 50,000 tons or so of the production will be taken up by the Soviet Union. This is the type of manufacturing plant which is critically required in India today, and this is the type which the Soviet Union is in a position to supply readily. We can obtain such equipment without casting a burden on our grave payments position or even diverting traditional supplies of export products. Even if after a few years the Soviet Union may not want to continue buying 50,000 tons of this line of production, we would have developed enough industrial capacity in our own country to absorb all this and other similar output. One can think of many such projects which offer possibilities of mutually advantageous collaboration.

Even without such 'tied collaboration', there is distinct economic advantage in negotiating for a larger supply of Soviet plant and machinery for projects which are today languishing because of the dearth of free currency reserves and falling western aid. Soviet aid is cheap (interest rates are nominal per cent), repayment periods long enough, about 12 years, and the details are usually adopted to suit Indian needs. The rupee payment basis can impart strength to our export drive.

Fears

The fears expressed in certain quarters that such sharp increases in Indo-Soviet aid and trade might cause a major diversion of exports, depriving India of much needed free currency earnings, seems to me rather unrealistic, almost academic. If our free currency reserves are falling, it is not because of exports to Russia; rather it is because the free currency areas are not paying a fair

75

price for our exports. They are also not buying as much and as many types of products as we have to offer. In some cases, jute for example, Russian buying has in fact provided major support.

The limits to our capacity to earn foreign currencies today are set, not by the Russian deals, but by the protection policies, the tariffs, quotas, and other restrictive moves of the free currency countries. In any case, an increasing proportion of our trade with the Soviet Union is now in the range of non-traditional items, mainly light manufacture and consumer goods, which the western countries are most reluctant to take in appreciable quantities.

It is about time, also, we shed the notion that all Soviet purchases in India are politically inspired. Whatever the earlier motivation, Soviet trade today has a distinct economic content.* Of course, the Russians will snatch what political dividends they can from the sale of a steel plant to us, or the purchases of manufactures from us. But the compelling motive today is to satisfy their economy's insatiable needs. If these needs cannot be satisfied by buying at an attractive price, or ease, in India, the Russians will naturally turn to other suppliers or alternatives. In the process, we will only be left with our illusions of augmenting free currencies and regret at the one eager buyer that turned away.

The Dangers

The dangers are real. The Russians are already planning for a sharp increase in the output of jute and kenaf (a substitute) in Uzbekistan, of tea in Georgia and trans-caucasian republics, of cotton, wool, skins, synthetic leather and other products in different parts of the Union. Today there is little impetus for achieving self-sufficiency in some of these products, but the risk is that our inhibitions may provide the pressure. Alternatively, we will brighten the chances of our rivals in whatever field we have rivals. In the case of textiles, for example, the Chinese are about to enter the Soviet Union in a big way.

* See Pryor, Frederick, *The Communist Foreign Trade System*, London, 1963, pp. 183–184.

In the larger perspective of competitive developments, the appropriate thing for us to do is to plan for increased capacities precisely in those fields of production where export possibilities are great—and real, not imaginary. The problem of diversion of surpluses may come if, alongside the plans for increased collaboration with the Soviet Union, we also have to adjust policies for increased trade with other rupee payment countries. But this should be a challenge for new ideas. Perhaps we may consider the feasibility of bringing all rupee payment agreements into some sort of a multi-lateral payment system. This would make our rupee a partially convertible currency within the framework of our trade in this particular bloc.

Note

The complete bibliographic information for this article is as follows:
D. K. Rangnekar, 'Economic Co-operation', *Seminar*, issue no. 73 (1965): 32–36.

9

North–South Divide

An Economic Analysis*

Today, the world is poised on the edge of radical transformatiom of the existing economic and political relationships. Because of the widening gap between the rich developed North and the poor developing South, tensions and contradictions of the system as a whole have surfaced and are giving a new dimension to a struggle for restructing the world economy.

T he continuation of old economic laws and big power diplomacy in a world beset by political cross-currents poses a dilemma for the 20th century nation states. On the face of it, it looks as if the West is vulnerable to economic dislocation at a time of political uncertainties and shifting alliances in the developing world covering the vast span of Asia, Africa, Middle East, and Latin America. Yet, in the last 30 odd years, the division of wealth, trade and power has become even more uneven than in the past. Countries which have gained from industrialisation in the existing international economic order continue to become rich, while developing countries are denied the benefits of world development. Countries with greater degrees of specialisation and greater division of labour have become richer. Maldistribution of national resources, the rapid growth of population limited savings

First published in *Business Standard Annual*, 1981.

and capital, all these have introduced a disturbing imbalance in the world economy. Separate and unequal, the rich nations are becoming even richer and the poor poorer. Subject to conceptual limitation, one might point out that the world GNP which was in the region of US $8.5 trillion in 1978 was shared so unequally that the rich countries of the North with roughly about 25 per cent of the world's population had 80 per cent of the total GNP, while the South which accounts for 75 per cent of the world's population had only 20 per cent. Income per head thus averaged $6000 for the North and $500 for the South. Millions have less than $200 per year.

In the first decade after World War II, the so-called advanced countries recorded rapid economic growth and social change stimulated by assistance from the U.S. Industrial expansion and technological innovation brought unprecedented prosperity to the countries. The new nations born during the same period embarked bravely on ambitious programmes of growth and social change, but found the going very hard. The international monetary system, based wholly on the strength of the US dollar, ensured swift recovery from the impact of the war and provided remarkable stability to the currencies of the rich nations. There was promise of sharing the fruits of development with the poor and the less endowed and the accumulation process grew in a sustained way. But to the disenchantment of the newly developing countries, the benefits of the world economic development appeared more and more distant, and severe trade imbalances appeared. The trading system itself came under severe attack and so did the monetary system, both of which contributed to tensions of development which got aggravated as the global economy assumed a new character when the economic boom of the 1960s came to an end. While the global economy was staggering, inflation and recession spread beyond national borders and assumed world-wide proportions. Bad weather and poor harvests in the early 70s contributed to world grain shortage and depleted food reserves hitting particularly the food-shortage developing countries. The rich industrial nations found that many of their concepts and assumptions of perpetual growth, stability, and plentiful supply of energy and materials were subject to challenge. The club of Rome and limits to growth theories represent the aftermath.

79

The poor countries grew increasingly restive operating under an economic and social system that seemed to deny them opportunities for progress and change in relation to the advanced nations, and more and more began to question the international economic structure and doubt if it could at all meet the challenges of the day. Fundamentals inequities exist in the structure of economic relations specially trade. The rich western countries have over decades created an economic pattern in which the ex-colonial and non-western countries are largely dependent for foreign exchange earnings on the export of a small range of products and materials. Recently oil and minerals have come into prominence. One well documented study of the international structure suggests a 60–90 per cent dependence on three to five products in 25 out of 37 countries surveyed. South Vietnam earned 90 per cent from two products, rice and rubber. Venezuela 98 per cent from oil and iron ore. Four countries, Iran, Iraq, Libya oil and Mauritania, earned over 90 per cent of foreign exchange on the export of just one product iron ore. Though marginal progress has been made in export diversification in some countries, only the OPEC countries can be said to have achieved any significant improvement in bargaining power.

The new long term projection of contemporary world trends i.e. a prolongation of economic policy with respect to international specialisation upon which is based the division between developed and developing countries shows that the relevant and absolute distance between the two worlds can only widen as time passes. In a period of flourishing developments, any society scores certain growth rates which affect its various sectors of activity and which can be compared with each other. But conditions for transition in the so-called Third World countries today are not the same as those the advanced countries enjoyed at the time of their twin demographic and industrial revolution. The industrial revolution was preceded by an agricultural one which played a decisive role in launching the industrial revolution at the very outset. Agricultural progress freed workers for industrialisation, fed them, opened up market for industrial goods and sources of supply of raw materials without which the industrialisation of the West was unthinkable. Now this pattern of development did not evolve within a closed national framework, but rather within the framework of the progressive system of capital accumulation and colonialism. It also thrived on flexible international monetary system and a relatively free flow of trade and capital. This system was not a national system, but was a collection of discreet countries following the same path and policies. It was indeed a system in which all these, mostly rich countries, were linked together, had an overall structure with inter-related parts and a definite sense of direction.

The overall structure operates in terms of the centre–periphery relationship. At the centre is the superpower, the US, with the greatest concentration of income, wealth and military prowess, and around it are the secondary colonial powers and allies, such as UK, Germany, France, Japan and Netherlands. Perhaps the second circle includes smaller, but richer western countries. And beyond this is the periphery of the Third World countries. The structure is, therefore, clear with lines of authority and distinctions all operating like a pyramid of power and wealth, though the transition from one position to the other is neither natural nor necessary. The nature of social formations preceded the integration of the periphery into the world system and that formation and stages have determined the forms in which these countries have evolved their agrarian and industrial structure. The traditional ruling classes of the Third World societies are usually the political classes to which the poor and the peasant usually pay a tribute in one form or another. This type of social formation came close to classical feudalism when it was evolved. In these formations, structured around a powerful state apparatus, the most widespread form borrowed by peripheral agrarian capitalism is the latifundist system.

This basically typifies all the regions strongly integrated in the world market, but it has 'bitten' only marginally into the enormous Asian continent. The recent 'green revolution' in certain areas of Asia, including India, is nothing more than an extension of this centuries-long process of transforming ancient aristocracies into capital based agrarian latifundist enterprises. The growing pressure on the land, which is not only the main obstacle to accelerated agrarian capitalism, but also the origin of spreading (or pressure for) agrarian reforms leading to the liquidation of latifundist capitalism to the benefit of middle-size farming capitalism.

81

This revolution is patently giving the whiplash to agriculture progress, and it is the origin of various examples of contemporary 'green revolution'. The limits of the green revolution (i.e. of capitalist middle-size farming's development process) are consequently inscribed in the principal contradiction of the system.

Looking back from the perspective of the 80s, it is evident that some of the worst fears about the global economy have been unfounded in the sense that no nation has collapsed under the weight of the crisis, though the capital accumulation process did not proceed smoothly either within the countries operating the system or as between them. Contradictions surfaced in the form of short recession, unemployment, and other crisis. For the most part the reverberations are felt in the periphery namely the Third World countries. The centre and its allies are invariably bailed out through the world mechanism of money and the institutions, which recycle a large part of the wealth flowing through it. Even so, the fact remains that the overall rate of growth of industrial production have tended to decline and had, at one point, come down to zero in some cases with chain reactions. True, the US, by virtue of its power, enjoyed the maximum benefits of the existing system through the international monetary mechanism, capital movements and trade. After all, Bretton Wood's did recognise the dollar and gold interchangeable until recently. The US could, therefore, afford to run huge balance of payment deficits, distribute patronage and at the same time draw on world sources of supply almost at will.

As problem of liquidity came to the fore following currency crisis in the last 10 years and IMF came under pressure and its arrangement loosened up, world economic environment changed qualitatively. Trade and development faced new threats, and exchange rate management and manipulation became a major weapon of attack on the Third World. Leading currencies were allowed to find their national level based on interaction of market forces. This speculation and money movement which resulted in freeing currencies of international obligations earlier enforced by the IMF, spelt economic disruption and hardship to the developing countries. "Pessimism about the dollar and the administration's economic management had become so rampant that the nation was on the brink of", in the words of a New York banker, "a nineteenth-century kind of financial panic from which a genuine depression could have developed".

Nevertheless, it is apparent that emergency measures that carried the world through one crisis after another in recent years are only the first faltering steps along the road to long term reform of the international economic system. Crisis management, however beneficial, is certainly not the answer to the ills that plague the global economy. Ever since the collapse of the European balance of power, the world production of arms has increased enormously. Competition between the Soviet Union and the United States both in the acquisition and sale of arms has also grown largely because of the preoccupation with the maintenance of military balance and security. This has accentuated the defence needs of the developed countries and also, indirectly perhaps, dragged in the developing countries through conflict of ideologies and cold war. There have been periodic pauses of these conflicts because of the continued search for a modus vivendi and the great interest shown by countries in peaceful cooperation and relaxation of political tension. However, the pauses have relaxation of political tension. However, the pauses have been very short. Other international factors (e.g. economic, political and social), have exercised an almost equal impact upon the strategic rationale of the world military powers. In the postwar era, the United States, the Soviet Union, Britain and France produced 90 per cent of the world's military material. Today, annual world defence expenditures are estimated at about $400 billion. The Reagan Administration's defence budget for 1981 was in the region of $194.1 billion.

Conflict of behavior in many parts of the world and the increasing dependence of the industrialized Western nations on external sources of raw materials, especially oil signalled the beginning of a new era. With the rapid integration and interdependence of world markets, the international monetary system shifted towards exchange rate flexibility to adjust to freer world trade. Higher oil prices, accompanied by a world recession and inflationary spirals in industrialized states introduced serious economic slumps. As a nation that rose from quasi-independent status to become the world's major industrialized power, the United State has always regarded trade as an integral part of its economy. In international commerce, the United States tried to establish, a mutual

advantageous relationship with the developing world. Liberalized trade, based on either bilateral or multilateral agreements,
and the expansion and preservation of U.S. investment overseas
have been for decades at the core of the American foreign trade
policy. Recognizing a growing need for a variety of raw materials, in recent years the United States has sought to improve
its access to forging markets on a competitive basis. Today the
United States pattern of trade with developing nations consists of
the important of raw materials and other primary products that
help to satisfy its internal consumption needs sustain American
economic growth.

In the developing countries, the situation is quite different.
In spite of the increase in defence expenditures in certain countries, estimates show that military expenditures are still on the
low side. It is estimated that in 1978–79 India devoted about
3.9 per cent of GNP to defence, African states about 3 per cent of
their GNP and Latin American states 2 per cent, while the USA
spent 5.2 per cent, the Soviet Union 11–13 per cent, the UK 4.9 per
cent and Pakistan 5.7 per cent (1978). The United States military
assistance program extended to many nations in Europe, Africa,
Asia and Latin America. In 1977 alone, some 77 nations together
with international organizations were the recipients of United
States arms sales that totaled some $11 billion. Although some
developing countries have developed arms production capabil-
ity, most developing countries are totally dependent upon arms
from abroad. Since United States' disengagement from the South
East Asian war, Iran, Israel, Jordan and Saudi Arabia, for instance,
have absorbed 60 per cent of United States military exports. NATO
countries, Japan and South Korea, have accounted for one-third of
United States military exports. Conscious of the adverse impact
of arms shipments 'B' on some developing nations, United States
policy on overseas transfers of arms has undergone some modification. The International Security Assistance and Arms Export
Control Act of 1976 have imposed congressional scrutiny on military assistance program and on arms transfers. More recently,
with the breakdown in détente and resumed cold war between
the two super powers, the United States and Soviet Union, competitive arms build-up in certain parts of the world has spurred
all round increases in military expenditures.

Big power rivalries and arms build-up have come nearer home in Pakistan and the Indian Ocean area. The United States is threatening to arm Pakistan to the hilt with a package nominally valued at $3 billion ostensibly to contain Soviet expansion. Past experience reveals that such arms have invariably been used against India (in at least three wars in three decades). But the scale of operations this time being enormously larger and accompanied by new bases in the Indian Ocean, the actual danger of militarisation beyond real security needs is great indeed. If the growth of imported arms countries its exponential courses, the developing countries will outstrip their ability to overcome economic, political and social handicaps. In their devotion to arms, civilian aristocracies and military elites will find themselves more isolated from people who prefer bread to weapons. Lacking democratic institutions and process of advice and consent, many leaders of the developing nations are convinced shortsightedly, that it is to their advantage to suppress by force the movements aimed at various reforms. Recent experience in Iran reveals the error of their calculations. Even a most modern army cannot depend on arms alone to defend itself against a popular revolt. Military power in the developing nations should go hand in hand with democratic processes if possible. The amelioration of internal ills, restructuring of the economic and social system, must be given priority over extensive arms imports, which only increase the possibility of deadly regional conflicts and immeasurably diminish the hopes of a developing world. Diplomatic initiatives to restrain international trade in armaments, together with negotiated solution of regional conflicts, would serve the interest of global peace. Tension has strained the economies of the developing countries and posed new problems of development.

Thoughtful men must ponder how far the West's post-war economic achievement, which has been to steer clear of major aid has rested fundamentally on the stimulant of its outstanding political and military threat. The short period of détente and the easing of the cold war tensions had seen a distinct hiatus in the momentum of the West's economic association as well as its military one. The casual connection cannot be slurred over. The relevant practical fact is that the tide of economic liberation has receded alarmingly ostensibly under pressure of economic recession. A constellation of external forces have emerged all so adverse to the developing countries and to the developing process. All indicators are negative. More recently there has been a decided shift away from liberal trade practices which were flaunted by some of the leading developed market economies as a fruit of free and prosperous system. The new wave of protectionism implies that a change in emphasis of protectionism methods and practices has taken place. Tariff, the traditional device, is only one of the several barriers, non-tariff and other barriers, to trade erected in blatant violation of the free trade policy embodied in the General Agreement on Trade and Tariff (GATT). Protectionist measures have been used even for political purposes and, with or without government complicity, have come to assume more importance than tariffs which periodically get reduced in various rounds of negotiations and horsetrading. With the onset of economic recession in the mid-70s, protectionism became fundamentally expedient allegedly to deal with fundamental domestic economic and structural problems. All this has retarded structural adjustments called for by international competitive forces. External imbalances, stagflation and inflation in the advanced countries have been associated with high degree of exchange rate instability.

To some extent, fluctuations in exchange rate have reflected changes in the pattern of relative inflation rates in the major trading countries. Mainly, however, they have been the result of speculative movements in the huge privately held liquid balances which at present overhang the international markets. These balances consist largely of deposits of transnational corporation and other private firms in the largely uncontrolled Eurocurrency market, and their growth has been fed by the very large United States payments deficit which has accumulated since 1976. Exchange-rate fluctuations have complicated the international adjustment process and have created disorderly conditions in international trade, thereby bringing increasing awareness of the need to establish a stable system of exchange rates. The range of measures recently announced by the United States Government to strengthen the dollar as well as the decision by the European Economic Community to establish a European Monetary System are evidence of this awareness.

The weakness of the recovery from the 1974–75 recession, combined with the emergence of substantial unemployment in a number of industrial sectors, has led many developed market-economy countries to extend existing protectionist measures, or to introduce new measures, against imports from low-cost sources. Developing countries have been particularly hard hit and, in effect, discriminated against, by these protectionist measures.

Protectionism has affected the rate of growth of world trade, over the 10 years up to 1973 world trade grew by 9 per cent a year in terms of volume; the rate of growth was slashed by one-half of the average during 1973–78. The rate of growth of world trade in terms of volume fell to a mere 1.5 per cent in 1980. The rise in average world trade prices however accelerated in the last two years from 18 to 20 per cent, so that the dollar value of world trade in 1980 at about $2000 billion was 21 per cent higher than in 1979. Actually the growth rate for 1980 is about the lowest for two decades. Moreover, the volume of world trade declined by about 3 per cent between the first and the second halves of 1980. The biggest single influence on world trade has been the restrictive policies pursued by advanced countries. There has also been a marked deterioration in the term of trade amounting to almost 15 per cent during the period 1974–78 representing a foreign exchange loss of over $30 billion. A further deterioration of 8–10 per cent is anticipated in 1980–81. Loss of trade attributable directly to protectionism would probably range between $30–50 billion though this estimate includes impact of restraint on Japan's exports. The current account deficit of the developing countries, excluding those in surplus, is estimated at $70 billion in 1980 and $90 billion in 1981. The net effect of the continuing economic crisis of the West has been to provoke major readjustments in the world economy and in the relative economic strength of the main trading countries and groups. What is generally not recognised in the important counter-cyclical role which trade with developing countries could play in supporting the economies of the advanced countries in time of recession in so far as the high import propensity of developing countries for manufactured goods and capital equipment could generate a sharp increase in the trade surplus of the developed countries. Such export (including semi-manufactures) from the West was estimated at $125 billion in

1977, approximately 23 per cent of the total exports of such products to the world.

The inner contradiction in the monetary system is now more than obvious but, incredible as it may seem, it is almost certain that this tacit recognition itself exhausts the area of agreement so that it will still not be accompanied by any specific and significant measures for radical reform. In any case the US and its allies have taken care to exclude the developing world from the nominal changes that have been brought about in the International Monetary Fund. The amendments of the articles of association of the IMF took effect on July 28, 1969 and the Special Drawing Rights (SDR) came into being in August of the same year. What is significant to note for our purposes is that in all the discussions to augment liquidity of the IMF in a way that would make it accessible to members was confined to the major powers of the West and developing countries were no where in the picture. The international agreement on SDR's and negotiations were within the Groups of Ten and with IMF officials, though ultimately the SDR system was opened up to developing countries also as full participants. This is yet another manifestation of the paternalism of the North.

Today the world is poised on the edge of radical transformation of the existing economic and political relationships. Because of the widening gap between the rich developed North and the poor developing South, tensions and contradictions of the system as a whole have surfaced and are giving a new dimension to a struggle for restructuring the world economy. The inadequacy of the existing system and the emerging imperative of a more just global community have come to the force as the developed nations press for a New International Economic Order (NIEO) and a greater say in the restructuring of the world economic system. The objective is to create a new and better environment for development so that the developing countries are to get the maximum benefits from development and transformation of their economies and societies. But the process of change is anything but smooth. The bold attempts to cut tariffs or remove them are lost in a thicket of disparities and exceptions. Equally disappointing is the West's stalling on aid to poor countries. Trade discussions have all along been heated and angry, and the West has cut a sorry figure particularly in the United Nations Development Conference. The US has not come verbally to grips with the main issue and appears to be reluctant to take a principled stand, and there has been lack of recognition of the threat that all this poses. Money has become tighter, and more and more countries are looking anxiously and primarily at their own balance of payments. In effect the North–South economic negotiations have, with minor exceptions, proved sterile.

The advanced countries have now and then offered baits of freer trade, more aid and so on; actually the structural problems of the international division of labour remains where it was and the NIEO seems as remote as ever. If one considered the various demands of the developing countries, none of them has really been accepted in the form in which they were presented. Some concessions have been made, the dialogue continues, and one need not perhaps been too cynical about the future. So far, however, few concrete steps have been taken toward the evolution of the New International Economics Order. Take the case of trade in labor-intensive manufactures. What the NIEO sought what the developing countries wanted—was free access for exports of their manufactured goods in developed country markets. A few tariff concessions—the so-called Generalized System of Preferences (GSPs)—have been extended by the developed countries. But this does not amount to much. Indeed, at the moment, the tide of protectionism is strong in many developed countries, including the United States. The second important trade issue concerns the stabilization of commodity prices. Here again, the developing countries demand for a common fund subscribed to by developed countries, for conducting buffer stocks operations in order to stabilize export prices of (and earnings from) 10 to 18 primary commodities has not been accepted in the spirit or from which it was originally presented. The need for stabilization is accepted in principle. Debate, however, continues on the rationale of a common fund for many commodities and on the issue of 'indexing'—maintaining price parity between the primary exports of developing countries and the manufactured goods imported by them.

On the third major issue—that of developmental aid to developing countries—there has been (until very recently) little progress; in fact, some deterioration has occurred over the years the original aid target for the rich countries was 1 per cent of their GNP of which 0.7 per cent was to 0.3 per cent of GNP of the donor countries. While aid flows have declined in real terms, the debt-servicing burden of the developing countries has increased. Consequently, the issue of debt redemption and debt rescheduling become urgent in many cases. Some influential American economists have been advocating a switch from official aid to direct foreign private investment into the developing countries. Indeed the relative decline in foreign aid and the countinuous growth of the debt-servicing burden have forced many developing countries to invite foreign investment on concessional terms and (particularly after the oil crisis) to rely on borrowings from European and commercial banking systems. These have raised fresh problems for the non-oil producing Third World countries. With US authorities becoming more and more unwilling to support multilateral non-military aid operations one doubts whether the volume of official aid-bilateral and multilateral will rise substantially in the future. Perhaps it is because aid has not been rising fast enough that the developing countries are seeking assistance in more indirect ways—for example, stabilisation and indexing of primary commodity prices, linking aid with liquidity creation, debt remission and rescheduling and other such devices.

In view of all this there is the need to revive or revitalize the discussions and negotiations pertaining to a reform of the international monetary system. It is already some years since some of the basic elements of the Bretton Woods system came to be seriously undermined. The basic requirements of a reformed system have been outlined on many occasions. They include the need for international control over the process of creating international liquidity and the corresponding need for the SDR to replace currencies as the principal reserve asset; the need—widely accepted but yet to be implemented—for the establishment of a link between the creation of SDRs and development assistance; the need for mechanisms that foster more symmetrical obligations as between countries with surpluses and deficits on current account; the need for more predictable and stable systems of exhange rates and for conditions that foster more orderly capital flows; and, not least, the need for developing countries to exercise a greater voice in the decision-making process.

The absence of a coherent system can imply a heavy cost to the international community. The problems of inflation, unemployment and slow recovery from recession that continue to bedevil the developed countries are not unconnected with the failure to reform the international monetary system. Nor are the problems experienced by many developing countries through losses in their terms of trade and the real value of their assets owing to fluctuations in the exchange rates of major currencies. Many features of the current scene could have, in fact, consequences of a seriously disruptive or disturbing nature in the future. These include the increasing tendency for the creation of international liquidity to be assumed by the private sector instead of the International Monetary Fund, the emergence of conditions for disruptive movements of short-terms funds, and the channeling of liquid balances by the private capital market to developing countries at excessively short maturities and high interest rates. If uncorrected, these features could severely undermine the prospects for sustained recovery and growth in both developed and developing countries and lay the foundation for deeper crises in the period ahead.

The NIEO has called for a radical transformation in the economies of the poor countries—a 25 per cent share of world industrial production by 2000 AD, which is a substantial increase from their present 7 per cent share. This would require not merely substantial domestic efforts on the part of the poor countries, but also massive resource transfer from the rich to the poor. The aid giving capacity of the richer from the rich to the poor. The aid giving capacity of the richer countries would depend considerably on their balance-of-payments position and their rate of growth. Income transfer from the rich to the poor through fiscal and other mechanisms are difficult enough within a country. In the international sphere such transfer are even more so. The confrontation between developed and developing countries aggravated in more recent years partly because of the sharp increase in oil prices and largely because of the sharp increase in oil prices. This has much to do with the revival of the cold war and keen competition for spheres of influence in the Middle East, South East Asia and Africa. This was manifest at UNCTAD V where the United States and some other countries took a stiff stand against the demands from the developing countries.

Hopes nursed by the West of the devastating import of the oil shock on the cohesion of the Third World countries have been belied. No doubt some developing countries have been enriched and some perhaps nearly ruined, but nearly all of them are agreed on the common call for a massive redistribution of wealth and power and a change in the world economic structure. The form and substance that the new order is the central concern of the newly emerging North–South conflict or relationship whichever way one might look at it but from the point of view of world development, the outlook is nearly as important in Washington as it would be in New Delhi or Accra. The strategy of the North to take advantage of the disparate interest of the South in order to down voice of wisdom must be defeated if the countries advocating NIEO are to bring about a qualitative change in the nature of the existing system and interdependence. The developing countries feel that global interdependence must be organized on a somewhat different basis than exists today if the growing income gap between the rich and the poor can be effectively bridged. On this issue—how best and how soon to bridge the income gap—there are still difference between the rich and poor countries, just as within a country the spokesmen of the rich and the poor direr on the same issue. Differences also stem from the manoeuvres of the big powers and the pressure tactics and some perhaps arise from disparate cultures.

Nevertheless the non-aligned movement has been gaining momentum and the South has as a whole shown that it has the necessary will and determination to strive for a better deal and seek negotiated change in the rules governing international economic relations. In this sense the non-aligned movement is only a political manifestation of the urge of the South to rectify the present ills and give the suppressed people a happier future and better destiny. Inevitably therefore, the most industrialised country in the developing world, namely, India has emerged a natural spokesman of the non-aligned countries and also of the developing world in general. In dealing with the North two other countries have also featured prominently and these are Nigeria and Brazil. These three countries enjoy a certain economic, strategic and geographic advantages which are being used to the maximum extent of promoting the cause of the Third World. Efforts to forge close ties have not always succeeded because smaller nations nurse suspicions of their larger neighbours and derive secret encouragement from the big powers of the North. But in the developing world as a whole there is growing realization that suspicions and regional bickerings must not be allowed to impede the emergence of the South and a new international economic system. There is also growing emphasis on regional cooperation. In spite of the divergent needs and interests the developing countries have recently shown a degree of cohesion.

Understanding among major developing countries is remarkably growing even in the field of peace-keeping on such tricky issues as Arab–Israeli conflict, nuclear rivalries, extra-territorial jurisdiction and above all on the need to establish peace and a new world economic order.

Understanding and unity on all these issues stem from a strong sense of injustice, exploitation and discrimination by the North. In South-East Asia geographical compactness, parallel history, similarities of conditions have prompted certain moves towards closer regional cooperation. In the context of protectionism in the West, some of these countries are looking towards one another for markets and supply of materials and manufactured goods. The past failure to exploit the enormous economic potential of the relatively backward areas through cooperation with the more advanced of the developing countries is yet another factor producing a sense of community in the South and promoting collective decision-making. Most developing countries realize that they failed to assert themselves earlier and use their weight and bargaining power effectively as a consequence of which the rich countries of the North have been able to maximize their gains and tilt the scales of power to their advantage. There is concern, therefore, about economic and political cooperation in the South and it is not unlikely that at least some of the leaders look forward to the day when Southern Hemisphere comes into its own with its superior resources, physical environment and human power. While in the long term perspective these convulsions may be irrelevant and unnecessary, trade and other economic relations have to continue to grow, whether regional or inter-regional, through policies and mechanisms which score over minor regional irritations. Even the OPEC countries which laid great store by the super money mechanism of the West are now having second thoughts. Though predominantly underdeveloped, but financially rich, the OPEC countries were suddenly flooded with oil revenues. Instead of converting these into resources for the resurgence of the Third World countries, the OPEC countries allowed themselves to be persuaded by Western powers to make the funds available to them through the IMF and otherwise. By the end of 1979 oil surplus funds were equivalent to US$236,000 million. Of the total, US$115,000 million was held in bank deposits, (US$68,000 million in US dollar denominations) US$58,000 million in portfolio and direct investment, US$17,000 million in US and British government securities, and US$46,000 million with the IMF and World Bank. By 1980 the balance would have risen to US$445,000 million. An economic document presented at the recent Arab Summit at Amman came down heavily against the OPEC policy of permitting the Western countries to retain oil surplus funds within their own monetary framework and exposed the paradox of Arab countries borrowing US$16,500 million from international money markets during the period of 1971–77 while accumulated by 1978. The problems of the OPEC countries got magnified as Western currencies depreciated and the banking system failed to provide either political or financial security. The US decision to freeze Iranian assets in U.S. banks after Washington fell out with rulers of that country posed the first doubts about the wisdom of continuing to invest petro-dollars in that part of the world.

The second factor in the shift of interests of OPEC countries was the Western attempt to split the Group of 77 by bypassing the onus for massive transfer of resources from the South to oil-surplus countries. All these and the deterioration in financial security have compelled OPEC nations notably Saudi Arabia, Kuwait, Bahrain to look for more stable and reliable investment links as, for example, with India. There have been several other attempts to split the ranks of the Third World and the Group of 77 which has been derisively described as "an international trade union of the poor, poor countries, not people." It is fallacious to assume that the unity of the Group of 77 or the Third World is fragile because they have different values, different needs and priorities. The fact is they all have some shared and converging interest, common historical background and mostly identical perception of the future. That explains the solidarity of the group of 77 and the non-aligned movement, though increase in membership has brought in some strains. The South, excluding OPEC countries, which had little or no significant regional economic ties 5 years ago has against heavy odds raised intra-trade flows to a level where they are today equivalent to 40 per cent of the 'South's trade with the North in value terms. This indicates an increase of 30 per cent in 10 years. The actual figures are comparatively higher for South-East Asia and Latin America. The flow of aid also within the South is now nearly one-half of the flows from North. The percentage of financial flows would appear to be even higher if one took into account OPEC resources recycled through the West. Technology transfer and the flow of skilled manpower are also on the increase.

India has been in the forefront of the Third World countries effort to develop economic cooperation. India has diversified the colonial system of trade it had inherited and, in step with its plans for self reliance, provided aid and technology to less-endowed members of the Third World.

The U.S. and the U.K. dominated India's trade at the time of independence. Ten years ago four countries, viz, US, UK, USSR and Japan together accounted for more than one-half of the country's exports. Today their share is down to less than 40 per cent. The fall is steeper in the case of the U.S. from 16.8 per cent to 12.6 per cent and in the case of the U.K. from 11.7 per cent to 7.4 per cent. As a result of deliberate policy of turning towards developing countries, India's trade with Asia and Africa today accounts for over 45 per cent of the total external trade-exports perhaps slightly lower and imports slightly higher. In view of the rising tempo and scope of development in these countries, India is keeping in mind the potential for expansion and diversification of this trade in its five year plans. The ESCAP region accounted for 26 per cent of India's global exports in 1979–80 and 23 per cent of imports. Exports of manufactures of African countries have been growing at a very fast pace and amounted to Rs. 353 crores of 1979–80. The Middle East and North African countries have indeed emerged as important participants in India's trade and development. By 1979–80 India had sanctioned aid totaling Rs. 113.5 crores by way of aid to South-East Asian and African countries. In addition 373 projects had been approved involving Indian technology, skilled manpower and management in enterprises in 35 countries. Indications are that policy in this realm is being liberalized permitting Indian corporate enterprises to participate in equity capital abroad.

Nevertheless, there are still wide areas of cooperation and operation, which are still not being fully exploited. Global forms of economic and technological cooperation in the South hold a potential threat to the North as OPEC demonstrated in the early 70s. The solidarity of the Group of 77 and the non-aligned movement carry with them the warning of more formal cooperation and collective action, which for one reason or another are progressing only slowly. While the basic responsibility for devising and implementing development strategies rests with developing countries themselves, the international dimension of development cannot be overlooked if policies are to succeed. It is now more than clear that economic problems are nearly universal and pervasive. Development is a process; it is not the result of altruism of the rich, nor can it be achieved by the organised effort of a single nation struggling at the poverty line. A new initiative is called for to restructure the world economy and the international monetary system, to eliminate inequities and promote growth and social change in poorer societies. It has been argued that the world economy can regain its momentum if the developed economies could, by lifting their growth rate, transmit expansionary impulses to the developing countries. But the fact is that the periods since the Second World War which saw a tremendous expansion and economic buoyancy in the developed market economies also coincided with a surge in the indebtedness of developing countries. Most of these countries were afflicted by balance of payment crisis which grievously affected their development programmes.

The new thinking proposes a shift from the present cheap energy sources to new energy sources and new technology and also a new division of labour as between the developed and developing countries. The developing countries would be encouraged to specialise in labour-intensive industries, probably also pollution—intensive industries, leaving the sophisticated and the research and technology—intensive industries to the developed market economies. Attempts are being made by certain interests to propagate this line of thinking in India also oblivious of the country's technological progress and industrial thrust. If India's trade payment problems remain unsolved the basic reason lies in the loaded value system of international trade. Also fitment into the new pattern of international division of labour was likely to destroy the domestic pattern of growth, particularly in the case of a large and newly industrialising country like India. The primary objective of development is to meet the basic needs of the population. This would entail and increase in the supply of foodstuffs and manufactured goods using technology appropriate to the resource endowment of the developing countries. The publicised concept of international division of labour now calls for specialization in the production of goods needed by the consumer-oriented developed countries. Surely, this would tend to distort the pattern of investment of the newly industrializing nations often leading to the adaptation of controversial projects on investments non-essential to the developing economy. Moreover, specialization oriented towards such a concept would expose to export of developing countries highly volatile forces of the market in developed countries.

The basic problem is really one of overcoming handicaps imposed by the institutional framework which today governs trade, foreign investment and external economy relations. The framework treaties, conventions and legal procedures and institutions ensure an unregulated operation of commercial forces of some of the rich countries. It is no easy task for the developing countries, singly or collectively to get round this framework. First, the compensatory finance scheme would have to be liberalized. Even trade with the rupee payment countries would have to be brought under the scheme. Indexation of commodities entering international trade will have to be seriously considered and supplemented by price stabilization-cum-product agreements to correct the adverse terms of trade impairing specialized exports like jute, tea, copper, zinc, etc. Reform of the international economic order on this scale would involve a search for new

97

methods of global management of resources in the long-term interest of all nations. In the short run developing nations will have already moved swiftly towards the pursuit of self-reliant and self-sustained growth. Countries like India which have already advanced in this direction will have to guard against excessive specialization under the published scheme of international division of labour in order to play an effective role in regional development.

Note

The complete bibliographic information for this article is as follows:

D. K. Rangnekar, 'North–South Divide: An Economic Analysis', *Business Standard*, Annual, 1981.

10

Today's Controversies—I

*Delhi's Attitude to Aid**

Desperation is not the word to describe the New Delhi atmosphere today. A charitable view of New Delhi's posture would be to say that we are all praying to God to save our economy, our values and our goals. On the face of it, the sense of desperation has led to many feelers and much confusion. But below the surface, there is a certain nervousness which is reflected in a persistent mixture of defence and apology in Government statements.

The Government is straining every nerve to rekindle American interest in India and to lure U.S capital. Yet important persons here keep protesting that they are doing nothing or have done nothing to seek U.S. aid. Not a day passes without some such denial or protestation.

But why? Is the quest of U.S. aid objectionable? Or, is there something else involved in the quest? All this seems strange.

Mrs. Gandhi, for example, is technically right in claiming that she did not go to the U.S. to ask for aid. She is also, perhaps, right in giving the impression that she did not discuss aid operations in depth. But nobody had expected her to do that either.

It is, however, difficult for any intelligent Indian, American or anybody else, to believe that there was anything more important than economic assistance which prompted our Prime Minister's

* First published in *The Economic Times* on 26 April 1966.

visit to Washington at this stage. If it was simply a matter of keeping the late Mr. Shastri's commitment, she should have gone to the U.S. in the first week of February according to the late P. M.'s original schedule. If it was a matter of courtesy, the visit could always have been deferred to a more convenient date.

Personal rapport between leaders of two great countries is always a worthwhile proposition. A sense of urgency arises if there are live issues and some pressing international problems. But India has become conspicuously insular since the death of Nehru, and there is hardly anything like a positive foreign policy line on any international problems today. If the Prime Minister was prompted to leave this country in the middle of a Budget session of Parliament, and amidst riots and unrest, it could only be because of some pressing urgency. And there was no particular urgency about high-level consultation between the U.S. and India, apart from, of course, the urgency of India's own economic crisis and the need for the resumption of American aid.

Mrs. Gandhi is also known to have carried a detailed brief on India's economic situation, plan and aid problems prepared by the Planning commission. The top-level discussions were almost wholly concerned with India's economic difficulties etc., which indicate that, at the other end also, the dialogue was intended to be held in the context of aid operations.

Two Reasons

I can think of two possible reasons why our Government is so seemingly unwilling to acknowledge that it is seeking U.S. aid. First, the publicity seems to have misfired. The continued aid freeze after Mrs. Gandhi's visit does not quite square up with the publicised success of the talks. The talks were, no doubt, cordial, but they could not have been otherwise. The cordiality may have been more noticeable for reasons of personality and also because both sides wanted to move to a 'thaw'. But cordiality at the personal level is something quite different from Government policy, and as yet, there is no indication of Mrs. Gandhi's impact on U.S. policy.

The second factor is perhaps a vague reaction to the suspicions and murmurs in the Congress Party about New Delhi's alleged 'sell out' under U.S. pressure. Criticism from the Left was expected. But criticism from the Right was unexpected. What seems to have unnerved the Government is the fact that no prominent Congress leader has yet come out strongly in support of the Government's new policy stance, not even Congress president Kamraj.

While the ideological and theoretical criticisms can be discounted, suspicions and uneasiness of ordinary congress M.P.s cannot be wished away. So, there is a persistent tendency to delink New Delhi's current posture from Mrs. Gandhi's visit to the U.S., and to apologise for every new move, and to make defensive utterances on all sorts of irrelevant matters except those that really matter.

One hears a lot about aid, about pressures, about Right wing swings in policy. Thus, the Congress Parliamentary Party meetings are told by self-appointed conscience keepers that the country has been "sold out" under U.S. and World Bank pressure, and the public is told that the Government is now accepting aid with strings. The prime Minister and other Government spokesmen vehemently deny these charges and, periodically and publicly, declare their continued commitment to the nearly forgotten congress goal of "democracy and socialism" and to "aid without strings."

But what does all this mean? Why should anybody protest about the acceptance of aid today, when aid has been accepted and many policies have been changed to suit that aid in the past couple of years? Was there some special expectation that Mrs. Gandhi will do something quite different from the late Mr. Shastri? And what does the Government mean by declaring that it will not accept aid with strings?

Strings Always There

Determination not to accept aid with strings may mean refusal to accept any aid today. Aid has always strings attached in one form or another. In some cases, the strings are less visible than in others. Sometimes the strings are pulled very hard; at other times, not so. And it may also be that, on occasions, the movement is far too gentle, almost subtle, to be felt or noticed. But the strings are always there, even if the quality and style of operation may vary.

Another point worth making is that no country in history that accepts aid can ever proclaim that it has done so with the full knowledge of strings attached to it. At least I have never heard South Viet Nam, South Korea, or Formosa declaring their grim determination to accept U.S. aid with strings. Nor have I heard any of the socialist countries having done so in the case of Russian aid.

The presumption that aid can flow in without any strings is project one's own emotional feelings in matters which are determine solely by cold economic and political considerations. Only the Pope can perhaps make an appeal for altruistic aid and school children may then give away their pocket money, and pious people a part of their hard earned wages, to prevent starvation deaths in this country. But Governments handle tax-payers' funds to further the nation's political and economic aims. Governments do not, normally and persistently, use these funds for international charity.

The U.S. Government has been financing aid operations for many years now. So have the Soviet Union, Britain and other countries. All of these countries have sought to further their political aims and influence policies, in various ways. To say that we have adhered to our path and that we have resisted pressures in the past, is not to deny the existence of pressures.

We cannot also honestly say that we have never reacted to pressures or that we have never shown any consideration to the susceptibilities of those who have given us aid. We can, of course, claim that we had in the past shown a keen awareness of our own national interest and managed to secure large amounts of aid without succumbing to external pressures.

But then we have been able to do so not merely by our strict adherence to non-alignment, but also by playing a positive role in world affairs, by acting to reduce tension between the Great Power blocs, by contributing to peace, by pulling some other people's chestnuts out of fire, and so on and so forth. All this admirably suited the interests of the big power at the time.

102

Both sides were engaged in some kind of a contest to tilt the world balance, and sometimes moved close to a head-on collision. It was India's influence and non-alignment which, sometimes, averted a catastrophe. Consequently, India itself appeared like a political prize coveted by both sides.

In a sense, without military power, but with a shrewd balancing of forces, we were able to provide, through our non-alignment, some kind of a recompense for the aid operations. In fact, it could be argued that this country received less aid than it deserved, for all that it did for the Great Powers in the fifties.

Today, we can no longer pretend to be what we were in the fifties. Nor is the world what it was. The situation has changed, and we have still not framed our own response to it. The External Affairs Ministry is groping for a policy. The present attitude is wholly negative, and reactions are delayed, half-baked and hesitant.

Timidity

An aspect of the present confusion in New Delhi is the premium placed on timidity. Many of those who talk of self-reliance, have made dependence their creed. Some nurse the mistaken notion that they can get all the aid that they want, if India is made to look helpless. There is also another peculiar notion that it is in India's economic interest not to take any active part in foreign affairs today. Some people imagine that they can get massive aid by appeasing the Big Powers, by pursuing a negative line and, at all cost, avoiding a direct confrontation.

This is one indication of India's retreat from the lofty historical perspectives which influenced New Delhi's policies, attitudes and postures under Nehru. I know of no case in history where appeasement, timidity and negative attitudes have contributed to beneficial national developments. But there are countless examples where such attitudes have contributed to tensions, irritations, waywardness, revolutions, unrest, turmoil and a loss of national personality. The state of economic affairs of some of these countries which have got large aid by pursuing negative policies should be an eye-opener.

103

But, consider pragmatically, should India shy away from its responsibility in international affairs, should it adopt a negative attitude to world events, and should it cease to be an effective leader of the non-aligned Afro-Asian world, what is there left of Indian influence, and what recompense can it offer to the competing Great Powers for their aid?

By becoming timid and negative, India will only encourage the Big Powers to seek a return for the aid in very tangible terms. When you are timid, you give the impression that you can bend. And once you start bending, you are forced to bend more, and it is a matter of time before you start crawling, surely, a great country like ours would not look nice in that posture! Those of us, who have participated in the nationalist movement under the inspiration of our departed leaders, are watching with horror and pain the present negative trends.

Time was when every time any politician or any M.P. referred to the "imperative need" for seeking larger aid to speed up development. Nehru used to jump up with anger in Parliament and lash out at what he would contemptuously describe as "aid mentality". His emphasis used to be on India's own scene of nationalism and spirit of self-confidence based on it. Aid was only a marginal element in financing import surpluses, never an element in India's strategy of development. Today, there is a premium on precisely the type of "aid mentality" which militates against nationalism and self-confidence.

It is a strange phenomenon to see important people denying quest of aid, protesting against strings, but championing planning based on large-scale aid. It is a contradiction in terms, a contradiction that can only flow from an intellectual crisis.

Qualitative Change

All these years of planning, foreign assistance was regarded as a temporary prop to the balance of payments to permit import of industrial equipment beyond the limits set by the country's current foreign exchange earnings. Today, aid seems to have become the main element in the strategy of survival, which is expressed in such contradictory terms as "larger aid to end all aid" or "aid for

104

self-reliance." Even if the mechanics of financing imports may be the same, the role and concept are certainly not. This is one indication of the qualitative change in New Delhi's attitude.

The accusations about a "sell out" are reckless and unfair. No Government can sell this country to anybody or any other country. Even if some of the leaders may be out of touch with the feeling and thinking of the ordinary people, it is unfair to suggest that the leaders are so callous and selfish as to humiliate the country left and right. It is nevertheless, true that there are some people who are over-anxious about their political durability and are apt to commit the Government to policies and measures which may not always be in the best interests of the people.

There is, for example, a visible tendency to seek electoral and political safety in ever-increasing import of PL 480 supplies. This is an easy alternative to the hard task of framing and implementing a national food policy designed to mobilise available supplies, regulate distribution and introduce a better system of production and distribution for the new seasons.

In this context, Mrs. Gandhi has done well to broadcast to the nation and spell out the Government's stand on certain issues in very broad terms. But the broadcast has come a little too late, and some of the main issues are lost in commitments to empty semantics such as "democratic socialism."

At a very early stage, perhaps before visiting the United States, or at least immediately on return, Mrs. Gandhi should have taken the public into confidence and told them the plain facts of the economic situation, about aid, and about Government policy on sensitive issues. Anyone who has faith in people knows that you cannot fool them; by the same token, you cannot make them believe by words what they know is not true by experience. If this simple truth had been kept in mind, the Government need not have been apologetic all the time, nor would issues have been so confused as they indeed are.

Pressure

I see no reason why the Government should keep claiming that it is under no pressure, when everybody knows that it is under tremendous pressure. The pressure is one of the dire economic situation of the country, and also of political argument and continued aid suspension. People who recognise this are apt to disbelieve when any Government spokesman stands up in Parliament or goes to the AIR to deny the existence of such obvious pressures. They are equally apt to offer spontaneous sympathy and stand by the Government if the pressures are recognised and the response honestly formulated and explained.

It is not extremely difficult to deal with the pressures of an economic situation. It is a question of guts and imagination. It is also not difficult to deal with pressures of argument. A good argument can be accepted, a bad one can be rejected. This applies to dealings with institutions in the normal course. But political pressures operate in government-to-government dealings and these are not always easily overcome, but they, too, can be met, as the history of this and other countries shows.

Ceylon was denied U.S. aid because of its trade policy in the fifties. Aid was suspended again because of a nationalisation measure in the sixties. But the country still goes on with imaginative policies without surrendering either to China or to the U.S. Pakistan also seems to have adopted our own history as a text book, drawing lessons for its own benefit.

It seems to me that we have exposed ourselves to great pressures because of New Delhi's inept tactics and its very poor grasp of the economy. The scare created about famine, and the second scare about economic aid, both weakened our bargaining position. The first has proved to be a humiliating substitute for a food policy, and the second now threatens to force down compromises which may eventually turn out to be harmful to the economy.

As in the case of food supply, so also in the case of maintenance imports, the Government had practically no knowledge of what was the actual position, prices did not rise when the Food Minister was crying about famine conditions, obviously because there were large supplies in the pipeline, similarly, factories did not shut down en masse and industrial output did not come to a standstill all these months again because there were large maintenance imports in the pipeline, which the Government did not borrow of.

If New Delhi's, policy-makers were in touch with the actual conditions of the economy, there would never have been any scare and subsequent humiliation, compromises and apologies. If the Americans are pressing us hard on policies or urging us to change our pattern of planning and social goals, this is so because they have always been wanting to do that. They have not found a congenial situation in the past because our political and economic policies were imaginative and New Delhi was in high spirits.

What is interesting is that the U.S. Government has not formally announced suspension of aid. Nor has it officially informed India about the cancellation of the Third Plan commitments. It has made its notings through the press. This is so because Washington does not want to write off India which is of great significance to American policy in this region. But it does want to use unannounced aid suspension for purposes of political leverage.

The quiet and informal cancellation of the Third Plan commitments by the U.S. Government was perhaps designed to give India some kind of a notice about America's continued displeasure at India's failure to bring about necessary changes in policy. The changes that interest the U.S. are not merely economic, though one hears a lot about these, but they also concern India's political policy, particularly towards Pakistan and Kashmir, even if Kashmir, for tactical reasons, may not be freely and openly discussed.

It is significant that, when the Indian Press carried reports about the cancellation of the past commitments, the Americans are understood to have urged the Indian Government to issue an official denial. When the Government sought a formal note from the U.S. Embassy contradicting the substance of the reports, the Americans pleaded inability to give it. This again confirms that the continued suspension of aid is a tactic for exerting pressure for wider negotiations.

Note

The complete bibliographic information for this article is as follows:
D. K. Rangnekar, 'Today's Controversies–I: Delhi's Attitude to Aid', *The Economic Times*, 26 April 1966.

11

Today's Controversies–II

*Fertiliser and Foreign Capital**

The controversy over the Government's fertiliser policy has distracted attention away from issues of far-reaching significance. The hue and cry about decontrol is really meaningless. The withdrawal of central control on fertilisers may do no harm to the cause of democratic socialism, whatever that may mean.

There is reason to believe that some of the ineffective controls are only harming growth and social change. This is something some of the professional Leftists cannot perhaps comprehend. They measure the degree of socialistic progression by the intensity of governmental control merely on paper. And they tend to equate any sign of decontrol with a right-wing swing.

Criticism of Government policy based on such superficial understanding of economic management tends to confuse the real issues at stake. The Government worsens the situation by its defensive, and sometimes unbelievable, statements.

The Government has, for example, aroused suspicion by being persistently secretive about the fertiliser deal and, worse, by denying major change in policy. Perhaps it could have got away lightly if it had seized the initiative, announced a new policy, if it wanted one, and produced pragmatic, plausible arguments. In a small way, Mrs. Gandhi's recent broadcast tried to make up for this very serious lapse in tactic and public relations.

* First published in *The Economic Times*.

Even so, the Government continues to deny that there is a change in policy. But why? Is change forbidden, something to be shunned or ashamed of? Or, is the Government embarrassed about something else, perhaps the circumstances and manner in which the change was brought about?

The old fertiliser policy did not work, partly because the Government lost confidence in its own industrial enterprise, and partly because distribution policy was inherently defective. The Central Fertiliser Pool was concerned only with nitrogenous fertilisers. Other fertilisers were free of control. But what is interesting is that the Central Fertiliser Pool made a tremendous profit (Rs. 43 crores) at the expense of farmers, when supplies should have been made available at a lower price.

No Total Decontrol

Even now, there is no complete decontrol of fertiliser distribution and pricing. The Government retains the option to take over 30 per cent of the private sector production, and, in any case, it will be in a key position controlling two-thirds of the local output. Marketing rights will be available for a period of seven years only to fertiliser plants licensed within the year ending March 1967, which means the policy is open to review a year hence. It can be scrapped if it does not work or extended if it does.

There are misgivings, however, because the Government has given the impression that the fertiliser policy is being changed under the pressure of the USAID and the World Bank. Here two points are significant. First, an exchange of letters between Mr. John Lewis of the Aid mission and the Finance Ministry, and certain communications from the World Bank urging foreign majority capital ownership, the grant of marketing rights to private foreign firms etc. preceded the Government's decisions.

Secondly, if the Government could decontrol fertiliser distribution and pricing now, there is a question why it could not have done so last year or any other time before the intervention of outside agencies.

Our own industrialists have been pressing the Government for a second look at the control system, but they have been rebuffed.

109

It would have been in good grace, and perhaps even beneficial to our economy and the national spirit, if the Government had shown greater respect to Indian opinion. In any case, misgivings could have been avoided.

There is also technically no violation of the Industrial Policy Resolution in allowing foreign capital participation in fertiliser production. Fertiliser is in schedule 'B' which lists industries open to public and private sectors. But there is, at the same time, a qualitative change in the Government's approach not quite in line with the spirit of the Resolution.

Fertiliser was regarded as a basic industry because of its crucial significance to our agriculture, economy and industrial development, as such, it was the Government's policy to allocate resources and promote fertiliser developments in terms of social costs and social returns. For that reason, the Government had, for almost a decade, refused to permit India's own industrialists to enter this field. Even recently when a few private ventures were licensed because of Government's boredom, the stand was tough. Several times the Government threatened to scrap licences or to take over the licensed projects. Nobody cared to find out why projects were not being extended. What is even more interesting is that the concessions, which are now being offered to foreign firms, were denied to Indian ventures.

If, against this background, the Government is willing to license foreign private ventures with the free marketing rights, and implying allocation of resources based on private costs and private returns, as distinct from the earlier investment criteria, there clearly is a change of policy and attitude, whether the change is good or bad is beside the point.

Capital Expenditure

Then, again, it has been the Government's policy, as a rule not to permit Indian industries to finance their capital expenditures from loan funds. Although because of the weakness of the capital market many firms have found it necessary to borrow money from banks, finance houses and other sources, thereby changing the ratio of equity to loan finance, the Finance Minister has frowned on this procedure of raising rupee resources. He has tried as hard as possible, through controls, pressures and procedures, to discourage and put a stop to this practice, if possible even at the early stage of scrutiny of the capital structure of new companies.

Now, the Government is willing to underwrite the rupee resources required by foreign firms which are shying about tying up with the Indian private sector on the ground that their collaborators may not be able to raise capital in the market. The implications are two fold. The Government can underwrite the rupee resource required by instructing its agencies to provide the foreign firms with loans. Alternatively, the Government will instruct the big State-owned institutions to take up equity capital in the foreign ventures. In either case, the commitment implies a change of policy.

If the Government gives loans, this means the foreign companies will receive an automatic privilege denied to Indian firms. If the state-owned ventures are forced to take up a minority part of the equity capital, this means the Government is accepting minority participation through the back-door, something in contradiction of its own decisions and public pronouncements.

These subtle changes have got completely lost in an absurd controversy about the role of foreign capital in fertiliser production. The critics are of two types. Those allergic to decontrol develop bile at a mere reference to foreign capital. There are others who are restrained, but value semantics of socialism more than the substance. They think it "unsocialistic" to allow foreign capital major participation, and any reference to this subject is considered new and a deviation from the Industrial Policy Resolution.

In the first place, the Industrial Policy Resolution has nothing to do with foreign capital. The Resolution was intended to set a pattern of industrial development which would give the State an overriding importance in determining the course of development and social change. The Resolution has enough loopholes for justifying almost the opposite, and it has not been implemented effectively in the spirit it was framed, in any case, so, there is no point in crying now when many deviations were made in the past by the implementing Ministry of Industry and accepted without murmur by Parliament.

111

It has never been the Government of India's stand that there will be no foreign capital allowed in this country, in fact, we inherited huge foreign investments when we became free in 1947. And although the nationalist movement was directed as much against foreign capital, as against foreign political rulers, since both were inter-linked, the Nehru Government did not start on a vendetta. He had the historical sense and the necessary perspicacity to see the immediate value of foreign capital and technology in speeding the pace of modernisation. But here, too, the emphasis in policy was always on Indianisation of development and the supremacy of the state.

A statement issued by the Ministry of Industry and Supply within eight months of freedom said:

"The Government of India agreed with the view... that, while it should be recognised that participation of foreign capital and enterprise, particularly as regards industrial technique and knowledge, will be of value to the rapid industrialisation of the country, it is necessary that the conditions under which they may participate in Indian industry should be carefully regulated in the national interest, suitable legislation will be introduced for the purpose...It will provide that, as a rule, major interest in ownership and effective control should always be in Indian hands; but power will be taken to deal with exceptional cases in a manner calculated to serve the national interest. In all cases, however, the training of suitable Indian personnel for the purpose of eventually replacing foreign experts will be insisted upon."

Foreign Capital

A year later, on April 6, 1949, Mr. Nehru made a detailed statement on foreign capital in Parliament which remains the only policy statement on subject to-date. In view of today's controversy, I might quote a few relevant extracts:

"The stress on the need to regulate, in the national interest, the scope and manner of foreign capital arose from past association of foreign capital and control with foreign domination of the economy of the country. But circumstances today are quite different...

112

Indian capital needs to be supplemented by foreign capital not only because our national savings will not be enough for the rapid development of the country on the scale we wish but also because in many cases scientific, technical and industrial knowledge and capital equipment can best be secured along with foreign capital... As regards existing foreign capital interest. Government do not intend to place any restrictions or impose any conditions which are not applicable to similar Indian enterprise. Government would also so frame their policy as to enable further foreign capital to be invested in India on terms and conditions that are mutually advantageous.

"... Foreign interests would be permitted to earn profits, subject only to regulations common to all... Remittance facilities would naturally depend on foreign exchange considerations. If, however, any foreign concerns come to be compulsorily acquired, Government would provide reasonable facilities for the remittance of proceeds.If and when foreign enterprises are compulsorily acquired, compensation will be paid on a fair and equitable basis as already announced in Government's statement of policy... As a rule, the major interest in ownership and effective control of an undertaking should be in Indian hands... Power will be taken to deal with exceptional cases in a manner calculated to serve the national interest... Government will not object to foreign capital having control of a concern for a limited period, if it is found to be in the national interest and each individual case will be dealt with on its merits... The Government of India have no desire to injure in any way British or other non-Indian interests in India and would gladly welcome their contribution in a constructive and cooperative role in the development of India's economy."

After the Industrial Policy Resolution was adopted, the Government issued another statement in August 1958 in the light of the boom of collaboration ventures which declared:

"Consistent with the Industrial Policy Resolution of 1956, Government have adopted a number of measures designed to reassure private investors, abroad particularly, with the scope and prospects open to them... Government have been following the policy of encouraging capital participation with Indian collaborations by foreign companies in respect of industrial enterprises

that have been approved—within the framework of the Plan—
by the Ministry of Commerce and Industry as being consistent
with the industrial development plans of the country, in principle, the cost of capital equipment to be imported is allowed, at a
minimum, to be financed from abroad. This is permitted as equity
participation itself or as equity and loans view combined, over
and above this minimum, while Government are of the view that
to the extent possible, majority control must be in Indian hands,
in suitable cases, and with due consideration to the existence of
arrangements by which Indian participants can exercise effective
influence on the company, particularly in the matter of development of Indian expertise and know-how, foreign investment as
bulk of the capital structure is allowed."

The Finance Minister gave, in April 1961, details of the principles and procedures governing foreign investments in India in the
context of new incentives. This statement said: "The broad principle on which the Government of India works is that conditions
should be created in India which will encourage the investment of
all capital, whether Indian or foreign. No special concessions are
offered to foreign private capital which are not offered to Indian
private capital excepting those which arise from the fact that the
owners of capital are not residents in India, e.g., remittance facilities for dividends and profits etc... It is seen that as far as possible
the majority interest in ownership and effective control of industrial undertakings in India should remain in India hands. Care
is taken to ensure that adequate provision is made for the training of Indian personnel for technical and administrative posts in
the enterprise in which foreign capital is involved. Often such a
provision is made a condition on which foreign investment is permitted. Foreign investment has to play an important role in the
development of the country and hence it is being allowed all the
facilities that indigenous capital enjoys."

Subsequent Government utterances on foreign capital have
revolved round these policy statements, which bring out two
significant points. First, there is progressive liberalisation of
approach to foreign capital. This is reflected in the change in
the substantive thought and in actual implementation of policy.
Secondly, the earlier negative attitude has been steadily giving
way to a positive quest of foreign capital buttressed by a series

of special concessions, including investment guarantees. These have been detailed in the Finance Ministers statement to the Informal Consultative Committee of Parliament on April 4, 1961, and brought up-to-date in a similar statement to a similar committee on September 18, 1964. There is also a recent Planning Commission's note on similar lines.

Those, who mistakenly believe that majority participation of foreign capital is a new trend, evidently never go through the lists of new enterprises involving foreign capital issued by the mid-Fifties and early Sixties, there was a sizable number of companies licensed with a high ration of foreign capital ownership—Parke Davis of India Ltd. (83 per cent.), Ceat Tyres (60 per cent.) and Henley Cables (60 per cent.), to quote a few.

The truth is that the Industrial Policy Resolution of 1946 and the Nehru statement on foreign capital of 1949 were of little significance to the actual implementation of policy, collaborators, who were not able to push through foreign majority agreements achieved almost the same objective by negotiating suitable management and other contracts. The end result was the same.

It may be that the process of liberalisation commenced with the acute foreign exchange crisis of the mid-Fifties. But it is also true that, judging by the very low priority and dispensable industries licensed with heavy foreign majorities, the consideration could not have always been the conservation of foreign exchange or the diffusion of new and highly sophisticated technology.

Yet, hitherto, the Government has not found it possible to sanction projects involving minority Government participation overtly or by the back-door. For example, Burmah Oil had to reduce its majority to parity in the case of the oil India venture. The Lube Project was held up for some years because of Esso's insistence, among other things, on majority ownership, and the project was sanctioned only recently on a 50–50 basis, in fact, there is a Cabinet decision, though not formally announced, that the Government will not accept minority participation in any venture, I presume this applies to back-door participation too.

Now, the licensing of foreign ventures for fertiliser production can be justified, as the Prime Minister has done, on the ground that we need the fertilisers very badly. It is quite true that the Government policy on fertiliser production has only created the demand without matching it with supply, and I mean supply at fair prices. If the foreign firms can produce this supply, well and good.

In passing, however, it may be mentioned that fertiliser manufacture is not a highly expensive proposition in comparison with steel or heavy machinery and other sophisticated industries. The foreign exchange involved is also comparatively small, and a Government that budgets for a fourth plan involving a foreign exchange outlay of Rs. 4,000 odd crores can afford to spend a few hundred crores for its projected fertiliser programme by entering into deals for new technology such as the one recently negotiated with Montecatini for the Durgapur and Cochin fertiliser plants. It is interesting to note that when the Russians withdrew from China, the Chinese concluded three contracts in 1963 with Italy, the Netherlands and Great Britain for the import of three giant nitrogenous plants (one a urea plant) of 100 TMT capacity. The average cost of each was only $6–8 million.

But there are a few points which need attention in the wider context of Indian development and policy. First, it is significant that those pressing for foreign majorities, marketing rights and other concessions for fertiliser ventures, have not questioned the resource allocation proposed for the Fourth Plan. Nor have they evaluated the fertiliser targets, or the alternative modes of conserving resources. These circles have not even questioned the role of the public sector or the formal commitment of the Government to democratic socialism, what is significant is that the foreign majority participation is sought in the public sector.

Secondly, the fertiliser deal can become a precedent. By itself, it can do no harm, but as a precedent, there is a possibility of harm. It can be used, after a period of time, as a basic argument for altering the structure of the plans, policy in other fields, the pattern of priorities and resource allocation etc. Then, as now, the emphasis may again be for a type of emergency development and policy which will permit a freer inflow of foreign capital and aid. India's own private sector may then start protesting that its scope and influence are affected.

On the face of it, as one official says, there is a tendency "to adopt anti-flood measures against a trickle". But once the underlying thought of this statement gets reflected in a policy, the logic of subsequent events can be expected to force major changes in attitudes, investment criteria, resource use, and long term economic and social goals. The question is: Is India prepared for this? Can the Congress afford to carry through this type of change and stay in power? Will such a change ensure political stability and desired economic and social progress?

One may argue, of course, that the Government of India is a powerful body and it can do this, that and other things to protect the national interest. Even if the good intentions are conceded, I do not think it is fair to rely too much on Government intervention to protect the national interest, once the process of change gathers momentum and brings about a deep economic involvement with many different countries. For that reason, the country ought to make up its mind whether it wants to go ahead with the type of planning it has accepted and the type of strategy it has adopted, or whether it feels the time has come for a fundamental change. I think, before the present Government commits the country so close to a general election, there ought to be a general debate on the subject because many long-term issues are involved.

Even purely from the economic point of view, the unconscious process of change impinges on the goal of self-reliance, the promotion of enlightened Indian enterprise, the development of a self-sustained industrial structure and so on and so forth. No suggestion has been made by foreign interests that any of these elements of national progress ought to be abandoned or changed. None is likely to be made. But changes do occur when one step leads to another and gets justified because of a shortage of foreign exchange or the availability of conditional aid.

Remittance Liabilities

I think a country like India which has been nursing balance of payments deficits, also has to bear in mind the remittance liabilities. The rate of profit in foreign controlled enterprises has generally been higher than in Indian enterprises. Consequently, the liabilities in respect of remittance of investment incomes, royalties, fees etc. tend to be high. Current payments on account of investment income has grown sharply from about Rs. 24 crores in 1956–57 to Rs. 47.3 crores in 1959–60, Rs. 61.9 crores in 1960–61, Rs. 80.4 crores in 1961–62, Rs. 94.1 crores in 1962–63 and Rs. 98 crores

117

in 1963–64. A good proportion of these represents payments in respect of service charges on loans. But it is important to note that the total investment income liabilities account for almost 30 per cent, of the external payments deficit on current account.

Full details of remittances in respect of foreign investments and collaboration are not readily available but the partial information which could be gathered indicates that remittance of current profits and dividends have nearly doubled since 1956–57. Remittances of dividends reached a peak of Rs. 22 crores in 1964–65, against Rs. 7.1 crores in 1956–57. The remittances indicated in the table accompanying account for over 17 per cent, of the payments deficit of 1964–65.

It is desirable, therefore, to examine closely the foreign exchange which may be saved by adopting a liberal policy to production units involving foreign capital and collaboration and also other likely gains in relation to the burdens of remittances, particularly because of our very delicate balance of payments position.

(Rs. crores)

	1959–60	1960–61	1961–62	1962–63	1963–64	1964–65
Current profits (excluding Burmah Shell's profit for 1963–64)	10.8	13.0	10.3	10.1	7.3	9.4
Dividends	11.7	12.6	18.5	20.9	17.0	22.0
Accumulated profits	5.6	6.7	6.2	9.2	4.7	4.7
Royalties	1.8	2.5	2.4	3.6	4.6	4.2
Technical Fees	5.8	5.5	9.6	13.0	11.5	16.2
TOTAL	35.7	40.3	47.0	56.8	45.1	56.5

Note

The complete bibliographic information for this article is as follows:
D. K. Rangnekar, 'Today's Controversies–II: Fertiliser and Foreign Capital', *The Economic Times*, 30 April 1966.

12

Trade Prospects*

When the cold wind of recession sweeps the rich countries the poor countries shiver. It has always been like that. But with the administration of effective economic power by oil-producing developing countries the air is full of commodity agreements, export stabilization schemes, stock-piles and buffers. Yet in the final analysis—and the participation in the dialogue between the rich and the poor realize—trade is the only virtuous and effective path to development. In effect what the developing countries have been demanding and what they have been politely and persistently denied is a better trading deal. World trade has been growing, in spite of worrisome shrinkages now and then. What is disconcerting is that the governments of the rich countries have made stupendous efforts to restrict that growth. There is disturbing evidence that along with expanding trade we are witnessing more trade curbing practices. In most of the western countries there are signs of a revival of economic activity after varying periods of recession. Indications are that the economies will continue to recover though perhaps less rapidly than before. In the normal course continuing economic growth should tend to prolong the revival of world trade. But new efforts to restrict trade seem to work against such a scenario. Such efforts reflect various domestic worries. One is a lingering concern in some countries that inflation may soon severely worsen. Inflation fighting programmes often tend to restrict the particular country's imports. France,

* First published in *The Economic Times*.

for example, recently instituted wide-ranging anti-inflation pro-grammes which included a continual scrutiny on import spending. Italy imposed a series of stiff rules including a requirement that Italian importers should maintain large interest deposits in the central bank. Britain with its chronic inflation problem has also moved to limit certain imports. Even in the U.S. there is an increasing protectionists' pressure, and if the trade deficit should continue to deepen protectionist moves are anticipated.

One of the main objectives of industrial planning in India has been to displace imports and reduce dependence on foreign aid. The strategy of import substitution pursued over the last two decades has brought in rich dividends. Industry has grown at a rate much faster than the economy as a whole. In the terms of physical output it is estimated that industrial growth has been one-third faster than the growth of the economy as a whole, though in recent years the rate of growth has been somewhat erratic. Even so, India is still crucially dependent on imports. It has been estimated that the share of imported machinery and equipment in gross fixed capital formation declined from 43.4 per cent in 1960–61 to 25.3 per cent in 1965–66 and 9.6 per cent in 1973–74. Yet the fact remains that in the Gross National Product the share of imports is higher (7 per cent) than that of exports (5 per cent), though this is much lower than in other developing nations like Philippines (24.6 per cent), UAR (23.3 per cent), Malaysia (39.6 per cent) and Thailand (22.9 per cent). The share of foreign trade in India's GNP must really be viewed in the context of India's large size, the domestic availability of resources, and development plans. India's vast natural and human resources provide a significant base for growth originating in domestic activity and supplies. India does not believe in isolationism, but is conscious of the need to exploit its own resources and reduce dependence on foreign aid and know-how. The basic strategy of development is indeed to increase national self-reliance. It does not mean autarky. It implies mutual benefits from trade and cooperation and a fairer redistribution of resources satisfying the basic needs. It implies reliance primarily on one's own resources, human and natural, and the capacity for autonomous goal-setting and deci-sion making. It excludes dependence on outside influences and powers that could use political pressures. It excludes exploitative trade patterns depriving countries of their natural resources for their own development. There is obviously a scope for transfer of technology, but the thrust should be on adaptation and the generation of local technology. India has, therefore, stressed increased international cooperation for collective self-reliance.

In effect what all this means is that the domestic rate of savings is expected to cover the desired investment requirement and part of such savings would, through exports, finance an increasing proportion of imports. These perspectives of development were spelt out in the Third Plan in the early 60s when it was declared that the economy would try to achieve increasing self-reliance so that India was able to support within a period of 10 to 12 years an adequate scale of investment from its own production and savings. In the wake of planning, import substitution has taken place in capital goods industries, basic metal and metal products, electrical and engineering, plant and machinery, chemical industries and in transport equipment and, to some extent, in electronics also. The process of import substitution was however interrupted and partially eroded by the oil crisis. Consequently, the draft Fifth Plan covering the period 1974–75 to 1978–79 had a defensive orientation. Its growth strategy was expressed in terms of tackling the balance of payment by 1978–79 in such a way as to meet the maximum amount of foreign exchange requirements, other than debt service charges, from our own resources. Exports then emerged as the key to self-reliance. Though the importance of exports was never played down in the earlier period of planning, the basic reliance for regulating the balance of payments has been on import control rather than on export growth. Import control has been a negative instrument which perhaps yielded results in the short run. This control in itself was related to earlier programmes of import substitution which originated in aid availability. If import substitution had been trade-based and not aid-based perhaps India's industrial structure might have been somewhat different.

When, in the mid-50s, the country embarked on planned development the direction and pattern of export trade was traditional. Traditional exports to the West however appeared to have reached a plateau. This period also coincided with the development of the concept of non-alignment by Jawaharlal Nehru which, in the

121

field of foreign trade, meant conscious diversification of India's trade relations. The concept of rupee payments emerged and a series of trade and economic agreements were signed with the Soviet Union, Yugoslavia and other East European countries. These agreements gave a calculated boost to India's export trade. In 1951–52 East Europe as a bloc accounted for a mere 0.6 per cent of India's exports and 1.2 per cent of imports. The figures for 1975–76 were to 10.6 per cent and 17.2 per cent respectively. The shift in emphasis was brought about by two important factors. First, the agreements provided for non-traditional exports. Second, the rupee payment facility induced large imports by India of a variety of capital goods and other essential equipment which, in turn, lead to Indian exports in terms of barter deals. In addition, there was recession in India about a decade ago when the iron and steel industry and the engineering industry made their first major thrust abroad. Deficient domestic demand inspired larger exports of a wide variety of goods including textiles. Even so this cannot be regarded as an autonomous growth. This was a part of India's plan strategy. The size of exportable surplus had also been consciously enlarged in the case of a number of products in order to achieve the purpose. Consequently, export of unmanufactured goods from India has risen by 12.8 per cent per annum during the 13 year old period 1960–61 to 1973–74. The share of manufactured goods in India's total exports during the same period rose from 48 per cent to 59 per cent.

In more recent years there has been a steady increase in India's export earning. For example, between 1970–71 and 1974–75 the rupee value of exports increased at an average rate of 21.5 per cent at current prices. This is no mean achievement. However, this rise must be seen against the perspective of inflation. The volume of exports, for example, increased at a much lower rate around 4 per cent annum. This would seem to suggest that an appreciable proportion of the gain reflected higher average unit value realization because of inflation. Even so, the growth reflected in better export earnings cannot be lightly dismissed. This has encouraged our planners to mark up the Fifth Plan export target. The annual export growth rate has been hiked to 8.5 per cent in real terms. This perhaps reflects, among other things, the new optimism generated by the rising sales of ready-made garments, engineering goods and leather manufactures. Japan and Iran have emerged as important buyers of iron ore. Iran is also importing Indian transmission towers and other manufactures. The EEC has become a major market for Indian goods. The uptrend in exports may continue especially if the Gulf countries continued to shop in India in a big way. Some of the turkey industrial and civil engineering contracts awarded to India are perhaps an indication.

But the question remains whether the volume of exports would rise at a fast enough rate and whether exports will outstrip the import bill. India's import bill will rose by 53 per cent in 1974–75 and 14 per cent in 1975–76, while export income increased by 32 per cent and 18 per cent respectively. The trade deficit was already large (Rs. 432 crores) in 1973–74 but the gap widened to Rs. 1,190 crores in 1974–75 and Rs. 1,216 crores in 1975–76. The planners have therefore had to revise some of their calculations. In the draft Fifth Plan exports were intended to cover as mush as 89 per cent of the projected imports during the Plan period. The revised Fifth Plan export target of Rs. 21,722 crores might probably cover three-fourths of the revised import bill of Rs. 28,524 over the five-year period. The proclaimed ideal of zero net aid appears to be receding beyond recall. The revised Fifth Plan envisages net aid of 9 per cent of the total Plan investment as against 3.1 per cent visualized in the draft. Institutional aid flows are tending to decline and there is the danger that developing nations may have to fall back upon expensive commercial loans which make the problem of debt servicing extremely acute.

In this context it is argued in certain quarters that in a country like economic growth must itself become trade-based. But then can a developing country regard exports as a leading sector in the developing process? A good deal has been written about export-led industrialization as an essential strategy for economic progress in developing countries largely based on the experience of small Asian countries like Hong Kong and Taiwan. But it is fallacious to argue that this strategy is suitable to all developing countries irrespective of size, domestic imbalances, resource endowment, etc. It is not conceivable that trade between unequal partners would tend to radiate a certain inequality and perpetuate economic imbalances if not underdevelopment. The examples of Hong Kong and Taiwan can often appear as false guide to countries like

India. There is reason to believe that attempts to promote export growth based on foreign capital and transnational participation could provoke protective sentiment in importing countries without conferring any tangible benefits on the poorer society. This is not to minimise the significance of export growth in the process of development. Perhaps the export sector deserves as much attention and development planning in a large country like ours. But it needs to be emphasized that a higher level of exports can only be sustained by a steady growth in the output of exportable products in order to protect domestic absorption, not by domestic denial. Export growth based on a squeeze of domestic consumption is not in the long run socially desirable or economically feasible. Export planning must, therefore, be directly related to production planning. In the final analysis we can hope for a sustained increase in exports only if we are able to ensure that there is a sustained growth in the national income.

But the moot question remains: can developing nations finance their development imports with exports in a value system in which the cost of their imports tends to leap-frog over their export income? Indian experience is telling enough. It brings out the severe impact of the loaded value system leading to deterioration in the trade balance. During the first half of 1976–77 India was able to narrow the trade gap mainly because of a slide in imports; the trend was reversed in the second half largely because of a spurt in PQL imports. The unit value index for PQL imports (base 1968–69) jumped from 334 in 1973–74, 736 in 1974–75 and 829 in 1975–76. But the cost of other imports also rose very sharply. Thus, for example, the unit value index for import of food and fertilizers shot up from 182 and 91 respectively in 1973–74 to 229 and 173 in 1974–75 and 276 and 167 in 1975–76. The terms of trade have recently shown further deterioration, and not merely because of the cost of POL imports. The terms of trade index which showed improvement in the first four years of the Fourth Plan fell steeply from 124 in 1972–73 to 106 in 1973–74, 77 in 1974–75 and 70 in 1975–76. In this context one can see that the impressive growth in India's foreign exchange reserves during 1975–76 recently has been to a large extent the result of appreciable inflows of private remittances through official channels following the government's severe measures against smuggling and illegal dealing in foreign exchange. The revised import bill in the Fifth Plan is, at Rs. 28,524 crores, Rs. 14,424 crores higher than indicated in the draft estimate. To this increase POL has contributed Rs. 3,200 crores (at Rs. 6,280 crores) and fertilizers and raw material for fertilizers Rs. 1,718 crores (at Rs. 3,168 crores). The increase on these two counts works out to less than 40 per cent of the total increase, and thereby hangs a tale.

The steep rise in the projected trade deficit from Rs. 1,350 crores in the draft and to Rs. 7,802 crores in the final version of the plan is not a phenomenon that is unique to India. Many developing countries are going into heavy trade deficits with the rich countries as well as oil producing developing countries. As a group the trade deficit of non-oil producing developing nations is placed at US $38 billion for 1975 as against a deficit of US $12.1 Billion in 1973. The non-oil producing developing nations have been severely hit by precipitate falls in terms of trade in the last three years. The size of the trade deficits would not have mattered were they to be entirely financed by better trading deals or other bilateral agreements. But invariably the deficits are financed by creditors who demand economic measures which have the effect of restricting trade of the developing nations. The consequent rise in external indebtedness of the developing nations reflects the underlying maladjustments in the world economy. In the context of the present international framework and inequality the efforts of individual nations to boost exports and to catch up with their escalating import bills often tend to result in frustration.

It has been argued that the world economy can regain its momentum if the developed economies could, by lifting their growth rate, transmit expansionary impulses to the developing countries. But the fact remains that the periods since the Second World War which saw a tremendous expansion and economic buoyancy in the developed market economies also coincided with a surge in the indebtedness of developing countries. Most of these countries were afflicted by balance of payments crisis which grievously affected their development programmes. Perhaps what is visualized now is not the traditional process of expansion. The new thinking proposes a shift from the present cheap energy sources to new energy sources and new technology

125

and also a new division of labour as between the developed and developing countries. The developing countries would be encouraged to specialize in labour-intensive industries, probably also pollution-intensive industries, leaving the sophisticated and the research and technology-intensive industries to the developed market economies. Attempts are being made by certain interests to propagate this line of thinking in India also oblivious of the country's technological progress on industrial thrust. If our trade and payments problems remain unsolved the basic reason lies in the loaded value system of international trade. Also fitment into the new pattern of international division of labour was likely to destroy the domestic pattern of growth, particularly in the case of a large and newly industrialising country like India. The primary objective of development is to meet the basic needs of the population. This would entail an increase in the supply of food-stuffs and manufactured goods using technology appropriate to the resources endowment of the developing countries. The published concept of international division of labour now calls for specialization in the production of goods needed by the consumer-oriented developed countries. Surely, this would tend to distort the pattern of investment of the newly industrialising nations often leading to the adoption of controversial projects or investment non-essential to the developing economy. Moreover, specialization oriented towards such a concept would expose the exports of developing countries to highly volatile forces of the market in developed countries.

The basic problems is really one of overcoming handicaps imposed by the institutional framework which today governs trade, foreign investment and external economic relations. The framework of treaties, conventions and legal procedures ensures an unregulated operation of commercial forces of some of the rich countries. It is no easy task for the developing countries singly or collectively to get round this framework. First, the compensatory finance scheme would have to be liberalized. Even trade with the rupee payment countries would have to be brought under the scheme. Indexation of commodities entering international trade will have to be seriously considered and supplemented by price stabilisation-cum-product agreements to correct the adverse terms of trade impairing specialized exports like jute, tea, copper, zinc, etc. Reform of the international economic order on this scale would involve a search for new methods of global management of resources in the long-term interest of all nations. In the short run developing nations will have to move swiftly towards the pursuit of self-reliant and self-sustained growth. Countries like India which have already advanced in this direction will have to guard against excessive specialization under the published scheme of international division of labour in order to play an effective role in regional development.

Note

The complete bibliographic information for this article is as follows:
D. K. Rangnekar, 'Trade Prospects', *The Economic Times*, Annual, 1977.

Part Three

Rope Tricks—
Planning India's Development

13

The Annual Indian Rope Trick*

Analysing India's budgets, D. K. Rangnekar says that budgeting today is an accountant's delight, not the economic exercise it was.

Any politician will tell you that the budget is a trick designed to hit the taxpayer without hitting the voter. The finance minister will tell you that it is a rope trick with him trying precariously to cover the excess of his disbursement over receipts. From his point of view, the reward to the citizen for saving money is equal to his ability to pay his taxes without borrowing. The marvel of all history is the patience with which human beings everywhere submit to burdens unnecessarily laid upon them by their government. India's budgetary experience, more recently at any rate, is that it is hard to fill up one hole without digging another.

In pre-Independence days the budget was merely a financial exercise, a description and analysis in the main of public revenues and public expenditures. The size of the budget was small because the role of the state itself was limited mainly to the administration of law and order. The budget was created by administrative expediencies and the policing requirements. The budgetary system had achieved a degree of stability, but it was thoroughly inadequate to cope with the basic task of development. But then the question of governmental intervention in the economy on a major

* First published in *Business Standard* on 20 February 1983.

131

scale simply did not arise. The philosophy and concepts of the day precluded the emergence of such initiatives.

Over the years there has been a sea-change in the role of the state and the impact of the budget. With the commencement of planning the state assumed a pre-eminent role in directing the flow of resources and the nature of development. Thus massive state intervention in investment, production and distribution became a major plank in India's strategy of development. And the budget emerged as the most significant instrument both to mobilise national resources and generate economic development. In a country where political propaganda had stirred the underprivileged masses, the budget became much more than a catalyst; budgeting itself became a social and managerial process of modernisation and social change. In this sense the budget indicated the nation's sense of direction, and the likely level of investment and development.

These tasks have inevitably cast new stresses and strains on the budgetary system and posed several grave problems, some defying solution. For one thing, the budget has been growing in size enormously, thereby generating at times undesirable pressures on economy. Secondly, the problem of financing ever-growing government expenditures has become complex both because of its sheer size and because of the country's division into separate states loosely joined into a federal system. Until recently, the central government managed to record surpluses of current revenues over current expenditure, while the state governments have consistently dis-saved, relying generally on crutches provided by the centre. But in more recent years, the centre itself has started dissaving, spending beyond its means and borrowing heavily. The current account deficit in 1980–81 was Rs 1,715 crores, in 1981–82 it was Rs 972.34 crores [B.E.], in 1982–83 Rs 626.43 crores [B E.]. The last figure is likely to be drastically revised when accounts are finalised.

The manner in which public expenditure is financed is important to the economy. If our government financed all its expenditures by borrowing, we would move headlong into serious inflation. If, on the other hand, the government sought to finance all its expenditures by heavy taxation, which restricted individual consumption, we could move into deflation and unemployment. These two extreme cases are only intended to illustrate the kind of problem a budget poses today, and emphasise the imperative need for a sense of balance in financing government expenditures. The need for a balanced approach has been frequently and erroneously equated with pessimism by certain finance ministers in this country. Where resources are mobilised and allocated in terms of priority planning targets and goals, such pessimism can be disastrous. An outstanding illustration of this defeatist approach is the obsession with inflation. At the slightest indication of a price increase, the finance minister torments himself and unsuspectingly walks into the trap of combating inflation and clamping on brakes when in fact it is time to press on the accelerator and clutch the steering wheel. At the other end, deficit financing has also been an easy way out for finance ministers who have no control over the surge of unproductive nonessential expenditures. In years of agricultural distress, excessive reliance on deficit financing has played havoc with the economy and society. The two extremes are reflected in the low level equilibrium India is lingering at in conditions where the economy is easily tilted into inflation and stagnation. This ding-dong is a major factor in India's slow pace of progress. With rare exceptions, India's finance ministers have shied away from bold experiments. There has been a certain reluctance to innovate and experiment, reflecting partly perhaps the conventional political philosophy of the Congress.

Of the finance ministers India has had, only three—Liaquat Ali Khan, T. T. Krishnamachari, and Indira Gandhi—showed any interest in new experiments, albeit on a limited plane. It was an irony of fate that India's first socialist budget was presented by a Muslim League leader, Liaquat Ali Khan, who became finance minister in the interim government. If one ignored the political motivation, it stunned the people with its radical fiscal approach. The country was in the throes of a crisis and facing the backlash of partition. But Liaquat Ali proposed new and drastic taxation—a business profits tax of 25 per cent on profit of Rs 1 lakh and over, a graduated tax on capital gains, and a super tax on income. He doubled corporate taxes. Significantly, the Muslim League leader made a tremendous gesture to Mahatma Gandhi by abolishing the salt tax. He also raised the minimum exemption limit for purposes of income taxation. The entire package of taxation was expected to yield slightly less than Rs 40 crores, a seemingly small amount today but a colossal tally for 1947. Liaquat Ali's socialist quest sent businessmen scurrying hither-thither. Stock brokers reeled with dizziness. The share and commodity markets went crashing. So sharp was the general reaction that a senior Congressman reportedly groaned: "The poor man has got his salt free; but the rich man has been sent to his grave."

Liaquat Ali's successors, Shanmukhan Chetty and John Mathai, were both engaged in what may be called a plain and simple holding operation. They sought to mollify businessmen who were bled white by Liaquat Ali.

They had to deal with a colossal refugee problem in the wake of the communal convulsions. The defence of Kashmir and police action in Hyderabad also posed a challenge to an economy already nursing the after-effects of colonialism and war. The challenge placed a premium on conventional notions and concepts of budgeting. Not surprisingly, some of these budgets came under sharp attack from the Congress party leadership, and it was not long before differences surfaced publicly between Nehru and Mathai. They reportedly differed on questions of payments of compensation for the acquisition of private property and the proposed creation of a planning commission.

Chetty presented free divided India's first full-fledged budget to the provisional Parliament. Mathai presented two budgets in 1949–50 and he was more noted for the biting, carping manner in which he dealt with his critics. When criticised for having ignored the poor man in the street by the late Durgabai (who subsequently married C. D. Deshmukh), he rebuked her saying: 'Madam, take my advice, don't take seriously every man you come across in the street.' C. D. Deshmukh has the distinction of having presented the largest number of budgets—six in a row.

Apart from the fairly long innings which coincided with the launching of the first five year plan, Deshmukh's tenure was noted for a relatively good economic turnout and sound management. One cannot possibly overlook the kindness of the monsoons and the promising climate which encouraged businessmen to produce more and go for expansion. In many ways the first plan was somewhat of a sham; most of the projects with the exception of community development had been designed and launched before partition. The stabilisation of food prices was helped, besides the weather gods, by an American wheat loan. The most glaring failure on the part of the government then was its inability to come forth with development oriented budgets. The actual story was one of missed opportunities. The government and leadership woke up rather late and sought to change gears in the second and third plans when food and foreign exchange difficulties had aggravated the situation, rendered difficult by two military conflicts. Increasing foreign pressures compelled a reversal of the plan strategy.

However, to Deshmukh's credit goes rectitude and prudence which won him accolades from the British. Reacting to the current inflationary crisis in the U.K. then, the *Times*, London, stated that the country needed a Deshmukh to handle its economy. Significantly, on one occasion allegations were made of a leakage of the fiscal scheme. Deshmukh promptly offered to resign. His integrity was impeccable and not surprisingly Nehru refused to accept his resignation. As an anti-climax Deshmukh resigned on the issue of the reorganisation of Maharashtra state, formed from the erstwhile Bombay province.

T. T. Krishnamachari succeeded Deshmukh. For intellectual competence, debating brilliance and long-term perspective, Krishnamachari had few peers. When he came on the scene in the mid-50s he created a minor stir by innovating the entire tax system on the lines proposed by Nicholas Kaldor, the Cambridge economist. This gentleman came to India to participate in a seminar at the Gokhale Institute, Poona, and later, presumably inspired by the rawness of the territory of economic management against the backdrop of a plan, persuaded C. D. Deshmukh to let him visit India again and look at the fiscal scheme. While Deshmukh obliged, being non-controversial, he placed the Kaldor scheme on the dusty shelf. Krishnamachari, who took an impish delight in springing a surprise on Parliament and the public, ferreted out the Kaldor scheme and clamped on the controversial expenditure tax, the wealth tax, gift tax and made drastic changes in capital gains taxes in 1957. Kaldor had suggested that if the expenditure tax were introduced the income-tax should be slashed. But Krishnamachari had his own mixture retaining income-tax at the prevailing high rates. When the Kaldor scheme of taxation as introduced by Krishnamachari failed to produce the desired results there was a hue and cry in the country and in a private conversation Kaldor disowned responsibility, saying he was unfamiliar with Indian social and economic conditions. Nevertheless, this phase saw a sharp step-up in plan investments, a good part originating in the centre's capital outlays and expansion of what is now called the public sector. Unfortunately, Krishnamachari got embroiled in the Mundhra scandal which rocked the political scene and attracted worldwide publicity. The finance minister, among others, had to pay the price. Morarji Desai who took over from Krishnamachari had the distinction of presenting four budgets none of which was really outstanding for innovation, reform and thrust. The main features of his budgets included the sharpest ever increase in defence outlay in the wake of the Chinese attack in 1963 and the introduction of the unpopular Compulsory Deposit Scheme and the gold control order. While describing CDS as temporary phenomenon initially almost every finance minister has found it convenient to continue it. The gold control scheme had merits but was clumsily implemented. How much of gold ornaments were collected ostensibly for armaments is not clearly known even today!

Desai's exit under the Kamaraj plan brought back Krishnamachari for a second stint. Promptly Krishnamachari withdrew Desai's Compulsory Deposit Scheme and the gold control order and introduced his own version of an annuity deposit scheme. Krishnamachari was somewhat jaded during this period largely because he resented the intrusion of the World Bank and its mission headed by Bell which was seeking to alter the direction of policy. This led to clashes with the late Lal Bahadur Shastri who was more receptive to the Bell mission's advice to restructure economic policy, devalue the rupee and so on. The brush with Shastri culminated in the premature resignation of Krishnamachari. Amidst rumours that Shastri proposed to hold an 'informal enquiry' into a charge-sheet submitted by some elements against the finance minister, Krishnamachari resigned barely a day or two before Shastri died in Tashkent. And in came Sachin Chowdhury, a distinguished lawyer from Calcutta but a relatively unknown figure in economic circles. He is better known for the devaluation of the rupee in June 1966 than for the budget he presented. His was a sorry plight.

His exit brought back Morarji Desai, who came for a second innings with the rank of a deputy prime minister in 1967, only to depart in anger on the eve of Indira Gandhi's radical programme which included bank nationalisation, abolition of privy purses and managing agency houses and the Congress split in 1969–70. With Desai's departure, the prime minister, Indira Gandhi, herself held temporary charge of the finance portfolio. From then on for a few years Mrs Gandhi took a keen interest in budgetary and economic policies. Though her budget in 1970 sharply pushed up taxation, she initiated drastic cuts subsequently in the marginal rate of taxation at the highest level from 97.75 per cent to 77 per cent and subsequently to 66 per cent. This operation reduction was pushed through by C. Subramanium who was otherwise non-descript. Pranab Mukherjee, the present finance minister, was then minister of state in the finance ministry.

Mrs Gandhi handed over the finance portfolio to Y. B. Chavan who had the honour of presenting four budgets. Chavan was on all sides and characteristically his budgets sought to please everybody. This period was not particularly conspicuous for any gain or loss. Subramanium took over from Chavan in 1974 and held on through the Emergency years.

The Janata regime 1977–79 was willy-nilly disastrous from the budget point of view. The only significant point to note is that H. M. Patel, who was the principal finance secretary in the heyday of Krishnamachari and unfairly figured in the Mundhra scandal, happened to occupy the finance minister's post. In a sense there was also another rather dubious feature of the budgets he presented, namely, the gold auction scandal. The Reserve Bank's gold stocks under the scheme found their way into certain bullion speculators' hoards and elsewhere. Parliament committees subsequently took very serious note of this bizzare operation.

Patel made way for Charan Singh when the rickety Janata coalition collapsed. His budget was an unashamed kulak attack on the urban upper and middle classes which allegedly supported the Congress. Sweeping concessions were given to kulaks and heavy taxes were levied on urban tax-payers. The last spell succeeded in bringing about a certain stagnation of the economy and exposing it to inflationary pressures.

R. Venkataraman and Pranab Mukherjee who succeeded him have not yet fully countered the full effects of the Janata and kulak budgets. These two finance ministers have also had to battle with three ignominious events—the Antulay affair, the black bearer bond scheme which was immoral from the word go, and the meek submission to the I.M.F. authorities in terms of an unwarranted loan arrangement. The budgets have been lacklustre affairs, though a combination of factors including the weather and planlessness have brought about a relatively better balance in demand and supply.

But then this is a negative satisfaction because we are back to a low level equilibrium. This is a shocking realisation considering the fact that the centre's budget is every year bulging. Among other things, there has been a steep increase in defence spending. In the '50s the defence expenditure was very small and even in the '60s was only in the region of Rs 400 crores. After the Chinese struck, Desai's budget provided for a staggering outlay of Rs 816 crores. In 1971–72 the defence allocation was Rs 1,240 crores. The provision for defence was marked up to Rs 4,600 crores in 1982–83. In relation to the semi-stagnant state of the economy these are formidable figures, almost prohibitive, though perhaps unavoidable in the existing geo-strategic situation. Yet one cannot help feeling that valuable resources are going away from development and mass prosperity. Non-plan spending has also grown sharply. In 1982–83 it was in the region of Rs 15,100 crores. With the burden of rising unproductive and consumption expenditures of the government, the public is denied the full benefits of its own contribution to the exchequer.

A sound budgetary system is expected to move resources to efficient purposes in order to ensure that every rupee is well spent. If this assurance is lacking, the public sacrifices in vain. One of the marvels of our social and political set-up is the people's limitless patience and their inexplicable tolerance of economic waste and dissipation of resources. Indeed, in recent years growth aims have been displaced by pure revenue considerations. Budgeting today is an accountant's delight, not economic exercise. Even though the expansion of the public sector has greatly slowed down, finance ministers in desperate search for revenues have had of late to place greater reliance on non-budgetary sources of finance to cover long-term capital expenditures and defence. Though the government controls the investment pattern of large financial institutions like the Life Insurance Corporation and more recently the banks and the provident funds associations, it has not been found possible to step up market borrowings to any appreciable extent. This has forced the government sector to rely increasingly on foreign aid, foreign borrowings and central bank credit creation (deficit financing).

The chart gives an idea of the steady increase in deficit financing.

The revised estimates for the centre's budget placed the overall deficit at Rs 1,700 crores in 1981–82. The figure for 1982–83 was originally estimated at Rs 1,365 crores. This has since been revised in the course of the debates in Parliament to Rs 1,371 crores. Current indications are that the real deficit will be much larger, though some window-dressing in the pre-budget days must be taken for granted.

Strangely, revenue considerations and the obsession with inflationary dangers have been cited as factors which restrain the government's developmental or capital expenditures. But this, in turn, has had the effect of dampening developmental activity all over the country. Consequently, recent budgets have been singularly unimpressive.

The lopsided approach to budgeting basically, however, reflected the pathetic inability of our government to widen and deepen the tax base and make it more equitable, on the one hand, and its inability to prevent leakage of incomes both on domestic and foreign account, on the other. The excessive reliance on foreign aid has cost the country dearly, even if it may have helped us, over a short period, to tide over the foreign exchange crisis created by distortions in planning and heavy defence commitments. The orientation of planning has undergone a change under pressure, the rupee has had to be devalued at the most inopportune time, export promotion developments have been retarded, and, finally, a process of deplanning has been forced down our throats.

I do not believe that India is heavily taxed in a general sense, but it is a fact that the ratio of tax revenue to GNP has been pushed up from around 7 per cent in the early '50s to around 18 to 19 per cent in the late '70s. But the tax burden falls unequally on a small segment of the urban population—around 40 lakhs in a country with a population of 70 crores. The burden of providing the government with a current tax revenue of over Rs 17.614 crores is carried entirely by urban citizens and businessmen. They pay direct taxes on income, wealth, capital gains and inheritance, apart from indirect taxes on goods and services. The indirect taxes include excise, sales tax and other levies on almost everything that goes into current consumption. Such levies account for over 80 per cent of all tax revenue. Here again there is a bias in favour of the farmer. There are no allowances for personal expenses, children's education, medical or other essential purposes as in other countries, and, consequently, the incidence of taxation appears to fall heavily on fixed income earners.

Though the exemption limit now has been raised, it is still on the low side, considering that the value of money has fallen.

There is a good case for increasing the exemption limit if only to free low-income earners from the rigorous of taxation. But there is no doubt that the aggregate burden of taxation is so heavy that evasion has become attractive and common. Today 'black money' is nearly as significant as white money, and is at the root of what may be called India's deplorable parallel economy. All this will continue to flourish so long as dairy, farming, forestry, vineyards and a host of prosperous agricultural activities are kept out of the tax net. While showing consideration for earned income, it is about time that agricultural incomes, which are multiplying several-fold every year, thanks to the sacrifices of the tax-payers, who have financed and sustained farm developments, is taxed in much the same way as any other current income. And if our Constitution stands in the way, the urgent need to rope in farm income is as justifiable a reason for its amendment as any.

Note

The complete bibliographic information for this article is as follows:
D. K. Rangnekar, 'The Annual Indian Rope Trick', *Business Standard*, 20 February 1983.

14

Nehruism and the Second Phase*

Many factors prevented Nehruism from becoming a fully effective doctrine of action in Nehru's lifetime.

Policy-making was so personalised that the meaning of policies was not easily radiated and not properly explained Nehru knew where he wanted to go and how, but others did not fully understand his intentions and ways. And since many of his colleagues did not sincerely subscribe to his philosophy and ideals, his policies and utterances came to be interpreted according to the proclivities of the interpreter.

The other vital gap in Nehruism was that the institutional aspect of change was neglected. If adequate attention had been paid to institutional reform, conditions today would have been much more favourable for a take-off into self-sustained growth and structural change. The task of Nehru's successors would also have been much easier and deviation so much more difficult. The absence of well-developed institutions and traditions is further evidence of the fact that Nehru's visions needed strategies and tactics which the men around him were intellectually and otherwise incapable of providing.

The failure to complete agrarian reform and to bring about the institutional changes necessary for mobilising resources and for channeling them into desirable uses is without doubt a crucial factor holding back the process of development. Without the necessary institutional support, the growth of the public sector cannot

* First published in *Economic Weekly* in July 1964.

possibly be dynamic. And without this dynamism the strategy of growth and modernisation envisaged by Nehru cannot become fully effective.

The political transition from the Nehru regime to the Shastri administration has been accomplished so deftly, that many people have tended to overlook one important implication of the change, namely, that India is now in the full tide of a second revolution, the elements and nuances of which are still quite unpredictable. The last 17 years of Congress rule represented in many ways a continuation of the political revolution which, under a succession of charismatic leadership, overthrew the British Raj. Pandit Nehru was the last of the old guard leaders, the sole survivor of the great men of the freedom struggle. He dominated the national scene by dint of his dynamic personality, exemplary character, heroism, mass appeal and eclecticism. He is gone, and his death marks the end of this phase of our nationalist revolution and the commencement of an altogether new experience in a new setting.

Under the spell of Nehru's magnetism and unchallenged authority, conflicting interests, petty rivalries, fundamental differences, all these and more had got submerged. The overpowering influence of Nehru's charismatic leadership evoked seemingly common response in all layers and interests, so that it was possible for the administration to complete three successful general elections, launch three Five-Year Plans, overcome tensions and, in a broad sense, project an image of a mature nation. Under Nehru, India at least gave the impression of having achieved a measure of stability, fairly effective leadership with a sense of direction, and a reasonably efficient administration seeking to hasten the process of social and economic change.

Revolution of Rising Expectations

To what extent was this picture real? We are too near the event to make an objective assessment of Nehru's contribution. But it is clear that with the end of his regime, all that latent urges, political differences, petty loyalties, caste lobbies and conflicting interests will now come to the surface and pose a new challenge to the establishment. Towards the end of Nehru's long career, the symptoms of the second revolution were already evident. The revolution of rising expectations had seeped down via the political propaganda machine of the Congress Party, the promises of the Five-Year Plans, the local political campaigns for rural redress, the new massive projects, and the message of the radio and the cinema. The spread of regional literacy and political consciousness had set off explosive forces of linguism, casteism, and local loyalties. New elites in the States and pressure groups had appeared and, by reason of their local affiliations, posed a threat to the High Command at the Centre. But Nehru's personal authority had the effect of preventing resurgent forces from becoming overtly destructive. It must be conceded that he had, at times, great difficulty in countering the pressures, and there have been instances in the recent past when the Centre has had willy-nilly to acquiesce in petty compromises or make concessions to parochialism in the name of "national integration".·

In a broad sense, however, it was possible for the Nehru regime to ameliorate feelings of alienation and provide a sense of unity, and inculcate a sense of commitment to planned development and progressive ideas even in unlikely sections of the population.

Beneath all the current tensions and problems lies the basic urge of an awakened people for material progress and social change. This urge was once latent; it is no longer so. Our people, who had been stirred by the message of nationalism, and who had been assiduously fed on the ideas of modernisation, patiently waited for years to see independence being made meaningful in economic and social terms. Now, under the burden of rising living costs and persistent postponement of social welfare, they are getting rather restive and frustrated. Bhubaneswar demonstrated that the revolution of rising expectations can no longer be contained. The recent agitation over rising prices shows that the crisis is deepening.

Thus, while the problems of unity and social progress have become almost desperately urgent, Nehru is no more on the political scene. The new leadership now has to meet the challenge without Nehru and without any charisma. This means the Congress High Command can no longer rely on emotive response, or the impact of a single dynamic person or even a group of individuals. It will be the actual doings of the leadership which will now count more than ever before.

It is fashionable these days to seek comfort in the thought that the basic foundations of modernisation, and social change have already been laid, and that, so long as the new leaders adhere to "Mr. Nehru's policies", there need be no feeling of void. Those who argue on these lines—and there are quite a few who do so—unwittingly deny creative possibilities in the higher echelons of the Congress Party today. That apart, in the first place, there can be no rigidity about any programme or policy. What really matters is the broad sense of direction, the social and political philosophy, the basic framework. Secondly, even the most well-conceived programmes in the world cannot be effectively implemented without a deep sense of conviction, and abiding belief in the underlying goals and an intellectual attachment to the experiment itself. Given such a framework, even an opportunist leadership, without the driving force of inherent conviction, could succeed in making an impact. A shrewd pragmatic leadership may excel.

Note

The complete bibliographic information for this article is as follows:
D. K. Rangnekar, 'Nehruism and the Second Phase', *Economic Weekly* (special no.) 16 (July 1964): 1235–1237, 1239, 1241–1242.

15

Second Thoughts on Indian Planning*

T he time has come for intellectuals to take an active interest in
the debate on social and economic issues.

If we are not to get lost in totally irrelevant questions, we
should go beyond whether the Fourth Plan outlay ought to be
Rs. 23,750 crores or whether Rs. 18,000 crores would be more
"realistic" and ask:

(1) Have we embarked on planning without being prepared
for it?
(2) Have we attempted to plan for economic and social transformation without sorting out carefully the factors which
are of crucial significance to the process of planning?
(3) Is planning for rapid economic and social change consistent with a parliamentary framework of the British
type?

Unless we give serious thought to our political institutions and
their functions, we may get deeper and deeper into a crisis which
might extend much beyond an inadequate rate of economic
growth.

Nothing can be more disastrous for planning than public apathy
and governmental indifference. But today planning has become
some kind of a bad joke to the public and an unwanted legacy

* Article first published in *Economic and Political Weekly*, Annual Number (II,
3–5), February 1967.

to the Government which cannot be discarded. If there was any conviction at all at the political level, it no longer exists in quarters that matter. To a certain extent, the climate reflects the slow-down of the economy and the impact of shortages and inflation. But there are also other factors behind the situation. These include the change in the quality and outlook of planners, the disenchant-ment of the administration with planning, the loss of morale of the leadership and its inability to get a grip over national currents, and, above all, the disappearance of men who commanded public opinion by virtue of their intellectual convictions and their faith in planning.

Yet, the decline in leadership and the near collapse of the Yojana Bhavan cannot be taken as the death warrant of the Indian experiment. Rather, it should make us all sit up and take note of the situation and remedy it, if possible. It is a sad commentary on intellectual activity in our country that, even today, after three plans, we should still be engaged in elementary discussions of whether a plan should be big or small, or whether we should have free enterprise or public sector in industry, or whether we ought to have controls or no controls, or whether we should permit or not permit foreign capital in certain industries, or what have you. These distract attention from the real state of the economy, the political compulsions of the present situation, the subtle, at times inadvertent, destruction of instruments and policies essential for achieving accepted objectives, and, more particularly, the intellec-tual bankruptcy and political opportunism of persons associated with planning and policy these days.

It seems to me that the time has come for intellectuals to take an active interest in the debate on social and economic matters so that they may provide the people with a proper focus. Largely because this is lacking, half-educated politicians tend to get mixed up in superficial issues concerning, say, the licensing of a fertiliser plant with foreign capital participation, or, occasionally, with the Nehruistic content of a particular phrase, or the lack of it in a par-ticular policy measure or decision. The big issues are missed, and one of these is that planning has, in this country, virtually lost its bearings, and so has the Government lost track of the facts of the economic and social situation in the country.

The Real Issues

Rationality points to the need for examining not merely the size of a plan's investment, but also priorities, social content, the scope and strategy for bringing about structural changes in society, the direction of policy and type of tools selected for speeding up the achievement of desirable goals. Unfortunately, now-a-days, none of these issues provokes any debate in the context of the prevailing situation, and the meagre discussion on the Fourth Plan has roughly been equivalent to isolated comment on the overall size. Even this is essentially a projection of the fraudulent division of opinion between the Finance Ministry and the Planning Commission. The mythical clash is really a smokescreen utilised by the planners (a) to gain political acceptance of a pre-determined investment target seemingly worked out after an elaborate process of discussion and compromise between the Commission and the Finance Ministry, the well-publicised controversy between the two wings of the Establishment and the subsequent agreement lending an air of "reality" to the planners' "ultimate" decision; (b) to divert critics away from the fundamentals and big issues, a public discussion of which might otherwise have been embarrassing to the planners.

Here, I should like to pose a few questions which, I think, ought to be examined carefully by thinkers and moulders of opinion. If we are not to get lost in totally irrelevant matters we should go beyond whether the Fourth Plan outlay ought to be Rs. 23,750 crores, or whether Rs. 18,000 crores or so might be more "realistic" (1) Have we embarked on a plan experiment without being prepared for it? (2) Have we aimed at planning for social and economic transformation without sorting out carefully factors and elements of crucial significance to the process of planning? (3) Is planned development for rapid growth and social well-being inconsistent with a parliamentary framework of the British style of democracy?

Looking back on the two decades of independence, it does seem that the country was neither prepared for full-fledged planning, nor was it prepared to abandon altogether the concept of planning which formed a part of the nationalist movement. The

forces released by political liberation had elements of social consciousness, but lacked direction and focus. Nehru in government
was a rather different person from Nehru the leader of a forward-
looking political movement seeking expression and fulfilment.
Consequently, even the socially-conscious elements could not find
free play after independence. After some initial fumbling with
radical ideas, Nehru, struck a characteristic compromise, giving
the country an institution called the Planning Commission, but
without anything like a philosophy of planning and well charted
strategy of development. Going through the documents of the
Commission, I find hardly any study which attempts an intelligent discussion of the political and economic issues involved in
planning in Indian conditions or projecting an appropriate, or
even a plausible, philosophy of development and indicating the
institutional and other changes required to make the planning
experiment successful. Except for Nehru's essay and Mahalanobis'
framework in the heyday of plan-consciousness in the early fifties, planning in India has been essentially an exercise in statistical projections and targets setting, isolated both from the original
framework, social perspectives, political conditions and the actual
state of the economy. One plan was difficult to fit into the next or
the preceding one, and the four have hung by themselves in mid
air, so to speak. In recent years, programming has been somewhat
more sophisticated, and so have been exercises and tools, but the
models are internally consistent only in a vacuum. Externally,
they come into conflict with almost every factor, every element
and influence, of practical significance to Indian economic development and social progress. This is why the institutional aspects
of planned development, for example, have come to be neglected
in this country. Much has been made of Panchayati Raj and the
co-operatives as instruments of change in the rural sector, but that
is a figment of the planners' imagination. The reality is that these
are no institutions, and whatever else they may be, they have
become a hotbed of political intrigue, seething with corruption.
Their contribution to growth and change is highly questionable.
Experience has shown that, If planning has to have any meaning in this country, the models, the programmes and the targets
must have an intimate relationship to the complexities of our real
life, including the extremes of poverty and wealth, the growing

148

disparities in opportunity, the social and economic distortions in the wake of earlier mis-investments and misdirection of policy and, more particularly, the social consciousness of an awakened, but miserably poor, people.

Isolated Half-planning

The isolated half-planning has led to an ideological tug of war sustained by the myth that this is a double controlled economy. The conflict can be identified with the factions that make the ruling party—the so-called Left, the equally so-called Right, and the innocent Centre. If the conflict had taken the form of a healthy constructive discussion, the few intellectual people in the Congress might have produced some new ideas to give a shot in the arm to planning. But, sadly, the conflict has been destructive, motivated, as it was, by factional expediency. In the absence of ideas, there was the Nehru "gospel" used by each side to justify or condemn things done in the name of planning. The result has been compartmental thinking, such as it is, the spread of illusions about the nature and content of planning and the creation of vested interests and rigidities holding up desirable changes in plans and policies and demoralising the forces of modernisation. The stultifying effects are there for all to see: There is no sense of direction, no perspective of long-term progress, no such thing as priorities, no courage behind policies, and no flexibility either, let alone the evolution of a set of distinctive concepts and philosophy.

Even programmes selected out of sheer pragmatism have been allowed to get shrivelled and lost or delayed. The fate of the steel plan is an illustration in point. But more damage has been done to the process and pattern of planning as also to its objectives.

Instead of preparing the nation for a forward-looking approach to planning, conditioning the people mentally to accept restraints and various types of disciplines, pushing ahead with imaginative development programmes and social and economic policies, the half-hearted partial planning has virtually dissipated the powerful forces released by the early nationalist fervour. Public sensitivity and response are confined only to external threats. A more comprehensive approach to planning from the start, with a clear sense

149

of direction and an equally clear strategy of development, might perhaps have avoided wasteful conflicts, controversies, and confusion encouraged by nervous bargains and constant retreats. The halting approach has actually developed contradictions which are now having a telling effect on the economy, particularly because no serious attempt has been made to find answers. Since mixed economy is glorified by rival factions for different purposes, even the partial planning has got mixed up about sectors, about financial and physical resources, and what have you. Priorities are set out, but seldom enforced. Physical targets are mentioned, but the detailed work, programmes and policies are all in financial terms. Even performance is measured in financial terms, which is absurd. But nowhere do the contradiction and weakness appear so glaring as in the scope of planning. Even after three plans, a major part of the economy is largely untouched. The planned sector still essentially remains what is oddly called the public sector. The private sector, which probably contributes 80–85 per cent of the national output, has not yet been properly brought within the scope of planning. In common parlance, the private sector is narrowly defined to mean private industry and business, but even these elements escape planning in the strict sense of the term. They are regulated and controlled, which is probably worse than real physical planning.

Thus, on the one hand, there is the spectacle of an enormous sector of the economy remaining unplanned, operating on its own laws, largely unmindful of the priorities, targets and objectives enumerated in plan documents; on the other, there is a fantastic structure of controls, regulations and the licensing system, largely operating on a negative motivation, seeking to hold, break up and deny. The planners talk of resource allocation, but this does not apply to the economy, it only concerns public finance. The organised private sector is a residue element in this picture. No resources are allocated to it; it has to fend for itself after paying its taxes. This approach has its corollary in the unimaginative pricing and fiscal policies. These are presumably a substitute for the proper planning of the private sector and have developed abuses and rigidities, frustrating growth and defeating whatever other objectives the planners might have had in mind. That is worse, none of these policies is related to actual performance of industry, or its cost trends, or even its "real" profitability, as distinct from the accounting concept.

In these conditions, the concept of resources and its allocation, on which the plans are supposed to be based, are not always unrealistic. The leakage of resources, for example, is a problem which the planners have not cared to take into account, though this is an important factor retarding development in this country. The projection of resources for the plans is not always properly related to actual development trends and potentialities. But what is really frustrating is that, even after so much experience, the plans have not evolved any techniques or policies to direct resources to priorities. Owners of resources can neither be compelled nor induced to do what the plans consider absolutely essential. Taxation and regulations are the main devices used in this field, but they make nonsense of priorities. Thus, for example, fertiliser factories may be licensed, but they may not come up, if profitability or other attractions are greater in producing sophisticated beverages, modern cosmetics or something else. Regulations and controls, being mainly negative, neither further the cause of growth and socialism, as some naive people imagine they do, nor do they permit desirable development of entrepreneurial skill or give an opportunity to genuine elements to generate output. But the country has got so enmeshed in this outmoded mechanism that even a slight relaxation of the control system creates political problems or economic distortions. Thus, our planning has added one more vicious circle to the conventional one of poverty retarding growth.

Results: Promised and Actual

Yet, the fiction of planning has given a new dimension to the political controversy about the virtues of planning vis-à-vis free enterprise in the current crisis. This is another manifestation of the lingering intellectual confusion which has made the concepts of planning and mixed economy, in the abstract form, sacrosanct, though neither has established any practical relationship

151

with the other. Some say that this permits us to have a little bit of everything and also nurse the illusion that planning, with a mixed economy and a British parliamentary system, is India's great contribution to the world. Only fools perhaps believe that the unplanned economies of the West are also mixed economies! Yet the continuing friction between the public and private sectors is becoming the enemy number one of development and mass prosperity. Investment programmes languish because neither the planners nor anybody else can show the courage to go ahead in the best possible way. Every time there has to be a debate on who can do the job better, and the debate is usually prolonged long enough for both, the public and private sectors, to lose interest in the programme or project. This has been going on for some years, confirming prejudices and compartmental thinking, much to the detriment of the laudable objectives of planning, making nonsense of priorities, programmes and policies.

Propagandists say that, in spite of all these deficiencies planning has produced commendable results. True, there has been considerable industrial development in the sense that we have now many new industries, and a complex structure is emerging. Some remarkable expansion has also taken place in power, roads, transport, atomic energy and even in certain areas of agriculture. Yet, how much of this would have come about in a big way and faster if we had a more comprehensive approach to planning, a more positive State interest, a more imaginative way of bringing the private sector within the purview of planning? In an article like this, it is not possible to evaluate achievements and analyse the contribution of planning. But I cannot entirely overlook the fear that our half-planning may not provide, from expedience, the answer to our poverty and the problems of modernisation. The mixed economy and the mixed-up planning, sustained by illusions and outmoded controls, have given us a growth rate of roughly 3–3$\frac{1}{2}$ per cent. There are better ways of achieving this rather inadequate rate of growth. And this lends an edge to the criticism one hears that modern capitalism could have given this country a much higher rate of growth. In any case, can we justify our pattern of planning which has given us a growth rate of only three per cent or so, and promoted the evolution of a "new"

152

feudalistic structure in the rural areas, intensified social stratification worse than that of the 19th century in the urban areas, besides thwarting the emergence of enlightened entrepreneurs as a force, while perpetuating and strengthening old-fashioned business with old-fashioned ideas? These results are different from the promises of the fifties, but they are so because there is a wide gap between the reality of our planning and the propagated illusions about it.

It may seem strange, but it is true, that even the illusions about the public sector are more frightening than the reality. Oddly, it is the inadequate development of the public sector which is an important factor behind the slowdown in the economy at present. So long as the state was pushing ahead with industrial and development programmes, there were large orders to share and equally large scope for related, peripheral and other new developments in the private sector. But with the decline in public sector development, many private sector industrial programmes and their profitability were affected. There have been certain avoidable limitations to the managerial and technical competence of some of the state enterprises, but because of this the positive aspects of the public sector have been minimised. Here, too, compartmental thinking and intellectual confusion have brought about the present situation. I have never been able to understand the need for an Industrial Policy Resolution, except as a weak supplementary instrument to half-baked planning. It was, after all, the product of a nervous compromise struck by the Congress Party which, being a platform of amorphous men without the necessary intellectual comprehension of the big issues, found commitment to planning at the earlier stage perhaps too much for it to take on and fulfil. This also explains why the first resolution of 1948 was watered down in 1956 and virtually abandoned, without saying so, in the last two or three years. But even the Resolution of 1956, if it had been fulfilled, might have made some difference to the state of planning and the economy. The Resolution had no time limit and left ample loopholes for opportunists to utilise. But the Government itself seems to have lost faith in its enterprise and capabilities soon after launching out on a number of projects in the first phase of enthusiasm.

From Underwriter to Undertaker

One suspects now the Government has lost faith in planning, as it was understood by Nehru. Today, the public sector, like controls and regulations, evidently has a negative function of taking over losing concerns from the private sector and entering areas where nobody else is willing to enter. This is not even an underwriter's function because underwriters at least make sure that they do not sink. This is nearer an undertaker's role, and in striking contrast with the original thinking which projected the state as a catalyst, an element in rapid growth, a focus of development, a radiating point for multifarious activities and developments in the economy. Doubts, ill-informed propaganda, and age seem to have had a telling effect on the Congress and on the Planning Commission, particularly after Nehru's deaths. The aid psychology now propagated from Delhi is a reflection of the new era of helplessness. The theme song of "defence and development", in itself a bogus concept, has now been effectively replaced by the new slogan "development with dependence". When we embarked on our development experiment, there was tremendous self-confidence and a certain pride in seeking development with our own resources. In fact, planning, by definition, presupposes, not other people's, the idea being to make the most economical and beneficial use of what you have and increasing your capabilities and resources in the process. Aid then becomes "aid", a temporary help, a supplement to co-ordinated national effort. Largely due to miscalculations by the planners and partly because of administrative failures, we moved into a crisis in 1956–57 resulting in the evolution of the Aid India Consortium for a rescue operation. But even with this mild shock and the creation of a new world institution, the Government had stood firm on certain essentials of national policy and economic and social objectives. Now the key to Indian progress, we are told, is aid, and the technique to get it is to project helplessness, to withdraw from active participation in foreign affairs and abandon plans and policies disapproved by our aid givers.

Now-a-days, we are told by our leaders and planners that we can do literally nothing unless we get aid—we cannot feed ourselves unless we go about with a begging bowl, and we cannot even have a plan unless our planners are told in advance by the donors how much aid they (the planners) will get if they are on good behaviour, almost like probationers! We cannot blame the donors, nor can we justifiably accuse the World Bank. They have their interests, outlook, strategies, and we should have our own. The Planning Commission has, however, lost the will to experiment, to evolve, to think, to propagate, and to face problems, and so has our Government. How can we have anything like a plan based on our own capabilities and potential, and a plan related to our own objectives and policies, if we cry ourselves hoarse that we can not do anything without massive aid? How can we have a plan if we start from the ridiculous premise that we now want more aid, not less, because we want less aid in the future and none when we are all dead? The inevitable outcome of this qualitative change in thinking is the involvement of external interests in India's policy-making and a retreat of the forces of forward-looking planning. The time has, therefore, come to face the choice—Do we want planning, or do we want to continue with the present farce? Do we want to go ahead with our ideas, or with somebody else's?

The Political Framework

If planning is to become realistic in this country, it must necessarily be comprehensive. If it has got to be comprehensive, it is clear beyond doubt that the present institutional framework is incapable of delivering the goods, because it has got too involved in farcical ideas and lost touch with the national currents. These ideas have only aggravated our crisis and brought us to the present state of humiliation, indignity and economic chaos. Even today, it has the illusion that liberalised imports will automatically result in larger industrial production, just as it appears to have taken for granted that, with devaluation, we would turn the corner.

But can we afford to have comprehensive planning? The objective conditions would suggest that we cannot afford not to have a bolder and a more effective way of planning. But the revivalism, the fall in quality and standards of leadership, and the political institutions and practices we have given ourselves, would seem to militate against any attempt to widen the area of planning or to change the diluted mixture of notions, illusions and the deteriorating reality. But should we not consider whether the British style of parliamentary democracy is unsuited to the compelling need for a more satisfying system of planned development in our prevailing conditions? Or, is one to assume that the British one is the only form of democracy in the world? From what I have seen of the working of our parliament, I fear that, unless given some serious thought to our political institutions and their functions, we may be getting deeper and deeper into a crisis which might extend much beyond the mere inadequacy of growth and intellectual confusion. I believe in democracy and values which go with it, but I do not believe in a system which converts democratic discussions into fish market outbursts, and the right of expression into a licence for abuse, and the system's continued survival at the cost of semi-stagnation and widespread distress. That apart, the wholly destructive approach of certain political parties and the sharp drop in the quality of politicians in the ruling party make it a remote possibility that the high standards, which go with the British parliamentary system, can be duplicated here in the near future. This is implicitly recognised by the Government over the years through the numerous amendments to the Constitution, the various legislative measures suspending or limiting fundamental freedoms, and the perpetuation of Emergency. My personal discussions with intelligent officials and parliamentarians also indicate that some serious thinking has got to be done on institutional reform at this stage to prevent parliamentary democracy from becoming an obstacle to India's rapid economic and social development, without which almost nothing, perhaps not even the Parliament House, can survive for long.

Note

The complete bibliographic information for this article is as follows:
D. K. Rangnekar, 'Second Thoughts on Indian Planning', *Economic and Political Weekly*, Annual, 2, issue nos 3–5 (February 1967): 273–278.

16

To Earn or Not to Spend

*The Taxing Question**

Since independence, the Centre's budget has grown almost ten times to its 6,000 crores (interim budget, 1971). All the money raised has not been spent for development and for mass prosperity. Our defence spending, for example, rose from Rs 278.74 crores in 1948–49 to Rs 1,182.83 crores in 1970–71. And how have successive Finance Ministers faced the challenge of poverty? Most of them shied away from bold experiments. As for taxation, while the farmer has been spared, the burden is borne mostly by the urban population.

Nobody enjoys paying taxes. Taxation almost always seems like highway robbery, and the Finance Minister, a glorified version of Robin Hood. To the lay public, therefore, the budget is a dreaded ritual and a yearly invitation to penance. The concept of social obligation sounds, at budget time, much too fanciful, and the profuse apologies for every tax hike the Minister may offer only provide cold comfort. Given a choice, the cynics—and their ranks are swelling—would do away with the budget. The frills of 'public good' make them weep year after year; the comic touches are mostly dubious; and there is no sense of popular participation and involvement. To the young, who look forward to the thrill of a new and bulging pay packet, the budget is a damper, a kill-joy.

* First published in *The Illustrated Weekly of India*.

Yet the budget is probably the most significant instrument available to a modern government to mobilise national resources and generate economic and social development. **In a country where political propaganda and electoral campaigns have stirred the underprivileged masses and beckoned them to a new economic and social order, the budget becomes much more than a catalyst: budgeting itself becomes a social and managerial process of modernisation and social change.** In this sense, the budget indicates the nation's sense of direction and the likely pace of investment and development expected in vital areas of the economy.

We in India have a long history of budgeting at the government level. When the first budget was presented 113 years ago, the British Raj had already evolved a serviceable system of public finance. After the political reform of 1919, this system was extended to every Province. Even so, the budget was, in those years, merely a financial exercise, a description and analysis, in the main, of public revenues and public expenditures. The size of the budget was small because the role of the state was limited. Indeed the budget had a very limited purpose and was guided, essentially, by considerations of administrative expediencies and law and order requirements. The budgetary system had achieved a degree of stability, but it was thoroughly inadequate to cope with the task of development. But, then, the question of any major state intervention in the economy did not arise. The philosophy and concepts of the day precluded the emergence of such initiatives. So long as the budget was an administrative tool for covering routine expenditures of the Government, financial outlays were insignificant, and so were taxation and public borrowing by the Central Government. Consequently, the budget made little or no impact on the economic activities of the country.

Over the years, there has been a sea-change in the role of the state. In the wake of the nationalist movement, novel ideas of modernisation have opened up glittering vistas of social and economic progress. The message of change has seeped through all layers of society. With the commencement of planning, after independence, the state assumed a pre-eminent role in directing and influencing the nation's economic and social development. It took on numerous new functions, besides the already complex task of stabilisation and distribution. In response to the nationalist upsurge, the economic system—and with that the budgetary system—started changing. Massive state intervention in investment, production and distribution has become a major plank in India's strategy of development. **The Government's budget has, therefore, the important tasks of providing for social overheads, narrowing inequalities of income and wealth, expanding developmental investments in terms of Plan targets, and generally aiming at the maximisation of output and social justice.** These tasks have inevitably cast new stresses and strains on the budgetary system and pose several grave problems which, 24 years after independence, defy solution.

For one thing, the budget has been growing enormously in size, thereby generating at times undesirable pressures on the economy. Secondly, the problem of financing ever-growing Government expenditures has been made complex both by the sheer size of the country and its division into separate States loosely joined into a federation. **While the Central Government has consistently managed to record surpluses of revenues over expenditures on current account, the State Governments have equally consistently dissaved, spent beyond their means, borrowed heavily, or relied on the crutches provided by the Centre.**

The manner in which public expenditure is financed affects the economy much more than is realised. To illustrate the point one can take an extreme case. If our Government financed all its budgetary expenditures by borrowing, we would move headlong into a serious inflation; if, on the other hand, the Government sought to finance all its expenditures by heavy taxation, which restricted individual consumption, we could have deflation and unemployment. This illustration is only intended to emphasise the need for a sense of balance in financing Government expenditures.

The need for a balanced approach has frequently, and mistakenly, been equated with pessimism by some Finance Ministers in this country. Where resources have to be mobilised and allocated in close relationship to Plan targets and social goals, such pessimism is disastrous; it much too easily gets tilted into inhibition. One manifestation of this defeatist approach is the obsession with inflation. At the slightest indication of a price rise, the Indian Finance Minister loses sleep, torments himself, and unsuspectingly walks into the trap of combating inflation. In the process,

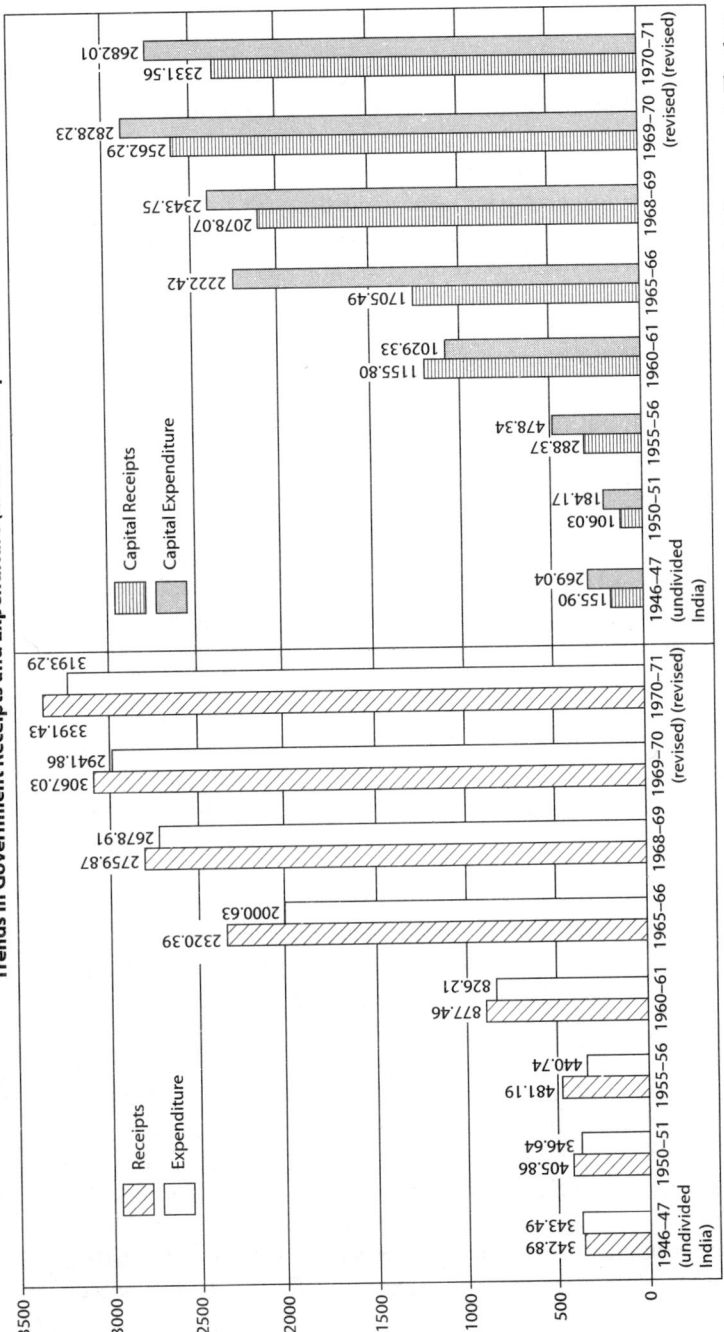

Trends in Government Receipts and Expenditure (in crores of rupees)

Capital Receipts

Year	Capital Receipts	Capital Expenditure
1946–47 (undivided India)	269.04	155.90
1950–51	106.03	184.17
1955–56	478.34	288.37
1960–61	1029.33	1155.80
1965–66	2222.42	1705.49
1968–69	2343.75	2078.07
1969–70 (revised)	2828.23	2562.29
1970–71 (revised)	2682.01	2331.56

Year	Receipts	Expenditure
1946–47 (undivided India)	342.89	343.49
1950–51	405.86	346.64
1955–56	481.19	440.74
1960–61	877.46	826.21
1965–66	2320.39	2000.63
1968–69	2759.87	2678.91
1969–70 (revised)	3067.03	2941.86
1970–71 (revised)	3391.43	3193.29

Indirect taxation on commodities and services has in recent years provided a major part of the total tax revenue of the Central Government. The share of these taxes in the total tax revenue of the Central Government rose from 72 per cent in 1955–56 to 80 per cent in 1970–71. On the other hand, the combined share or direct taxes on income, corporation, etc., declined from 28 per cent to 19 per cent. Taxation of "property and capital transactions" has, however, remained stagnant, accounting for one per cent of the total throughout this period.

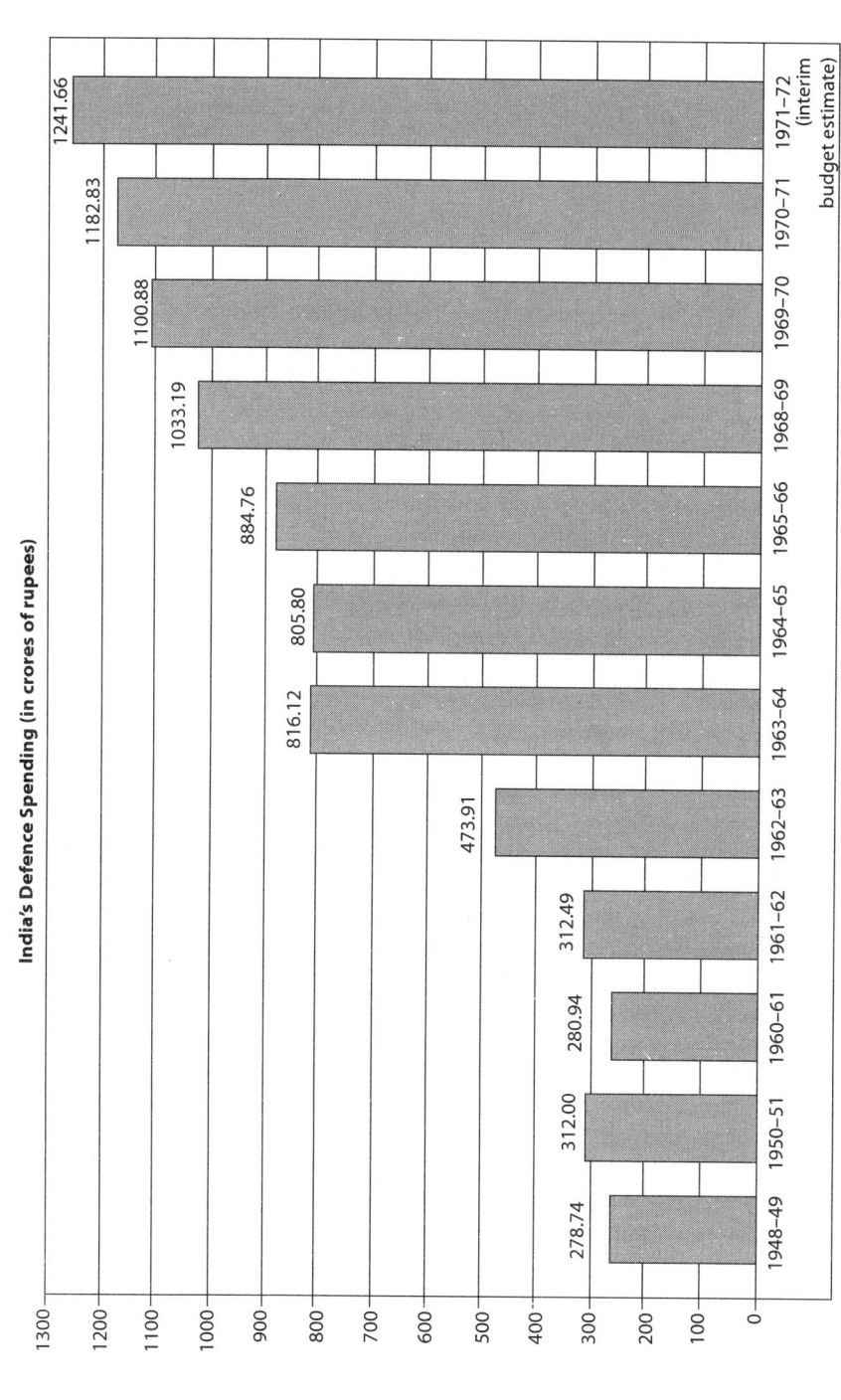

India's Defence Spending (in crores of rupees)

Year	Amount
1948–49	278.74
1950–51	312.00
1960–61	280.94
1961–62	312.49
1962–63	473.91
1963–64	816.12
1964–65	805.80
1965–66	884.76
1968–69	1033.19
1969–70	1100.88
1970–71	1182.83
1971–72 (interim budget estimate)	1241.66

he clamps on brakes when he really ought to press the accelerator and clutch firmly at the steering wheel.

No Bold Experiments

Apart from the treachery of the monsoon gods, the chicken-hearted behaviour of some Finance Ministers has been a major factor in India's slow pace of progress. With rare exceptions, our Finance Ministers have shied away from bold experiments. There is a certain reluctance to innovate, reflecting partly perhaps the conventional political philosophy of the Congress. Of the eight Finance Ministers we have had since the end of the British Raj, only three—Liaqat Ali Khan, Morarji Desai and T. T. Krishnamachari—have shown some interest in new experiments (albeit on a limited plane). **Ironically, it was Liaqat Ali who gave India its first "socialist" budget (ignoring, of course, his political motivation).** It was not development-oriented—the Interim Government was in 1947 preoccupied with problems of partition—but it stunned the people with its radical fiscal approach. Liaqat Ali Khan proposed some new and drastic levies: a business profit tax of 25 per cent on profits of Rs 1 lakh and over, a graduated tax on capital gains, a super tax on income. He also doubled the corporation levy. Simultaneously, the salt tax was abolished and the minimum exemption limit raised. The entire package of taxation was expected to yield slightly less than Rs 40 crores, a seemingly small amount now, but a colossal figure in 1947, considering that taxation earlier was insignificant and the rupee was worth very much more than it is today. The socialist twist hit business profits, and sent business men and stock brokers reeling. The share and other markets came crashing down. So sharp was the general reaction that a senior Congress leader said: "The poor man has got his salt free, but the rich man has been sent to his grave." After Liaqat, the next two Finance Ministers, Shanmukham Chetty and Dr John Matthai, were largely concerned with some kind of a holding operation.

They were faced with a two-pronged challenge. They had to rejuvenate the stock brokers and business men, who were bled white by Liaqat Ali; and they had to provide for the rehabilitation

162

of refugees. The communal convulsions after partition, the defence of Kashmir and the police action in Hyderabad—all these posed a challenge to an economy already nursing the after-effects of colonialism and war effort. The challenge was much too great in a set-up that placed a premium on conventional notions and traditional concepts of budgeting. Small wonder, then, that the first few budgets came under severe attack within the ruling Congress Party. And it was not long before differences surfaced between Nehru and Dr Matthai. They differed on the question of payment of compensation on Government's acquisition of private property and also on the proposed creation of a Planning Commission.

First Plan a Sham

C. D. Deshmukh, who succeeded Dr Matthai, had a fairly long innings, which coincided with the launching of the First Plan. Deshmukh pursued a moderate line which preferred consolidation of gains to expansion. He kept taxation relatively low and emphasised the creation of an infrastructure. The relatively good economic turnout of the period was usually attributed to Deshmukh's economic management. But one cannot possibly overlook the kindliness of the monsoons and the promising economic climate (also reflecting the good monsoons), which encouraged business men to produce more.

In many ways the First Plan was some what of a sham; almost every project, with the exception of community development projects, had been designed and launched before partition. The stabilisation of food prices was helped, besides the weather gods, by an American wheat loan. The most glaring failure of the period was the inability of the Government to come forth with development-oriented budgets. Economic conditions then favoured a surge of industrial and Plan investments. But the actual story was one of missed opportunity. We woke up rather late, and sought to change the gears in the Second and Third Plans, when food and foreign exchange difficulties tended to aggravate a situation already rendered critical by two military conflicts and growing foreign pressures for reversal of our Plan strategy.

163

Centre's Receipts from Selected Taxes
(in crores of rupees)

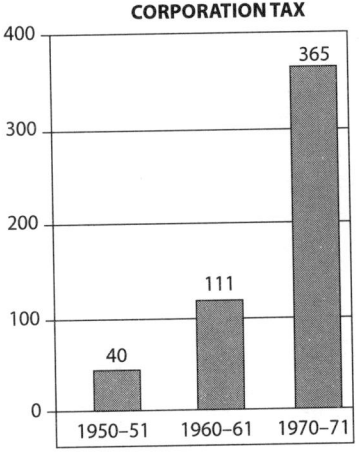

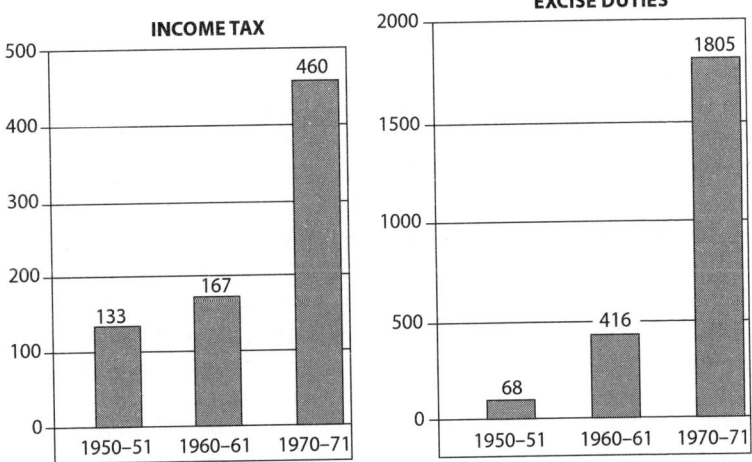

T. T. Krishnamachari, who came on the scene in the mid-'fifties, created a minor stir by introducing taxes on wealth, expenditure and gifts, partly on the lines proposed by Nicolas Kaldor, a Cambridge economist. When this scheme of taxation failed to produce the desired effects, Kaldor, a naturalised British citizen, sought to disown responsibility by saying that he did not know local conditions. This phase saw, nevertheless, a step-up in Plan investment, a good part originating in Government's capital outlays and expansion of what is called the public sector.

Since independence the Centre's budget has grown almost ten times to a staggering figure—Rs 6,000 crores by 1971. But this gives an exaggerated idea of the state's role in the economy and of the pace of investment and development. First, Plan investments in recent years have been static. Development and expansion are even now on a low key. Plan outlays are around seven per cent of the national income as compared to 8–11 per cent in the

Size of the Public Sector

Government domestic revenue (G.D.R.) and expenditure (G.E.) relative to the gross national product

Country	Year	G.D.R. (a) % of G.N.P.	G. E. (b) % of G.N.P.
Burma	1956	14	23(c)
	1963	18	29(c)
Ceylon (d)	1959	18	19(c)
	1965	20	19(c)
Taiwan	1956	20	26
	1964	17	22
India	1955-56	9	12
	1962-63	12	16
Pakistan	1960-61	9	13
	1964-65	11	19
Philippines	1956	9	12
	1965	10	11
Thailand	1957		12
	1965		15
Malaya States	1962	22	23

(a) *Excluding current transfers from the rest of the world.*
(b) *General Government consumption expenditure and fixed capital formation of general Government, state enterprises and public corporations.*
(c) *Expenditure includes changes in inventories.*
(d) *Excluding public corporations.*

mid-'sixties. Secondly, defence and non-development expenditures weigh heavily on the budgetary scheme.

Defence Spending

There has been a steep increase in defence spending, following the conflict with China in 1962, and the short Indo-Pak war of

Distribution of Individual Income Assessed to Tax
(in percentages)

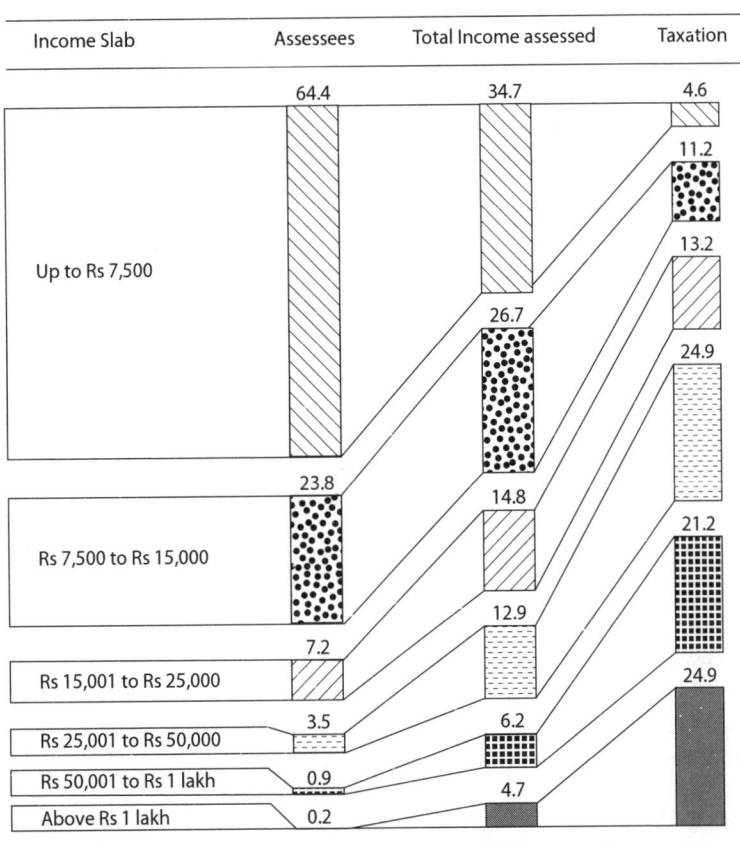

Income Slab	Assessees	Total Income assessed	Taxation
Up to Rs 7,500	64.4	34.7	4.6
			11.2
			13.2
		26.7	
			24.9
Rs 7,500 to Rs 15,000	23.8	14.8	21.2
		12.9	
Rs 15,001 to Rs 25,000	7.2		24.9
Rs 25,001 to Rs 50,000	3.5	6.2	
Rs 50,001 to Rs 1 lakh	0.9	4.7	
Above Rs 1 lakh	0.2		

1965. Until then, in the 'fifties, defence expenditure was pretty small. Even in the early 'sixties, it was only in the region of Rs 400 crores. After the Chinese struck at the borders, Morarji Desai, who was then the Finance Minister, had the embarrassing task of presenting a budget with a staggering defence outlay of Rs 816 crores. In the interim budget for 1971–72, defence is allocated Rs 1,240 crores, a figure, which in relation to our national income is prohibitive, though perhaps unavoidable in the prevailing circumstances. **One cannot help feeling that valuable resources get diverted this way from development and mass prosperity. Non-Plan budgetary commitments have also mounted. Expenditure on administration, current outlay on defence services, police and public debt servicing has swollen over the years to reach well nigh Rs 1,000 crores.** Every Finance Minister has made sacramental offerings at the altar of prudence and pledged to enforce economy in spending; but more often than not, he has failed to keep his promise. It is non-developmental extravagance, and not investment, that needs to be kept in check.

Even after all this, the States' role in the economy and the hold of the public sector as a whole are relatively small in India, contrary to propaganda and belief. Planning can play a crucial role in national development only if it gives greater push to investment and growth than is possible without planning. Many people in this country have false notions of the magnitude of our effort. Though one can concede that, in relation to the chronic poverty of the majority of our people, we have saved and invested creditably in the past, the fact remains that the present trend of policy is apparently unfavourable to investment on the basis of the long-term view of the economy. The accompanying table, with all its limitations, illustrates that even Burma and Ceylon and Taiwan are currently engaged in a relatively much larger effort than ours.

With the burden of unproductive and consumption expenditures of the Government soaring, the public is denied the full benefits of their own contribution to the budget. A sound budgetary system is expected to move resources to efficient purposes in order to ensure that every rupee is well spent. If this assurance is lacking, the public sacrifices in vain. **One of the marvels of our**

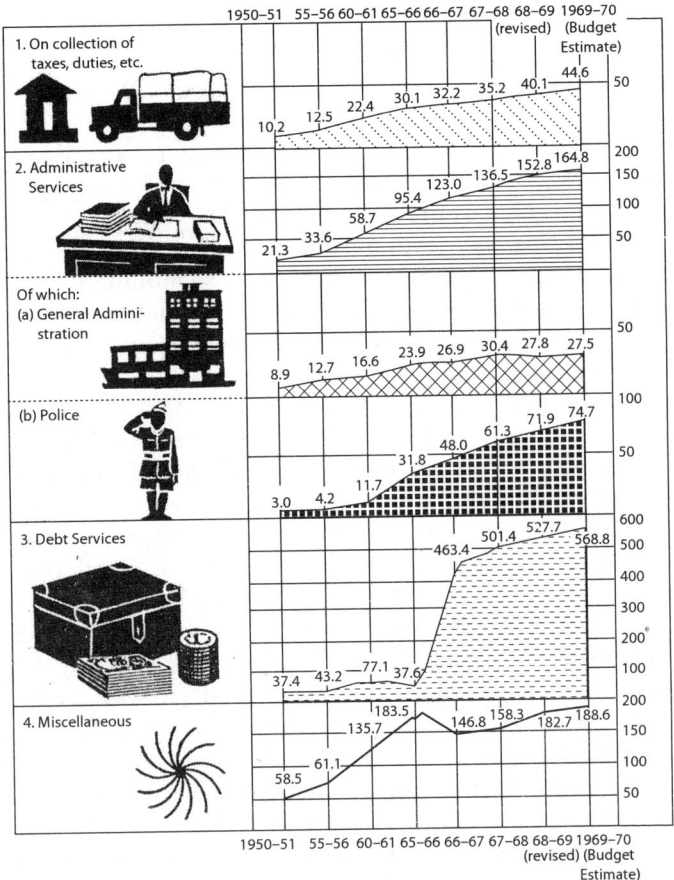

**Non-Development Expenditure of
the Centre (in crores of rupees)**

social and political set-up is the people's limitless patience and
their inexplicable tolerance of economic waste and dissipation
of resources. Indeed, in recent years, growth aims have been
displaced by pure revenue considerations. And even though the
expansion of the public sector has greatly slowed down, Finance
Ministers, in desperate search for revenues, have had, of late,
to place greater reliance on non-budgetary sources of finance to

cover long-term capital expenditures and defence. Though the Government controls the investment pattern of large financial institutions, like, for example, the Life Insurance Corporation, and more recently the banks, the provident fund associations, etc., it has not been found possible to step up the market borrowings to any appreciable extent. This has forced the Government sector to rely increasingly on foreign aid, foreign borrowings and central bank credit creation (deficit financing).

Tax Base Not Widened

The lopsided approach to budgeting basically, however, reflected the pathetic inability of our Government to widen and deepen the tax base and make it more equitable on the one hand, and its inability to prevent leakage of incomes both on domestic and foreign account on the other. The excessive reliance on foreign aid has cost the country dearly, even if it may have helped us, over a short period, to tide over the foreign exchange crisis created by distortions in planning and heavy defence commitments. The orientation of planning has undergone a change under pressure, the rupee has had to be devalued at the most inopportune time, export promotion developments have been retarded, and, finally, a process of deplanning has been forced down our throats.

Deficit financing has increased from about Rs 46 crores in 1969–70 to about Rs 230 crores in 1970–71. There was no reason to feel alarmed about this, if it meant deficit finance had something to do with increased productive investment and was accompanied by well-conceived production policies to step up the supply of essential goods and materials. Unfortunately, on this score one is not reassured. Strangely, revenue considerations and obsession with inflationary dangers have served to restrain the Government's developmental or capital expenditures. But this, in turn, has had the effect of dampening developmental activity all over the country. Consequently, recent budgets have been singularly unimpressive with one possible exception—Morarji Desai's budget for 1963–64 when he raised Rs 260 crores in taxes, the highest on record. Though he abolished some of the Kaldor levies, he pushed up direct taxes on personal and corporate incomes and lengthened the list of excise levies. More significantly, he introduced the controversial gold control order and a compulsory deposit scheme. But his commendable effort was short-lived. Krishnamachari, during his second innings, promptly cancelled both the schemes, and went back to the expenditure tax, proposed an obnoxious annuity scheme, and made some far-reaching changes in capital gains tax, estate duty and gift tax. Of the last three budgets, Mrs Gandhi's essay was interesting mainly because it, for once, left the tax structure largely undisturbed.

A Few Points for Chavan

Looking ahead one might hazard the guess that unlike other Finance Ministers, Y. B. Chavan is on a good wicket. The economy is in better balance, industry is ticking again, revenue receipts are looking up, buffer stocks of food and materials are promising. He can present his budget with the confidence that a bold economic and fiscal approach could give just that push to investment, employment and growth that the Congress has inspired the people to look forward to. But a few points are worth bearing in mind. First, if planned outlays are to grow, as grow they must to generate employment and output, the growth of current and non-Plan outlays must be held in check. Second, the slow growth of national income will inevitably check the rate of growth of income and corporation tax revenues. That goes for other receipts too. So the Finance Minister will have to look for increases in the level of tax revenue from other sources. One such is domestic loan finance. With suitable institutional changes, it may be possible for the Government to tap a large share of private saving. **With the marginal rate of tax on income pitched high — it has gone up steadily from 70% to 93% — the incentive to evade tax is at its peak.**

I do not believe India is heavily taxed in a general sense — the ratio of tax revenue to the GNP is quite low, around 13 per cent, as against 21 per cent in Malaysia and Brazil, 19 per cent in the U.A.R. and Ceylon, and 18 per cent in South Africa. **But in India the tax burden falls unequally on small segments of the urban**

How the Centre Spreads Its Tax Net

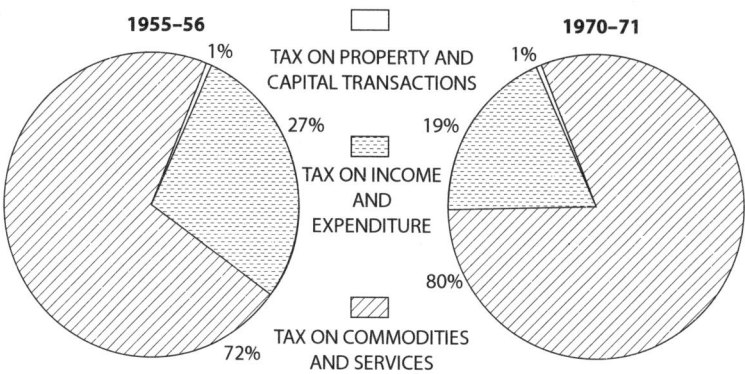

1955-56   □   1970-71

1%

TAX ON PROPERTY AND
CAPITAL TRANSACTIONS

27%   19%

TAX ON INCOME
AND
EXPENDITURE

80%

TAX ON COMMODITIES
72%   AND SERVICES

population, 30 lakhs in a country of 54.7 crores. In fact, the burden of providing the Centre with a current revenue of the order of Rs 3,000–3,400 crores is carried entirely by the urban citizen and business man. They pay direct taxes on income, wealth, capital gains and inheritance. The total contributed this way now exceeds Rs 830 crores. In addition, the urban tax-prayer also has to pay indirect taxes, excise levies, sales tax, etc., on cigarettes, petrol, garments, tea and almost everything that goes in the current pattern of consumption. The burden of indirect levies has been growing—such levies account for roughly 80 per cent of all tax revenue. Here, too, there is a bias in favour of the farmer. There are no allowances for children's education, medical or other essential purposes as in other countries, and, consequently, the incidence of taxation appears to fall heavily on fixed income earners. Though the exemption limit now has been raised to Rs 5,000, it is still on the low side, considering that the value of money is down.

Parallel Economy

There is a good case for increasing the exemption limit if only to free the low-income earners from the rigours of taxation. **But there**

171

is no doubt that the aggregate burden of taxation is so heavy that evasion has become attractive and common. Today 'black money' is nearly as significant as white money, and is at the root of what may be called India's deplorable parallel economy. All this will continue to flourish so long as dairy, farming, forestry, vineyards and a host of prosperous agricultural activities are kept out of the tax net. While showing consideration for earned income, it is about time that agricultural incomes, which are multiplying several-fold every year, thanks to the sacrifices of the tax-payers, who have financed and sustained farm developments is taxed in much the same way as any other current income. And if our Constitution stands in the way, the urgent need to rope in farm income is as justifiable a reason for its amendment as any.

Note

The complete bibliographic information for this article is as follows:
D. K. Rangnekar, 'To Earn or Not to Spend: The Taxing Question', *The Illustrated Weekly of India* (30 May 1971): 8–14.

Part Four

Industrialising India—Follies and Policies

17

India

The Emerging Industrial Power *

Modernisation of one-fifth of mankind is not the easiest task in the world. In a country which at times is a formless confusion, a world in itself, the task certainly becomes super-human. But ageless India set out to disprove the pessimists. The vision and courage of Jawaharlal Nehru and the dogged determination of the people have paid rich dividends, and today one can speak of India as an emerging industrial power. India's poverty and food shortages of the earlier years were so efficiently advertised by well-meaning people that India's impressive strides in different directions and particularly industry and technology appear almost startling. It is not as if India has overcome all its problems, nor can one say that a miracle has been at work. But the mere fact that India has been able to terminate the era of dependence on imported food supplies and produce enough food to feed its own people—and even export some to friendly countries—has brought about a sea-change in the outlook and attitude of the people. Besides, the massive investments made over the years in a variety of large industrial complexes are now bearing fruit.

* Article first published in *TIME* on 20 November 1978.

Signposts of Change

In the wake of these developments, the entire face of the country is changing, slowly perhaps, but surely. Industry and business are emerging as an important element in the nation's social system, though agriculture still remains the dominant factor. The magnitude of the change underway is not yet fully reflected in either the statistics or documents, but the visual impact is there for all to see in the growth of large and small cities, the emergence of new townships with big and small factories dotting the landscape once predominantly rural, and in the mushroom growth of unenumerated, unregistered business and small workshops all over the country. The ancient landmarks are fast disappearing, the old signposts giving way under the stress of new industrial developments. The old economic and social ties are being torn asunder. Science and technology are disrupting the old social order, and the traditional family-bound individual is now face to face with the inexorable pressure of change. India suddenly finds itself suspended in the midst of an incomplete industrial revolution and the defiant resistance of its hallowed ancient cultural civilisation. The ferment among today's younger generation is symbolic of the general impatience of a society in quest of new values, new attitudes and a new cultural synthesis. With the spread of social consciousness, we see the emergence of new forces and pressure groups. Trade unions are, for example, getting better organised and more effective; village-level associations are playing an increasingly important role in the local social and cultural development, and farmers' lobbies are active in national politics. And modern concepts of marketing and management, and methods of improving productivity are catching on.

Industry and business contribute today more than one-third of the national income as compared with a mere five per cent, or so before independence in 1947. The decennial rate of urbanisation is now nearer 40 per cent as compared with about 25 per cent in the fifties. The volume of India's national income today is much larger than that of Austria, Denmark, Norway, Portugal, Sweden and Switzerland put together, five times that of South Africa and almost three times that of Australia. This achievement is dwarfed by India's massive population, lingering poverty, and social disparities. India has created over the last three decades, first, a climate conducive to rapid industrialisation and, second, a process of technical change which has picked up its own momentum, something which cannot now be reversed. The basic foundations of a self-propelling development have been laid, covering manufacturing programmes, defence mechanism, and even highly sophisticated industries and technology, including the nuclear field. In terms of aggregate physical output India today ranks among the first ten industrial nations in the world. In the field of nuclear development, India is perhaps among the first six nations. It has the third largest scientific and technological manpower in the world. Thus, over the years, India's industry has emerged as a vulnerable tool which can be used for achieving the nation's basic social and economic goals.

Political Transition

When one bears in mind that, after independence in 1947, India has started off with a tense atmosphere, a torn economy, a disrupted labour force and an explosive political situation, one can truly realise what it must have taken the leadership, the government and the people to settle down to the constructive task of transforming the economy and the society. The transition from a disrupted economy to an ambitious modernised society brings about its own distortions, but the disruptive forces were contained by the systematic manner in which the economic processes were directed and policies evolved and implemented. Indeed, India's stable political system is in striking contrast with the emergence of military or benevolent dictatorships and bloody coups in some of the developing countries. India's political system today is a combination of tradition and modernity. To say this is not to suggest smooth sailing all along the line. Troubles and tensions there have been in plenty, reflecting mostly the backlash of democracy and social conflicts. The poor and the awakened are also growing impatient with inequality and social injustice. States with different political persuasions are also pressing for social change.

But all are one in the single-minded pursuit of industrialisation, technological advancements and social progress.

The basic strategy to industrialisation and development was really formulated in the wake of the national struggle for independence. Business leaders in those years, notably Mr. J.K.D. Tata, Mr. G.D. Birla and Mr. Jamnalal Bajaj, gave the Congress party strong support in its struggle for independence and in the evolution of ideas and concepts of development. Since the earlier industrial revolution had bypassed India, the political leaders felt that a large and potentially powerful nation like India could miss its destiny unless it adopted a more modern and dynamic policy of development. Opinion gained ground among intellectuals also that government intervention was necessary to cope with the huge task of pushing through an extensive industrial programme in a short period of time. Businessmen supported this strategy of industrialisation. They did not feel that there was necessarily a conflict between the strong central role of government envisaged by the Congress leaders and other intellectuals and their own business interests.

Before independence the only industries of any significance that existed in the country were jute and cotton textiles, tea, coffee and rubber plantations, a few engineering shops, and some coal mining which functioned closely in association with the development of the railways. The pioneering industrialist, the late Mr. Jamshedji Tata, set up India's first iron and steel works in 1911 but he had to battle against prejudices. Mahatma Gandhi's "Swadeshi" (Buy India) movement provided some stimulus to Indian private industry. But the war brought out India's dependence on imported manufactured goods and, because of the disruption to normal trade, stimulated local production in a number of engineering and chemical industries and saw the birth of India's machine tool industry. Yet, the results remained unimpressive.

Mixed Economy

With the widespread endorsement of the concept of mixed economy, the new Congress government, on assumption of power, set up the Planning Commission and enacted the Industries Development & Regulation Act acquiring wide powers for regulating production and development of industries. But public sector investment did not take off in the First Five Year Plan, nor did private investment. Much of the emphasis was on the utilisation of existing excess capacities created during the Second World War and the Korean War Boom. The experience of the first five years of planning prompted the government to modify its approach and strategy and a new Industrial Policy Resolution (IPR) was adopted in 1956, partly to reassure the private sector, but largely to set out realistic guidelines to the subsequent plans. The IPR has been accorded the status of "an economic constitution" and, indeed, it remains even today the basic statement of industrial objectives and the framework for the second and the subsequent plans. The objectives and procedures outlined in the IPR had a very broad basis of support. The threat of imminent nationalisation was eliminated, even though apparently the responsibility of the state had been enhanced. Thus the IPR and the Second Plan (1956–60) gave a spur to public sector investment in several directions and in its wake brought about massive private sector expansion. Indeed, this was the period of an investment boom in the economy that probably remains unmatched even today.

There was a marked change in business outlook both from the point of view of the potential growth rate and the attitude of the government. The basic directions and tools of policy appeared to have been well formulated, and the private sector saw the way to partnership with public enterprise. The resultant buoyancy of private investment and the planned increase in public investment, together with inevitable errors in reckoning, created a foreign exchange crisis from 1957–58 onwards. This period also got coincided with droughts and acute food shortages compelling India to seek foreign aid and food imports. Foreign exchange thus emerged as a principal constraint on rapid industrial developments.

During the Second and Third Plans, industrialisation policy was dominated by short run balance of payment problems. Aid came to finance almost one-half of imports. The government was compelled to adopt strong measures to minimise foreign payments. Import of products which could be feasibly produced in

India was banned. This critical balance of payment situation saw the birth of India's import substitution strategy. Perhaps, this may not have been a deliberate choice, though self-reliance has been a national goal.

With single-minded devotion, the government and the private sector combined to displace imports by local products rather than by relying on an export strategy or a combination of the two. Imports and foreign exchange control guaranteed near absolute protection to Indian industry. This has brought about a remarkable degree of self-sufficiency and a highly diversified range of industries.

While seeking to provide protection for domestic industry the scope for transfer of technology was fully recognised. But the thrust was on adaptation and the generation of local designs and technology to ensure autonomous growth and development. India was more fortunate than several other developing countries in experimenting with this multi-pronged approach to modernisation. For one thing, India's internal resources were massive. India did not lack in entrepreneurs. With centuries of trading experience behind them, the old entrepreneurial communities had emerged as a powerful force in the society, and the switch from trade and finance to industrial production and distribution was quick enough. The second and third generation of entrepreneurs with specialised training in engineering and the humanities brought a new element of dynamism. A middle class with deep roots in scholarship and education, with a large element of westernised training and thinking, provided the professional element in management and organisation. The shift from traditional forms of financing to organised commercial and industrial finance was not as easy and rapid. Here the national government assumed the key role and constituted special institutions and geared the banking system. Industrialisation was not impeded by scarcity of labour either, in the sense of its growing real cost to entrepreneurs.

Various tools of economic policy were evolved and used. Investment planning was essentially based on the Five Year Plans, and the related industrial progress set out output targets, estimates of investment and capacity, indicating preferred priorities in providing guidelines to the administration. In the process, the government acquired powers on matters such as industrial licensing, determination of location and size of plants, pricing and distribution controls, incentives, allocation of resources including foreign exchange etc.

In the light of experience, the government adopted a pragmatic approach and proceeded step by step to liberalise the industrial licensing system. Several industries were freed. Investment projects upto specific limits were delicensed. Industries of importance to the national economy, those having direct linkage with the core sector, and those with long-term prospects for exports were all considered, as basic, critical and strategic for the growth of the economy. Large houses were eligible to participate in any of these listed industries. Licences were issued to private sector units in areas which were exclusively reserved for state ownership or where further expansion was intended to be in the public sector.

Investment Boom

With the streamlining of policy there was a virtual boom in industrial ventures, many with foreign collaboration. As against 1,580 industrial licences issued in the First Plan period, a total of 14,479 were issued in the subsequent two decades ending 1977. Besides, the boom attracted entry of several multinational companies. There are 171 subsidiaries and 482 branches of multinational companies operating in the country today. This period is also marked by a tremendous increase in registered small units from about 3,500 to over 200,000, many run by trained technologists and engineers in consumer or light engineering fields. The development of small-scale units was partly induced by the government's decision to prohibit entry of large-scale industries in certain areas. All this had a stimulating effect on the industrialisation process. The growth of the large-scale industrial sector, measured in absolute physical terms, was truly impressive. In fact, net manufacturing output grew faster than the economy as a whole since the First Plan. Outlays on planned development have grown nine-fold in the last two decades. Government's direct investment in industry was less than $38M in the early years of planning; today the figure is in the region of $14B in 145 enterprises. This and the government's pragmatic economic policies prompted a surge of private sector investment. Much of this reflected the growth of modern and sophisticated industries. This is perhaps the main qualitative development which has acquired large infusion of new management, skilled labour and technical expertise. In practical terms it meant the emergence of new industries and projects to cater to the newer requirements of the economy and also to displace imports.

Though foreign aid and capital did condition the pattern of investment in the earlier years of planning, in more recent years, investment has come mainly out of domestic savings. For example, in 1975–76, aggregate net investment was 16.1 per cent of the national income at current prices, of which domestic savings accounted for 15.5 per cent and net inflow of foreign reserves 0.6 per cent. In 1976–77, net aggregate investment was 14.3 per cent with domestic saving accounting for 15.7 per cent. Contrary to the general impression, a very large proportion of the industrial investment—50 to 60 per cent—would appear to be originating in the corporate, other private and household sectors in recent years.

With the earlier thrust of government investment several public sector enterprises came to the fore and among India's top 101 industrial corporations 52 were government-owned companies accounting for 79.3 per cent of the aggregate assets of these corporations and 74.4 per cent of sales. Three of the public sector enterprises, Indian Oil Corporation, Steel Authority of India Limited and Bharat Heavy Electricals figure in the list of industrial giants outside the United States compiled by FORTUNE. This is apt to give the impression that the public sector is a dominant element in the industrial economy. This perhaps deserves a caveat. For one thing, public sector investment remained on a plateau for several years after the big push of the late fifties and early sixties and recovered somewhat recently. Secondly, all public investment is concentrated in steel, heavy engineering, heavy electricals, machine tools, electronics, fertilisers, petroleum, etc.

In the aggregate, therefore, without minimising the productive achievements of the public sector, an assessment of India's industrial performance over the last two-and-a-half decades becomes in essence an evaluation of the performance of the private sector, particularly because there are virtually no public enterprises in the consumer goods sector and not many in the intermediate sector. Approximately two-thirds of the manufacturing investment since the sixties would appear to have been in the private sector. This is reflected, for example, in the impressive growth of the private sector corporations and big business houses, some of which have grown in size four to five times since the early sixties. The top 71 large industrial houses would seem to have increased their assets by as much as 50 per cent in just three years from 1972 to 1975. Even after taking into account price changes, the increase in assets of these leading industrial groups would probably work out to 46 per cent in three years. Tatas and Birlas appeared to be growing in terms of assets at an average rate of $125M every year. These 71 industrial houses covered a total of 899 industrial undertakings with assets aggregating $7B in 1972 and $10.5B in 1975.

During the First Plan, i.e., in the fifties, India depended on import for most of its requirements of manufactured goods. Today, India's range of production has gone beyond all expectations and most of the industrial imports have been displaced. India is now completely self-sufficient in the manufacture of plant and machinery needed by some of its major industries like cotton textiles, jute, sugar, chemicals, paper, cement and a wide range of consumer goods. Its range of manufacture includes ships, automobiles, locomotives, machine tools, power generators and transmission towers, tractors, trucks, turbines, boilers, high precision ball bearings, heavy electrical plant, centrifugal pumps, gas cylinders, drilling equipments, gear and gear boxes, construction equipment including aircraft, frigates, radar, tanks, guns, missiles, electronics and a variety of software. A beginning has been made in the production of satellites and rockets. Major electrical items for domestic and industrial use are now manufactured in the country. Small beginnings have been made in the field of computer systems and other electronic equipment like consumer and professional electronics. Many of the basic drugs and heavy chemicals which used to be imported even in the sixties are now produced in the country. India has three shipbuilding yards and a fourth one is under construction, and in the process the country has emerged as the second largest ship-owning country in Asia and perhaps the 16th in the world.

Steep Climb Up

Over the years India has kept pace with global development as a whole even though burdened by financial constraints and material shortages. In a number of industrial products India is now among the world's top producers. India is the largest producer of cotton yarn in the world, second largest of scooters, it stands fifth in the production of coal, sixth in lignite and sugar, eighth in rayon and acetate filament, ninth in pig iron, ferro alloys, manganese, caustic soda, nitrogenous fertilisers and cement, 10th in soda ash, 13th in crude steel and aluminium, and 14th in sulphuric acid and tyres. All this development was made possible because the planners devoted considerable attention to the creation of infrastructure facilities. In electricity generation India today ranks 12th in the world. Basic and capital goods industries now account for over 40.3 per cent of the value added in the factory sector, intermediate goods industries account for 28.8 per cent and consumer goods (durable and non-durable) account for 30.9 per cent. Import substitution in the manufacture of consumer goods is virtually complete and imports, if any, do not constitute much more than 0.5 per cent of the market. In the case of capital and intermediate goods, import substitution has been rapid, but some imports of material, components and machinery still continue.

Industrial production has shown an uninterrupted increase during the first fifteen years of the planning period. The rate of growth averaged seven per cent per annum in the first decade (1950–51 to 1960–61) and increased further to nine per cent per annum in the next four years (1961–62 to 1964–65). Thereafter the rate of growth has been erratic and generally below expectations. The growth rate declined to 5.3 per cent in 1965–66 and remained stagnant for the subsequent two years, spurting thereafter to 7.4 per cent in 1969–70, only to fall back to around 3–4 per cent in the next five years. However, the index of industrial production spurted to 10 per cent in 1976–77. Thus, the annual growth rate was about six per cent during the period 1974–78.

The exogenous shocks which affected the industrial growth rates included the war with China in 1962, the war with Pakistan in 1965, the devaluation of the rupee in 1966, the Bangladesh war

184

of 1971, successive drought years from 1965 to 1967, the repetition of bad crop years during the period 1971 to 1973, and more recently the oil crisis which pushed up the import bill for petroleum products from about $255M in 1972–73, to $700M in 1973–74, $1.5B each year in 1974–75 and 1975–76 and $1.8B in 1976–77. But the government achieved a considerable measure of success in tackling the energy crisis, first, by switching to coal (resources of which are abundant) and other substitutes; secondly, by an intensified oil exploration drive on-shore and off-shore, and by control of consumption. Still the industry plunged into a state of recession three times in 1966–67, 1970–71 and 1975–76.

A part of the explanation is to be found in the slack in governments expenditure on power, industry, transport and communications which had earlier been the prime stimulant for demand. Inequalities of income and wealth have acted as a damper, apart from distorting the structure of investment and generating an elitist pattern of consumption. Fluctuations in agricultural output and their effect on economic growth also tended to depress demand. Demand weakness and other imbalances need not have become so acute if India had pursued a flexible policy for developing export potential or rather linking up a growing export market with expansion of the domestic economy and the market. With the acceleration of India's repayment liabilities—debt servicing accounting for as much as 16–17 per cent of total exports—the quest for export growth assumed a new dimension. Thus exports emerged as the new key to self-reliance. Significantly, this development coincided with a series of good crop years boosting food and agricultural production. Also there has been nothing short of a revolution in the production of fruits, vegetables, dairy products, poultry, fisheries, etc. All these and the rising rural incomes created a cumulative effect both from the supply and demand sides generating a new sense of confidence.

Assisting Third World

With its tremendous technological and industrial accomplishments behind it, India began to feel that it could share its experience and lend a helping hand to the third world countries. The neighbouring Asian, African and Middle East countries lacked the capacity to produce capital goods, but had the necessary agricultural or oil potential to provide a basis for developmental partnership with India. Conditions for such partnerships in their development effort were also highly favourable. For one thing, India had a store of technical know-how and skills waiting to be tapped. Secondly, India had a well developed infrastructural base and a still existing, though perhaps diminishing, underutilised industrial capacity. Proximity also favoured India as a supplier of goods and know-how. That apart, India had an obvious comparative advantage in a range of capital and intermediate goods and other manufactures which it was willing to test in open competition with the more developed countries. Apart from offering plant, machinery and equipment of a high quality at attractive prices, India was also in a position to cut down on costs of the importing country by offering skilled and unskilled labour needed for installing and maintaining the equipment.

India's success went much beyond the frontiers of the third world as its engineering and other sophisticated goods found ready acceptance in the western markets, notably in the United States, Britain, France, West Germany and other EEC countries, besides the Soviet and East European countries. In the process exports zoomed. Export earnings showed a steady uptrend, and today we can speak of India as having achieved a breakthrough in the foreign trade and balance of payment situation. This has moved the economy from a highly constrained to a favourable foreign reserves position.

The soaring non-trade receipts over the past few years have given India a shot in the arm. Generally known as remittances from abroad, these represent, among other things, income transfers arising out of India's brain drain—the migration of highly qualified technologists, scientists, engineers, doctors, economists and others. The spurt in remittances reflects partly the firming up of the value of the rupee vis-à-vis the pound and partly the new policy measures adopted by the government to reduce smuggling and liberalise investment facilities for non-resident Indians abroad and migrants. The inflow has brought about an incredible improvement in India's foreign exchange reserves which exceeds $5B by April 1978.

The value of India's exports which was 22.5 per cent in 1972–73 rose to 28 per cent in 1973–74, 31.9 per cent in 1974–75, falling thereafter to 21.4 per cent in 1975–76 and rising again to 27.2 per cent in 1976–77. This performance is impressive indeed considering the annual average growth rate of a little over one per cent in the first plan period, around two per cent in the second plan period, and between four and five per cent during the third plan period. However, the rise must be seen against the perspectives of inflation and changes in exchange rates, etc. In real terms, exports were projected to grow at an annual rate of 8.5 per cent at constant prices during 1974–79. But this target was exceeded and the growth of exports averaged 10 per cent a year at a constant prices. In 1977–78, the growth is expected to be around 8–9 per cent. Even taking into account unit value variation and the increase in the quantum of export, export earnings rose from $3.2B in 1973–74 to $4.6B in 1976–77 indicating a growth rate of 27 per cent per annum compound.

This reflected a substantial growth in the export of a variety of manufactured goods. The share of manufactured goods, including sugar, which was 47.1 per cent of the total value of exports in 1960–61 rose to 55.2 per cent in 1970–71 and 63 per cent in 1976–77. The dynamic element here is India's engineering industry. From less than two per cent of the country's exports in the early sixties, engineering exports now account for well over 11 per cent of the total. The export of plant, machinery, equipment and other engineering goods which was a mere $17M in 1961 rose to $163M in 1970–71 and multiplied five-fold in the next four years to $69.3M. In 1977–78 the aggregate export of engineering goods has shown a rise of 13 per cent to $781M. This has prompted the industry to set a target of $1.3B by the turn of the current decade and $2.68 by 1984–85. Other new products include iron and steel, railway wagons, petroleum, plastics, chemicals, leather manufactures, garments, food products, fruits and vegetables, consumer durables, jewellery, silver and gems, etc.

The diversification of India's export basket brought out how well India was equipped to provide a wide range of equipment and services including sophisticated technology. Names such as Bharat Heavy Electricals, HMT, TELCO, TEXMACO, etc. were, relatively unknown to the outside world, but by making inroads in the new markets of the Middle East, Asian and African countries, these and other corporations have compelled the western world to take notice of India's emerging industrial prowess. Many of these industrial giants of India have managed to achieve high levels of productivity, quality, and even an edge in competition with other suppliers. This is reflected for example, in the textile machinery deal in Tanzania won by TEXMACO and Star Textile Engineering, and a machine-tool contract in Algeria by HMT. Tata Export House, a pioneering venture in exporting consumer goods and durables besides capital goods and engineering products, has been able to push up its exports from $17.5M in 1971–72 to $131M in 1977–78. There has been a marked uptrend in the export of commercial vehicles. Ashok Leyland exports of $0.75M in 1974 went up ten-fold in one year and now stand at $12.5M. TELCO's exports of vehicles and other equipment reached $466M in 1977–78. Exports of steel products by Tata Steel have been in the region $433M. Export of packed and bulk teas by one of the reputed companies has shot up from $124M to $144M and that of Bombay Dyeing from $225M to $266M during the same period. Exports of engineering equipment by another well-known Indian company, Crompton Greaves, almost doubled between 1976–78 to $60M.

In the wake of these developments there has been a spurt in the export of Indian know-how, technology and consultancy services. Starting with Iran and the Middle East countries, some of the consultancy service organisations have gone to the very door steps of the pioneers in the field of computer and software technology in the west. For example, Tata Consultancy Services has won big contracts not only in the Gulf and Middle East countries, but also in Latin America, the United Kingdom, Poland, the United States, etc. averaging a value growth rate of 30 per cent per annum.

New Export Culture

All this represents the evolution of a new export culture assisted perhaps by fortuitous factors such as the commodity boom and world inflation of mid-seventies (when India was more competitive with lower inflation rates) and the partial floating of the rupee in 1975. The new culture is to be seen in the conscious nursing of industries with export potential, strict adherence to quality control, the setting of targets, market research, demonstrations and flexibility in production planning and adaptation of new technology. The Trade Development Authority, Trade Fair Authority, Engineering and other Export Promotion Councils have played an effective role in arranging buyer-seller meets and promoting exports. Export credit facilities and the proposal for setting up an export-import bank all fall in the same pattern. The Electronic Export Processing Zone set up in Bombay with 23 units in production and 69 applications underway and the free trade zone in neighbouring Kandla are among the new ideas floated. The newly acquired economic and financial strength has encouraged India to evolve a foreign aid programme, which totalled $754M by March 1977, mostly in the form of grants. The initial beneficiaries include Tanzania, Sri Lanka, Indonesia, Nepal, Bangladesh among others.

In the light of the new found dynamism in industry and exports one might have expected considerable optimism in planning for future developments. However, the draft sixth plan has been rather cautious. The average rate of growth of national income is projected to be around 4.7 per cent between 1978–83. In absolute terms, public sector outlays on large and medium scale industries and minerals will be stepped up from $12B to $16.76B during the next five years, 1978–83, but its share in the total public sector outlay on development will fall from 25 per cent to 19 per cent. Though significant expansion is proposed in a wide range of mass consumer goods, intermediate and capital goods industry, the main emphasis is on better utilisation of existing capacities and expansion of employment-intensive activities including agriculture and irrigation. Since power supply has emerged as a major constraint a substantial increase in investment is proposed in this area. On the assumption that private sector investment will pick up in the wake of development outlays, the planners forecast an industrial growth rate of seven per cent per annum. Aggregate exports during 1978–83 are projected to grow at an annual rate of seven per cent at constant prices, on the assumption that it may not be possible for India to continue exports of food products and steel.

With so much of industrial development behind it, India cannot afford to miss opportunities of the next decade or two, those which will come its way as the more advanced countries shift to very advanced technologies, what are called "knowledge-producing" and "knowledge-processing" as against goods-producing forms of employment. There exists a potential for absorbing a substantial proportion of India's rising foreign exchange reserves for investment financing, though in the long run a high level of investment will depend on the domestic saving rate. With the use of food and foreign exchange reserves it should be possible to push the investment rate to about 19–20 per cent and, with a judicious allocation of resources, exceed the growth rates of national income and export envisaged in the draft Sixth Plan, which has still to be endorsed by Parliament and may undergo modifications. Though export development has been spectacular, the fact remains that exports still account for only 6–7 per cent of GDP and about 10 per cent of aggregate industrial output. The marginal export-output ratio is, however, higher than the average.

Since India desires to assist in the development effort of the neighbouring Asian, African and Middle East countries in an effective way, the development strategy that is being evolved seeks to establish a specific relationship between development and social objectives, on the one hand, and investment rate and growth of export, on the other. The success of this strategy is reflected in the structural changes in industry and the emergence of India as a technological force to be reckoned with. In term of its past performance and its future, India realises that the scope goes beyond the conventional range of production and export. With an appropriate mix of technologies India hopes to enter new markets in technology-intensive and more sophisticated lines of production. A gradual shift in the pattern of industrial development in the next decade or two is already foreshadowed as new concepts and ideas catch on. The economy has already become much more resilient than ever before, and as India enters more sophisticated areas the success of Indian enterprise will reverberate far and wide.

Note

The complete bibliographic information for this article is as follows:

D. K. Rangnekar, 'India: The Emerging Industrial Power', *TIME*, Supplement on India, 20 November 1978.

18

Crisis Today–I

*Failure to Stem Structural Deterioration**

There appears to have been a radical shift lately in the focus of political discussion in India. Earlier it used to be concerned with personalities, programmes or policies. Now it obsessively turns to issues of credibility and continued economic drift.

Desperation is not the word to describe New Delhi's atmosphere today, a charitable view of New Delhi's apparently neutral stance on crucial matters of economic and social policy would be to say that all Congressmen are praying to God to save the economy and the system. The immediate task of economic management has become the most outstanding casualty of dithering. The leisurely pace which at present seems to be the limit of government hope is matched only by a range of uncertainties down the line in spite of protests to the contrary. The manifestation of non-policy making is to be seen not only in the relentless inflationary pressures, but also in the structural crisis, the growing army of landless labourers and seething urban discontent.

If today the country is passing through a traumatic experience it is because the social crisis has deepened, inequalities have increased, unemployment has become chronic and the gains of years of sacrifice and investment have been cornered by ill-deserving, power-hungry groups, elements which have no integrity and no sense of social responsibility. There has been very

* First published in *Business Standard* on 24 August 1981.

191

little structural change in this country in spite of three decades of planning. This is one of the key factors behind the crisis situation today. All that has happened is that the share of agriculture has fallen from over 50 per cent to around 43.9 per cent at constant prices. But the increase in the share of the industrial sector has been very small. In fact, the growth rate of the commodity producing sectors, both primary and secondary, has lingered behind the growth in administration, defence, services and other sectors.

In recent years, manufacturing in particular, has perhaps given way to real estate, finance, banking, defence, administration, hotels, transport and communication, all representing the lifestyle of the elite classes. While the share of the secondary sector in the composition of the net domestic product has stagnated around 21–22 per cent, that of real estate, finance, transport, hotels, etc., would appear to have gone up to 34 per cent. The structure of industrial production also appears to be oriented towards the demand and consumption pattern of this class.

In spite of the so-called green revolution, the overall growth rate of agricultural production as well as productivity per hectare has failed to get accelerated beyond the levels achieved in the 15-year period prior to 1965–66. In fact, the most striking feature of the green revolution and agrarian change in recent times is the continuous growth of rural wage labour in its working population. This represents eviction, dispossession and deprivation of what was one time a class of small, marginal property cultivators.

Between 1961 and 1971 the total number of agricultural workers increased by 11 per cent from 118.29 to 129.16 million. But during the same period the number of workers under agricultural labour households soared by 70 per cent. This reflected (a) a dispossession of land held by tenants; (b) distress sales of land by poor farmers; and (c) peasants with concealed tenancy. The Agricultural Labour Enquiry Committee which submitted its report in 1978 showed that the proportion of farm labour households with and without land had increased sharply, probably reflecting the pressure of inflation and living costs compelling small and marginal peasant farmers to supplement their incomes by working on other people's land to the extent where wage displaced farm income.

However, as a factor responsible for the pauperisation of small peasants, inflation which has benefited the rich farmers and businessmen may be relatively more than important. In an economy like ours where acute inequalities in income and wealth distribution and abject poverty and malnutrition of masses coexist with the relative affluence of a small section of the community, the norm of average per capita income is a meaningless statistic. More important are the composition of growth, real income increases, structural transformation of the economy in furtherance of such socioeconomic objectives as elimination of poverty and unemployment, and more equitable distribution of income and wealth.

But what we are witnessing today is a further structural deterioration. And this is to be seen very largely in the area of shortages of essential goods, the relating abundance of luxury goods, the maldistribution of what is meant for the average citizen, the slowdown in the anti-poverty programmes, the retreat of the economy from the declared goal of self-reliance and a shift to renewed dependence of the economy on foreign aid and supplies.

It is not as if structural problems did not dog planning in the earlier years, but clearly they appear to have been accelerated in the last ten years or so. In the initial period, there were compensative factors in the form of higher growth of per capita income, investment and employment and organized industries, relatively better fiscal management and some quest for technological self-reliance. The increased poverty of a larger proportion of the population is an important manifestation of the complex dualism between the growing importance of the commercial sector and the lingering poverty of the farm sector.

The system operates in favour of the landlords, traders, moneylenders and the political satraps for reasons which political leaders feel least inclined to alter. India's inability to abolish poverty and ensure overall economic and social transformation has brought the dilemma of planning in a mixed economy to the fore. The class consciousness has increased and this, in Indian conditions, mingles with caste consciousness. The problem gets magnified in a caste-ridden society as it is associated with cumulative inequalities of status, income and power. The caste hierarchy and class superiority are linked to ownership of land and other assets and traditional social status. Poverty and inequality combine to exclude the vast majority of the people from the economic and political developmental processes.

The gravity of the problem of poverty varies with the type of definition one chooses. On the basis of consumption expenditure, the percentage of population at or below the poverty line would appear to be large, in the region of 51 per cent in the rural areas and 38 per cent in urban areas.

A more direct estimate of poverty based on nutritional deficiency in relation to a calorie norm of 2,300 calories and a protein norm of 57 grams per day made in the Sixth Plan indicates that 28.8 per cent of the population in rural areas and 36.2 per cent in urban areas are poor. These figures, though lower than the poverty percentages indicated by the relative share of consumer expenditure are, nevertheless, high enough to cause widespread concern. Nutritional deficiency is aggravated in times of drought and floods, neither of which are uncommon.

In general, one could say that a large proportion of the population has to go without even the most essential needs of daily life because, first, the national income (and hence, aggregate consumption) is too small relative to the enormous size and growth of the population, and, secondly, the distribution of this income and consumption is very uneven. If poverty is unrelieved by 2000 AD, 300 million Indians would be at or below the poverty line and another 125 million would perhaps eke out an existence. The pressure grows as population control has got bogged. The 1981 census revealed an increase of 24.75 in ten years to 683.81 million. At current rates India's population would probably be in the region of 1000 million at the turn of the century.

The structural crisis has affected the rural poor even more because production of certain crops, notably pulses and inferior cereals, has shown a decline, while the production of commercial crops appears to have gone up. The production of jowar, maize, bajra and pulses has been more or less static or falling in recent years. The yield per hectare of pulses, for example, has gone down from 539 kg per hectare in 1960–61 to 385 kg per hectare in 1979–80. In the case of gram, the principal source of protein to the masses, the decline has been sharp from 674 kg per hectare in 1960–61 to 480 kg per hectare in 1979–80. The net availability of pulses which was around 56 grams per day per head of population is now down to 30.1 grams. Economic policy has failed to identify the critical constraints on the growth of agricultural output which are also related in part to the unwillingness of government to interfere with the fundamental production and property relationship in agriculture.

India's inflationary problems has, in the context of the abject poverty of the masses, been more grievous than in some other countries, and that in a period when sobriety in the conduct of the value of money, the inevitable function of economic management, was more needed than elsewhere. Price inflation in India has been unabated and, in more recent years, almost alarming, except for two years of remarkable stability. And the gravity of the inflationary situation comes home when one realises that the recent price rise is superimposed on the increases of earlier years.

Rising prices do not by themselves cause any real change within an economy if all prices rise at the same time and at the same rate. This means nobody is seriously hurt if prices of current production factors and prices linked with other commitments rise at the same rate and time. Difficulties arise because economic and social relationships are not evolved with a neat and simple correlation. Not all prices rise at the same rate nor at the same time; some rise faster than others, and some not at all. In an economy with a rapid rate of growth of output and a sophisticated policy mechanism to protect the interests of fixed income earners, the gap between increases in incomes and increases in production generally tends to be smaller than where production lags behind and grows only slowly. How to distribute a national cake whose dimensions do not grow with demand? This is indeed a dilemma.

Great harm is caused to the economy also by sharp changes in the rate of inflation from year to year. This generates a psychological belief that prices will continue to rise perhaps at a faster rate. And so inflation feeds on inflationary expectations. Though there are cases where industrialisation and economic growth have been achieved in conditions of rapid inflation, there is no causal relationship as such. It is now widely recognised that chronic inflationary pressures stem, not from the processes of development, but from internal, social or political tensions created by different social groups. Almost certainly a stable Indian currency would have led to a more rapid economic growth than we have had over the last 25 years of incessant inflation.

In the earlier years of planning, stability was equated with stagnation in a simplistic manner. It was believed that it was worth putting up with a little bit of inflation, if that was the price of a significant reduction in unemployment and increase in production. After the apparent success of initial planning our leaders felt that it was worth putting up with a lot more of inflation, if that could bring about a real improvement in employment and the distribution of income. But then the inflation that plagued the Indian economy has been devoid of any positive aspect of progress. What began as a tolerable inflation creep developed into a menacing inflation gallop with arbitrary and painful effects on individuals, groups and also on the economy.

Inflation has had no pay-off in reduced unemployment, but has rather coincided with the highest level of unemployment since independence. Inflation associated with government policies has had the effect of making the distribution of income more rather than less unequal. Planners discovered at some cost to their strategy that gambling with inflation was no way of achieving social and economic transformation. Yet the change over has not been as nearly complete at government level as among economists.

From the point of view of the economy as a whole, inflation has (a) led to a reduction in the level of real income because of mis-allocation of resources resulting from the artificial distortion of relative prices and (b) resulted in a redistribution of wealth from people whose income or assets or both do not change as prices change to those whose income and assets do. If inflation could be correctly anticipated all financial and labour contracts could be adjusted accordingly and wages, salaries interest rates, pensions etc., would, in money terms, all be higher though not relative to one another. But inflation occurs in an uncertain world in which nobody can correctly decide future prices and contracts cannot be continually altered to offset changing expectations of inflation. Salaries and wages and other contractual arrangements may take long, several years, to catch up with inflation—and may never do so. Meanwhile incomes get eroded and so do savings linked to fixed interest. Redistribution of income and wealth goes on in an arbitrary way with the transfer of purchasing power from the weak to the strong, from those who do not have capital to those who have, from those who cannot afford debts to those who can, and from those who cannot dictate terms to those who can.

In India the more serious impact of the prolonged inflation is to be seen in (a) the surge of business profits and unaccounted incomes, (b) decline in real wages of the working population, (c) maldistribution of national income and the emergence of the *nouveau riche* class as a major factor in social and political life, (d) consumer and labour unrest, (e) incentives to divert increased money incomes to non-essential consumption, (f) excessive protection and subsidies to industries breeding sellers' markets and inefficiency over a wide area and (g) slowing down of exports and diversion of exportable goods to the high priced, sheltered domestic market. All these and the disincentive to invest with rising prices and incentive to divert money incomes and potential saving to consumption or speculation only add further to the inflationary pressures.

Government policy has also failed to protect the weak members of society against the most flagrant distributive injustice resulting from inflation. In prevailing conditions it is the working and middle class people with fixed incomes who have been brutally squeezed by the inflationary pressure on the one hand and unrestrained exploitation by the new rich operators on the other.

Not much attention has been paid to the impact of emerging technology on the economic situation. Under the impulse of science and technology, some kind of a chasm is developing between modern technology sectors and the relatively traditional ones. Electronics, petro-chemicals, the chemical processing industry, pharmaceuticals, sophisticated machine tools, plastics, polyester and other synthetic fibres, aircraft manufacture, television, computer and other business machines and a host of other industries are not only capital intensive but also research or technology intensive industries. These industries are constantly in search of economies of scale and new processes based on R&D. They tend to gravitate towards multiproduct or multi-industry management and sources of capital. The inter-inking arrangement is unobtrusive but of an order which makes analysis and policy formulation in response to such development either difficult or ineffective. The multinationals figure prominently in such areas with subsidiaries and interlinking (but seemingly independent) enterprises.

The relevance of such developments under the impulse of science and technology to the inflationary phenomenon lies in the fact that massive capital expenditures are involved in the never-ending search for better productivity and greater efficiency with no commensurate contribution to essential supply flows. Apart from generating inflationary pressures, the massive expenditures tend to grow as the technology-based sector becomes more and more powerful and increasingly immune to competition and government policy. Competitive pricing is the first victim and the oligopoly theory the second.

In the science-based or technology-based industries pricing is the function of inter-firm price-setting arrangements. And these agreements may even cover small units operating under the facade of an independent name or label. Competition is maintained only through the media of advertising, packing and occasional product differentiation, but all these submerge under the integration of production and distribution agreements and common access to capital resources, R&D financing and marketing systems. Occasionally, there may be concealed mergers, capital participation by foreign firms, technical collaboration ventures, common export houses, overseas linkup etc.

The government's fiscal, monetary or economic policies designed to influence the economy as a whole are limited in their effects on this sector. If the operation of the technology-intensive sector were beneficial even in the long run all this might not have mattered much. But unfortunately what is happening is that in a country where basic necessities are not within the reach of the common people we find more and more capital being pumped into technology or science-oriented enterprises catering to a small segment of the elitist population and operating under price setting agreements as between themselves and even with smaller units whose marginal costs are much higher. As in the case of competition with marginal influence on prices it is the need of inefficient or artificially curtailed scale of operations which determines the price policy.

Finally we come to the dismal truth that black money has taken full command of the market mechanism, now allowed free play, and has practically submerged what may be called the official economy. Black money is eroding our basic values, corrupting public life, and converting almost every conceivable scheme, project, organisation or idea into a source of benefit to the black-income elite that today dominates the Indian way or scene. The development of new concepts and tools of economic management has been abused so as to strengthen the growth and power of black money. The controls, curbs and measures have been undermined, violated or manipulated to extract unfair economic advantages and surreptitious incomes by unscrupulous elements among businessmen, government servants, contractors, middlings and politicians.

The enormous size of black money incomes which accrue to people engaged in speculation, clandestine deals, trading in the black market or indulging in more sophisticated accounting malpractices is large. It is difficult to estimate black money income, but there is no doubt that the proportion of national output which finds its way into the parallel economy which in turn fuels inflation and inflicts social hardships on fixed income groups, has tended to increase in recent years. As the aggregate spending of the economy grows so also does tax evasion. The availability of unrecorded or undeclared money incomes to defiant contractors, fixers, middlings, manipulators and an entire group of parvenus has indeed become the bane of India's economic and social crisis today.

What we are witnessing today is not only a growing polarisation, inherent in the structural crisis generated by black money, but—to multiply the dangers of black money power—also the weakness or near breakdown of a whole series of safety valves which have sustained us so far and played a vital part in the development of India and its democratic system. The forces that are undermining the power of consensus politics and strategy of development are as dramatic as the growth of black money. The 'summits' of the various kinds of 'black' business are like the tops of unexplored mountains, much more than the parts below, inaccessible operations of seemingly unknown potential contrasting sharply with the humdrum life of honest tax-payers and the law-abiding citizens.

Because of its accelerated growth in recent years, black money has rendered virtually ineffective the Reserve Bank's restrictive credit and monetary policy. Black money has virtually broken the nexus between the RBI bank rate, and credit policy and interest rate structure of the monetary system. Available on tap, black money switches from one commodity to another on demand. The dearer money policy has been virtually frustrated by this third— the other two being the organised money market and the conventional unorganised market—super-sensitive money market where returns are very high and quick.

Note

The complete bibliographic information for this article is as follows:
D. K. Rangnekar, 'Crisis Today–I: Failure to Stem Structural Deterioration', *Business Standard*, 24 August 1981.

19

Crisis Today–II

*Anti-inflation Follies**

> If a thing's worth doing, it is worth doing badly.
>
> —G.K. Chesterton

T he sensitivity of the general public to inflation in India is understandable as prolonged and sharp price increases not only create social problems but aggravate inequalities and halt the development process and employment generation by eroding financial resources. Therefore, public policy must attach the highest priority to curbing the rate of inflation. But this must be done with full awareness of the forces at work in the economy.

Even a cursory glance at the policy package of the government of India will reveal that this awareness is lacking. The government's response to the developing crisis has been too simple by half. The much publicised anti-inflationary package comprises (a) a ban on strikes and threat of punitive action, (b) an increase in prices of petroleum products to raise resources for the Centre's budget, (c) massive imports of foodgrains, edible oils and sugar, (d) increase in bank rate, etc, less publicised and perhaps the most significant crisis management measures has been the secret negotiation with IMF for massive borrowing.

Strike ban: The strike ban is a concession to the aggressive employer's lobby, but it also stems from a misconceived notion that

---

* First published in *Business Standard* on 25 August 1981.

201

Indian inflation originates in 'wage push', strikes, and labour indiscipline, all resulting in reduced production, low investment and high costs. This is absolutely fallacious. The labour department's statistics show that total number of mandays lost in 1980 owing to strikes and lockouts was much lower than in 1979— 12,346,204 as against 43,865,277. In the first two months of 1981, for which figures are available, mandays lost owing to strikes and lockouts were even lower, a mere 26 per cent of the corresponding period in 1980.

What is significant, but ignored by policy makers in New Delhi, is that the mandays lost owing to layoffs and lockouts by employers is steeply on the rise, from 20 per cent in 1979 to 46 per cent in 1980. In this context it is strange that the government should imagine that by banning labour agitation it can stimulate output. Apart from being one-sided, this measure can be counter-productive. Collective bargaining will be eroded, striking at the root of industrial peace. The ban on strikes looks like a prelude to the reported move to impound the dearness allowance of all government staff to start with. This is most unfortunate, even if it complies with IMF discipline, because as it is wages are either static or eroded by inflation. Real wages are already lingering behind growth in productivity. In contrast our study on giant companies suggested that profit after tax had grown by as much as 40 per cent in one year. The National Accounts Statistics 1981 so revealed that the rate of growth of compensation to employees had fallen, whereas profits had risen. New Delhi should realise that measures are called for to protect the real income of workers and discourage layoffs and lockouts.

Monetary policy: This has been performing a highly irrelevant function in the government's scheme of things. Monetary policy has really been on the shelf, in spite of the one per cent increase in bank rate, and marginal increase in statutory liquidity ratio and cash reserve ratio from August 21. These measures have very little to do with the growth of liquidity. The nexus of the bank rate and the interest rate structure has long been broken.

Today banks are flush with funds and an increase in cash liquidity ratios can have no impact on the flow of funds to the private sector. Banks have been able to keep their own borrowings from the HBI within limits and augment their cash reserves and investments. An increase in the banking rate would have had some effect if it was steep and if interest rates down the line were increased and margins on larger advances pushed up. The major reasons why banks are in a strong financial position are (a) a decline in official procurement financing and (b) more generally, increased deficit financing by the government in the last several months. The permissive regime which allows the business sector to borrow freely from the public in the form of deposits, debentures etc, and from the banks in the form of credit has made nonsense of demand management. This also encourages the flow of black money in speculative and manipulative operations. The poor and short-sighted management of public finance has only added to the liquidity in the system through reckless borrowings from the banking system. Thus the so-called package of measures for credit restrictions have no bite left in them.

Rise in administered prices: The attempt to raise the prices of petroleum products is another ham handed attempt to mobilise 1600 crores to narrow the budget deficit which, thanks to the tyranny of spending, has reached the gargantuan level of Rs. 3,300 crores. The increase in prices of petroleum products for the second time since January has come as a rude shock to the people, reeling under inflationary pressure. For one thing, price increase in items like kerosene has the same effect as an indirect tax. Secondly, a price increase in items like diesel could have a 'cost-push' effect. The underlying implication of this policy is also unfair in so much as the huge amount of collected revenue need not be shared with the States. The burden of manipulation of administered prices falls heavily on shoulders least able to carry them. In fact this measure means denial of the normal pattern and volume of consumption.

Inflation itself is in the nature of an indirect tax on money and the rate of hidden tax is the rate of the rise in prices. The people, with a certain stock of means of payment and as a reserve for unforeseen liabilities steadily find the purchasing power of the rupee eroded by the rising prices. In order to maintain the same level people have to expand the amount of means of payment. This means they have to acquire and hold more money to have

the same purchasing power as they had before the inflation set in.
But this is easier said than done.

Cutting taxes: The increase in public revenues over the years has
been accompanied by a parallel rise in current public expenditure
so that over a period of the savings ratio has been eroded. Mainly
because subsidies have been growing at all levels and resulting in
higher profitability for the business sector, public investment has
been lagging behind targets. The momentum of plan expenditure
has also little relevance to social priorities today. Apart from the
fact that infrastructure developments have lagged behind requirements, even the low level of public sector investment in recent
years has turned heavily on borrowings from the banking system,
direct taxation was a major source of revenue to the government
before and in the earlier years of independence. But steadily the
tax system has changed in such a way that the ratio has declined
from 34 to 35 per cent in the mid-50s to less than 20 per cent now.
Correspondingly, indirect taxation has been going up and covering nearly all items of mass consumption.

With 80 per cent of the revenue coming from indirect taxes and
less than 20 per cent from direct taxation, there is the impressive
lobby not only of businessmen but also of former bureaucrats,
now nearer the seat of power, who argue in favour of dismantling
whatever is left, of the direct tax structure. This argument finds
the surging business profits inadequate and pleads for more fiscal concessions. Unfortunately this line of argument overlooks the
plight of the masses who are already paying heavy taxes on items
of mass consumption including textiles, edible oil, sugar, medi-
cines, kerosene etc. But the point is lost in the present lobby for
indirect taxation regardless of the fact that this is both iniquitous
and regressive.

Import of food articles: The decision to go in for massive food
imports has virtually set at naught the proclaimed drive towards
self-sufficiency. Only the other day we were shouting at the top
of our voices that India had crossed the hump; today we are scan-
ning for supplies in the American market. In reality, the decision
to import wheat, sugar and edible oils is essentially a concession
to the rich farmers and traders of Punjab and Haryana. And more

significantly, it is the direct consequence of New Delhi's decision to devalue the procurement and public distribution system and hang by the market. It is no longer possible for the government to conceal the fact that it has consciously lagged behind its procurement targets for wheat as the marketing season comes to a close. As against the target of 9.5 million tonnes, purchases by government agencies will be nearer 6.3 million tonnes, a shortfall of 3.2 million tonnes. The targets for Punjab and Haryana were deliberately lowered (from 4.7 mt. to 4.4 mt. and 1.7 mt. to 1.4 mt. respectively) and even so actual procurement in Punjab was 3.7 mt. and Haryana 1.1 mt. It is clear enough that rich farmers and traders have been allowed to comer the bulk of the wheat crop. And to placate business interests, who have a vital stake in the cost of food, imports are being planned and that too in a year when the government itself claims that the total procurement production would be a record 133 mt. including an all time high in wheat. The decision to go in for imports is also scandalous because of the avoidable drain of foreign exchange revenues.

Note

The complete bibliographic information for this article is as follows:
D. K. Rangnekar, 'Crisis Today–II: Anti-inflation Follies', *Business Standard*, 25 August 1981.

20

Crisis Today–III

IMF Borrowals—Perils of Economic Chaos*

Perhaps the most controversial policy decision the government has taken is to go in sackcloth and ashes to IMF. Clearly this is New Delhi's attempt to borrow its way out of trouble. Contrary to proclaimed democratic precepts, the public has been kept in the dark and a free and frank national debate has been pre-empted. The undue secrecy surrounding the negotiations with IMF has aroused suspicions that there is something disconcerting about the whole affair, and also that New Delhi was buckling under.

The projected volume of borrowing has escalated over time. India is now seeking a loan of 5 billion SDRs, which would in terms of dollars mean a little over $6 billion. The government's move has evoked widespread resentment for three major reasons.

First, it is feared that the soft option of seeking IMF cover is no way of tackling the balance of payments problem it only postpones the imminent crisis, and could magnify it as time passed. Secondly, any style of economic discipline imposed by IMF could halt the process of social change and cause economic disruption. Thirdly, massive borrowing from IMF could foreclose India's options both in the field of domestic strategy and also external borrowing from other sources.

* First published in *Business Standard* on 26 August 1981.

It is not clear what kind of policy changes and economic discipline IMF is insisting upon. But reports suggest that these include devaluation, a cut in food and other subsidies, reordering of plan priorities and a more drastic anti-inflationary package with monetarist slant. It must be noted that not all borrowings from IMF carry such 'conditionality clauses'. There are certain types of borrowings which indeed carry no strings. India's IMF quota over a period of three years is 1717.50 million SDRs. India could borrow 4.5 times its quota over a period of three years. It could borrow 100 per cent of the quota under compensatory financing, 50 per cent under buffer stock facility and 25 per cent under the reserve tranche. Today India owes the IMF $300 million, borrowed under the compensatory financing facility. It could also borrow another $70 million to $80 million to bridge its balance of payments gap without any preconditions.

The IMF economic discipline is clamped on beyond these prescribed limits. The 'conditionally' becomes applicable when large loans like the present Indian request for 5 billion SDRs are negotiated for. The larger implications of 'conditionality' must be viewed in the context of what happened in the mid-60s when the Fund Bank pressures and Washington played havoc with the Indian economy. 'Conditionally' then forced Indian to devalue the rupee on June 6, 1966 and initiate a reversal of public policies in the name of 'adjustment and corrective policies'.

The pressure to devalue and disband the process of planning followed the visit to India of the so-called Bell Mission. The Bell Mission, which submitted its report to the then World Bank chief, Mr. George Wood, made out a strong case for altering India's economic and social framework and devaluing the rupee. The government, which had earlier, in the wake of the war with Pakistan in 1965, suspended all aid to India, played a behind-the-scene role. Mr. Chester Bowies, who was then Ambassador in Delhi and Mr. L.K. Jha, who was then secretary to the Prime Minister, the late Mr. Shastri, were in constant touch with each other.

The Bell Mission report was torn to pieces by the then finance minister, the late Mr. T.T. Krishnamachari (TTK). From what I recall of a personal conversation with TTK, Mr. Bell was rebuffed, and Mr. Krishnamachari said that so long as he was finance minister he would not give in. "Who is this Bell to tell me how to run my finance ministry", he asked. "This Bell, big or small, does not ring here." He even went on A.I.R. to reassure the country and Parliament. He argued strongly, among other things, that the external demand for Indian exports was inelastic. He also feared that the Fund-Bank-Washington-prescribed regime was likely to put the plan in jeopardy and distort the entire cost-structure of the economy.

The Bell mission episode occurred in 1965 and at that time the proposed borrowings from IMF were very small. The economy, disrupted by the war with Pakistan, was hardly likely to provide a fertile ground for an about-turn. But Mr. Krishnamachari fell out with Mr. Shastri on this and other issues, and he was neatly eased out in December 1965. Later on there came a string of personalities favourably disposed towards the Washington package. These included "socialist" Ashoka Mehta (minister of planning). The architect of India's PL 480 revolution, Mr. C. Subramanium (minister of food), Mr. L. K. Jha, ageing bureaucrat now near the seat of power again, and others. Mr. Jha is reported to have canvassed for devaluation in the name of "bold leadership". Lal Bahadur Shastri and his secretary, Mr. L. K. Jha, were obliging to Mr. Bernard Bell in 1965. In fact there is reason to believe that these two had paved the way for devaluation, though it was the kitchen cabinet that clinched the issue.

The case of the new-fangled kitchen cabinet was that devaluation would prompt the US administration to resume aid which had been suspended in 1965 in the wake of the war with Pakistan. The actual borrowings from IMF were then as low as $127.5 million at the start of the Third Plan and had gone up to $325 million by March 1965.

Yet the government sought to give the impression that devaluation was some kind of panacea for India's economic ills. A purely monetary measure thrust down a poor country's throat was sought to be invested with some mystic elements, something which could only aggravate the people's sense of frustration. The devaluation of June 1966 plunged the economy headlong into an acute crisis the result of which was prolonged recession, distortion of costs, inflation, unemployment and demolition of the planning process. Even the World-Bank-sponsored Aid India Consortium's decision to allocate $900 million by way of aid did not save the economy from near collapse.

It is significant to recall that in 1966, senior spokesmen of the government loudly denied having surrendered to the Fund Bank authorities; they had denied also that they were considering devaluation. Yet devaluation followed such denials!

One wonders whether India has even recovered fully from that telling blow of 1966. In retrospect it is clear that the drastic decision, taken in a great hurry without adequate prior preparation, had adverse repercussions on the economy. The preconditions to aid not only enjoined devaluation, but also a plan holiday. This devaluation and prolonged plan holiday not only disrupted the development process, but set the clock back for India.

The moot question now is whether the government has really examined the options open to it. Are there any alternatives to the proposed borrowing of $6 billion under the enlarged access facility subject to strong adjustments which could conceivably impose a severe strain on the economy and the poor people?

To put the present critical phase of India's balance of payments in perspective it has got to be realised that (a) export contributions to import capacity have fallen dramatically, particularly because of the eroding impact of the terms of trade which have declined; (b) the unthinking liberalisation of imports over the last three years, including import of equipment, technology and capital goods, has drained reserves.

The reluctance to accelerate import substitution, mobilise domestic resources and slash the import content of output appears to be at the root of the balance of payments crisis. The table shows a sharp decline in exports' contribution to import capacity.

Net external assistance as a per cent of imports has dropped sharply from 16.6 per cent in 1976–77 to 5.7 per cent in 1978–79

Trade trends year	Exports as per cent of imports
1976–77	101.4
1977–78	89.7
1978–79	64.1
1979–80	73.0

and 7.8 per cent in 1979–80. The current assessment of the government reflects, on the one hand, an excessive reliance on the theory of import inflexibility and wishful thinking on export promotion, on the other.

The theory of import inflexibility is largely based on the soaring bills of petroleum products. The truth of the matter is that the government has not at all seriously considered ways and means of curbing non-essential consumption of petroleum products. It has relied wholly on fiscal instruments to generate disincentives (which at the same time being in revenue). This policy has clearly failed. The saving possibility is actually limitless but not seriously considered by New Delhi. The Petroleum Conservation Action Group has indicated industrial fuel saving of 33 per cent and smaller saving down the line. New Delhi has also neglected the development of alternative facts and infrastructural facilities— coal for oil substitution has been given a backseat, something that could bring about a 20 per cent cut in oil imports and slash the import bill by over Rs. 1,000 crores. Imports saving would grow if the Petroleum Conservation Action Group's recommendations were implemented.

New Delhi's memory is proverbially short. It has forgotten that before coal and power started causing problems, India was exporting a large number of items which are now on the import list—steel, cement and paper, to name a few. It requires far less investment and no drastic policy change to end shortages of these products as also of fertilisers, food, oilseeds and sugar where shortages are artificial. A closer look at the export-import arithmetic is, therefore required if only to trim fat and eliminate unnecessary pressure on foreign exchange reserves.

Surely the import of foodgrains has much to do with the politics of low procurement and that of sugar is a concession to the pampered sugar lobby? At any rate the balance of payments situation does not permit a continuation of the present liberal import policy. The fact that imports are today growing at 50 per cent per annum and export at a mere 5 per cent carries with it its own warning.

Given the long term nature of the changes in world markets, including trade cycles and protectionism, the most urgent need for India is to promote the adjustment of the Indian economy to the changing parameters of world trade and price relatives. A programme aiming at such structural readjustments should focus on redirecting resources in terms of a strict order of national priorities. The restructuring must include also a concerted programme of import substitution, particularly in areas where world market changes have increased the cost of major imports and also in areas where India's competitive advantage in production has improved. The failure in this area has landed us today in a sorry plight. Instead of pursuing a policy of self-reliance the government has at the behest of lobbies and erroneous advice recklessly drained foreign exchange reserves on wasteful imports, including playthings of the rich. Worse still, even today foreign collaboration is freely encouraged in areas where Indian know-how is well established. Why, for example, should India import know-how for the hotel industry when the Taj group and Oberois are big names abroad? If self reliance came into its own, nonessential imports were controlled, and petroleum conservation also streamlined, the balance of payments problem would appear manageable. And we would not at any rate be placed at the receiving end.

The hurry-scurry also appears somewhat strange when India's own foreign exchange reserves are in the region of Rs. 4000-odd crores and receipts keep coming in. There is also a sizeable proportion of unutilised foreign aid. The Aid India Consortium has been quite generous even this year. The scope for alternative external borrowing has also not been fully explored. A new development which does not seem to have received much notice here is the gradual switch of OPEC funds away from the U.S. In fact OPEC countries, perhaps as a reaction to the freeze of Iranian assets, are looking for alternative countries to place their surplus funds. India must be regarded as an attractive proposition. But this calls for initiative, diplomacy and inducements.

It would not be fair for the present government to saddle the present nation and its coming generation with a huge foreign debt and a package of policies which the people at large may reject in a free referendum. The aid positioned the government is already daunting. The outstanding public debt was Rs. 39,584.33 crores at the end of 1980–81. Of this, the external debt was Rs. 10,607.91 crores. External debt servicing already absorbs well over Rs. 900 crores per annum. The government would, if it pursues the path, force the Indian economy and the people into a formidable external debt trap.

Any recommendation to devalue the rupee has no validity in present day conditions. Even though there is only wild speculation about this issue, it bears pointing out that the Indian rupee is already floating. The rationale of a system of floating rate in relation to a basket of currencies is to ensure regular and automatic adjustments in the world value of the rupee. Devaluation under a floating regime has therefore no relevance. The exchange rate is fixed daily on the basis of the value of a weighted basket of currencies. This basket includes currencies of India's major trading partners. In theory at any rate fluctuations in the value of the relevant currencies are taken care of and the rupee value adjusted accordingly. The only question is whether the basket of currencies is rationally determined. It is arguable whether the basket of currencies is a proper amalgam of currencies and whether the present system of adjusting the value of the rupee is satisfactory.

But on the basis of the RBI rates between January and August the rupee appreciated by 14.6 per cent against the pound sterling and depreciated by 13.52 per cent against the dollar. In terms of the trade weighted exchange rate there appears to be a depreciation of a mere 1.18 per cent during the same period. Devaluation even by the backdoor can in this context confer no benefit on our exports nor make them more competitive. It could only end up by introducing a new 'cost-push' element via imports to the economy.

Any rational approach to the current crisis will have to include several elements. Besides measures indicated in earlier sections, priority should be given to a policy that sets out to curb drastically conspicuous consumption at all levels, including business and political. This might also include a ban on entertaining more than 25 persons and also a ban on ostentatious ceremonials, including weddings. At the other end, the public distribution system should be enlarged to cover all essential items of consumption besides, food, and this should be made an integral part of the policy to protect the masses against inflation.

Secondly, an elaborate scheme to tap black money. The permissive bond scheme has only resulted in offering the parallel economy a parallel currency where bonds are fetching premiums. The government should also (a) intensify searches and seizures,

(b) publicise the names of persons raided and the results of the raids and (c) publicise all details of the final settlement.

Thirdly, a reversal of the present permissive import regime is called for and a new emphasis on import substitution, R&D and technological self-reliance.

Fourthly, one way of curbing liquidity and black money is also to enforce a ceiling on family holding of currency and precious metals and stones, including jewellery. No family should be allowed to hold more than Rs. 15,000 worth of money and jewellery.

Fifthly, monitoring system should be evolved to check the flow of funds in the exchange and commodity markets where speculative forward trading goes on despite bans. It is estimated that a sum of Rs. 4,500 crores was recently involved in speculative operations in sugar, edible oils and wheat.

The income tax department should be equipped at all major centres with an elaborate valuation department. Wherever undervaluation is involved, the property in question should be auctioned and the excess value appropriated. It is a mistake to assume that black money is involved wholly or mainly in real estate. However, since black money deals are booming in real estate in Bombay, Delhi, Bangalore and other centres it is necessary to make by law all property transfers conditional upon income-tax evaluation and registration.

Sixthly, the procurement and public distribution system should be enlarged to cover not only foodgrains but other essential consumer goods, and this should be made a prominent and integral part of the public policy. This should cover not only the metropolitan cities but also other urban areas.

Note

The complete bibliographic information for this article is as follows:
D. K. Rangnekar, 'Crisis Today–III: IMF Borrowals—Perils of Economic Chaos', Business Standard, 26 August 1981.

21

Industrial Policy*

India's basic approach to problems of industrialization has been conditioned by the Industrial Policy Resolution of 1956 and also by the philosophy and thinking popularized by Nehru and other Congress leaders before independence. The industrial Policy Resolution has generally been accorded the status of "an economic constitution". It remains today the most important declaration of the basic approach and of the principal objective of industrial planning in India. Without doubt it has been the guiding star of the country's five-year plans since 1956 and the touchstone for assessing industrial projects or determining priorities. It is this resolution that committed India to State intervention in order to enforce a certain pattern of industrial development and a certain manner of utilization of real resources. In a sense it carried forward the preparatory work done for drafting the Industrial Policy Resolution of 1948 very shortly after independence.

The resolution of 1948 was preceded by the statement of Government's industrial policy (April 1945) which sought to give greater precision to the principle of industrial reconstruction embodied in the second report on reconstruction planning. This statement was essentially in the nature of an answer to the persistent demands from the private sector for a clear enunciation of Government's policy of industrial development after World War II. The need for a conscious industrial development policy for India was visualized by the national leaders long before the

* First published in *The Economic Times*.

214

release of formal statements. The Congress party's national planning committee had, at a meeting in 1938, set the tone by explicitly declaring the need to have State-owned or controlled key industries for the pursuit of the general objective of rising income and national self-sufficiency. This committee also took the view that the establishment of heavy and basic industries was necessary as a strategic measure in a plan for industrialization without, however, including the development of cottage or small industries. This view of the national planning committee was endorsed at the subsequent meeting of the Advisory Planning Board. It is likely that the widespread support for coordinated industrial planning to bring about rapid increase in standard of living and fundamental changes in the economic and social structure persuaded Government's Planning and Development Board to release a statement of Government's industrial policy in 1945 which was largely accorded with the views of the politicians.

The industrial policy statement of 1945 made a radical departure from the laissez faire economic policy pursued by the British Raj. This statement provided an entirely new approach and a new thrust to economic policy in the country. It advocated, for example, explicit Government control of 20 key industries and ownership of many heavy industries. Basic industries of national importance were to be nationalized if adequate private capital for their development was not forthcoming. The candidates specifically mentioned for this treatment included aircraft, automobiles, tractors, chemicals, dyes, iron and steel, prime movers, electric machinery, machine tools, electro-chemicals and non-ferrous metals. The statement proposed the use of licensing and other controls achieve a multiplicity of objectives including prevention of monopolies and regional concentrations, the setting up of a system of targets to determine "the correct lines of planned development and thus also to prevent private capital going in the direction of excessive profits." The statement also indicated that these measures were intended to secure fair wages and security for industrial workers among other objectives, elimination of excess profits and improvement of quality of goods.

There is really very little to distinguish this statement of intentions from the Industrial Policy Resolution of 1948. It is likely to have guided the actual scope of Government intervention in the heyday of planning. The first Industrial Policy Resolution of 1948 was essentially modeled after Jawaharlal Nehru's thinking and the general tenor of debate in the Congress party's sub-committee which prepared an economic programme for the new Government. It is interesting also to be noted that the industrial policy of the Government preceded the establishment of the Planning Commission. The resolution of 1948 stated that a mere redistribution of existing wealth would make no essential difference to the people and would merely mean the distribution of poverty. The dynamic national policy was, therefore, to be directed to a continuous increase in production by all possible means side by side with measures to secure equitable distribution. The resolution established six industries in which the state will be exclusively responsible for new undertakings—coal, mineral oils, iron and steel, aircraft manufacture, ship building and telecommunication equipment. The Government reserved the right to take over existing private companies in these areas. The resolution also established three Government monopolies—arms and ammunition, atomic energy and the railway. Eighteen other industries were subject to central regulation and control. Excepting for the specified industries, the rest of the field was left open to private, individual co-operative enterprise, though participation of state on a competitive basis as well as State intervention, where necessary, was not ruled out. It is in this resolution that the Government made its intentions of establishing the Planning Commission explicit. The two instrument of this policy were the Industries (Development and Regulation) Act of 1951 and the Companies Act 1956. These laws conferred on the Government, through a licensing procedure, the power of regulating production and expansion of industries. The spirit of the Industrial Policy Resolution of 1948 and the Industries Act of 1951 clearly favoured the deliberate acceleration of industrial growth. Indeed the first exercise in planning began with a strong emphasis on the strategy of industrialization. The 1948 resolution had, in effect, committed the country to deliberate industrialization and also to a concept of mixed economy with spheres allotted to the public and the private sectors. This concept, though modified by subsequent events and developments, still lies at the root of the Government's economic thinking. The Constitution had codified almost a similar

216

theme and directed that policy should ensure that the economic system did not result any concentration of wealth and means of production to the common detriment. The 1948 policy held away until 1954 when the policy premise started shifting to a declaration in favour of a "socialistic pattern of society". This concept was again a modification of the earlier objective of a welfare State enunciated at the Nasik session of the Congress in 1950.

A clear enunciation of the socialist goals emerged from the Avadi session of the Congress. The Avadi resolution of 1955 made it clear that "the State will necessarily play a vital part in starting and operating big projects through...overall control of resources trends and essential balances in the economy...with strategic control over the private sector to prevent the evils of anarchic industrial development." Bolder measures towards industrialization thus became the king-pin of planning and the new orientation found fuller expression in the Second Five Year Plan. The commitment to socialist objectives and also to accelerated industrialization necessitated a fresh statement on policy on industry. Accordingly, the Parliament adopted the second Industrial Policy Resolution on April 30, 1956. The Second plan and the second Industrial Policy Resolution of 1956 were supposed to reflect the ideological position of the Congress since Avadi.

The second Industrial Policy Resolution differed from the first in a number of ways. In the light of the disappointing performance of the private sector between 1948 and 1955 there was a greater emphasis on the expansion of the public sector. The exclusive responsibility of the State was enlarged from 6 to 17 industries (schedule A). A further category was introduced (schedule B) which listed a dozen other industries in which the state might take the initiative. More significantly, the threat of imminent nationalization which the 1948 resolution contained was eliminated. Instead, the private sector was guaranteed plenty of opportunity to develop and expand. The Industrial Policy Resolution of 1956 set out some of the principles of Nehru's philosophy, though it retained sufficient ambivalence to placate the uncommitted elements. The Resolution declared that "the State will progressively assume predominant and direct responsibility for setting up new industrial undertaking and for developing transport facilities. It will also undertake state trading on an increasing

217

scale". An important sector of industries was exclusively reserved for the State and the intentions of the State to enter other fields indicated. As the resolution explained, "the adoption of the socialistic pattern of society as the national objective, as well as the need for planned and rapid development, require that all industries of basic and strategic importance, or in the nature of public utilities, should be in the public sector. Other industries which are essential and require investment on a scale which only the State, in present circumstances, could provide have also to be in the public sector". But to underline the concept of mixed economy, all industries other than those included in the specified schedules, were left open to the private sector, with or without State participation.

For the period and conditions, the formulation of the Resolution was an admirable attempt to surge forward without too much pain. Yet there was no time limit stipulated for the fulfilment of the Resolution, which seemed rather odd. It is significant to note that several years after its adoption, the Resolution had not even been fully implemented. Planning and industrial administration tended to be too slow, and as a result the development of State enterprise fell far short of the expansion visualized by Nehru and outlined in the two Industrial Policy Resolutions. The policy and goals had not been strictly adhered to, and deviations from the prescribed norms were not uncommon. The truth was that the conviction with which Nehru approached matters of policy or goals was not fully shared by all his ministerial colleagues. Also, much distance separated Nehru's scientific rationalism from administrative expediency. In actual practice the ambivalence and loopholes in the resolution, which offered comfort to the reluctant elements, came to the fore faster than expected. The loopholes and exceptions were indeed more readily availed of by the administration and businessmen. In the case of the Industrial Policy Resolution, for example, the basic concept of socialism and the underlying goals were glossed over. Licences were issued to private sector units in areas which were exclusively reserved for State ownership and control or where further expansion was intended to be in the public sector. These included coal, oil, fertilizers, chemicals, engineering etc. Proposals for setting up State-owned steel mills were held back for years (in the earlier phase) in preference to the expansion of the private units. Schemes for setting up public sector units in new fields were watered down under pressure for private sector participation, association or continuance. Thus, for example, three Western oil companies were granted permission to establish refineries. The proposal for setting up a public sector steel mill in the First Plan was shelved under the weight of criticism from those who favoured the expansion of the existing private sector steel plants. Even after the initial jitters were shed, the Government preferred mixed enterprises. Thus we saw, in the fifties, the Government signing a deal with Stanvac (later ESSO) for oil exploration. It subscribed minority share capital in the prospecting companies formed in Assam. It was initially willing to grant $33^1/_2$ per cent of the share capital to Krupp-Demag in the proposed new steel project. It was only in the Second Plan, when Nehru saw through the game of foreign capital and multinationals, and took firm command, that some of the notions were abandoned and public sector steel plants and other projects were pushed through. Public sector investment then surged; from a very low level, it doubled by the end of 1957 and trebled by 1958 (at 1960–61 prices). After some hesitation, when investment levelled off, there was a spurt in public sector activity from the middle of the Third Plan. Investment rose steadily to a peak of Rs. 260 crores in 1965–66 (1960–61 prices). Thereafter public sector outlays reached a plateau or fell off. In more recent years there have been some renewed activities, but not on the earlier scale.

The most significant contribution made by the two Indus‑ trial Policy Resolutions is indeed to be seen in the new thrust of industrial investment in the economy as a whole. Private sector investment zoomed in the wake of public sector expansion. Before independence, the only industries of any significance that existed in this country were just jute and cotton textiles. A small beginning had been made by Tatas in setting up an iron and steel mill and there were a few engineering shops and some coal mining functioning closely in association with the development of the Railways. Apart from that, the only activity of note was in the field of tea, coffee and rubber plantation. All these were oriented essentially towards the export of jute, cotton, tea and other primary products. Tatas had to battle against prejudice and a discouraging Government. The swadeshi movement started by

Mahatma Gandhi had provided some stimulus and, because of the national movement, some stray development in the field of engineering and chemicals took place here and there. The great opportunities provided by the Second World War remained un-utilized because of the prejudicial attitude of the alien rulers. With independence and planning, there has been a sea change, and industry and business have emerged as an important element in the nation's economic and political system. The magnitude of this change is not fully reflected in Government reports, documents and statistics. But the visual impact is there for all to see in the growth of large and small factories dotting the landscape which was predominantly rural, the growth of big and small workshops, business and stores and a whole range of unregistered and une-numerated workshops. Private sector investment had reached its peak level by the end of the Third Plan (1956–66). Thereafter it began to falter. It probably fell off sharply in more recent years.

Even so, what is particularly noteworthy is the fact that we have created over the last two decades a climate which is infi-nitely more favourable to rapid industrialization in the years to come than what we had when we achieved independence. Today we have a powerful technical base which simply cannot be destroyed. The process of technical change has its own momen-tum which cannot be reversed. Thanks to the farsightedness of the Government, today we have laid in this country the basic foundation of a big defence programme and prepared the nation for a leap towards self-reliance, apart from increasing produc-tion for the benefit of our people and for improving health and social standards. Thus it is clear enough that the Government's industrial policy has helped considerably in diversifying the industrial structure and also in directing investments to newer industries. Apart from the expansion of large units, there has also been a tremendous increase in registered small-scale units from about 3,500 in 1961 to nearly 2,00,000 by 1973. But the growth in small-scale units has not been dispersed. Maharashtra and Tamil Nadu dominate the scene. In regard to dispersal of industries, it is doubtful whether industrial policy has really been effective. All States did not adopt a positive and helpful approach in the early years of planned development to foster and develop indus-tries in their respective area. In providing infrastructural facilities, such as power, communication, land, water and financial assistance through the State finance and development corporations was a delayed realization in many States. The net effect was that policy at State level did not induce dispersal. The Central Government had, therefore, to restrict the entry of large industries in order to encourage small-scale units in the countryside in as many as 55 industries later raised to 121.

The basic soundness of India's industrial policy remains unquestioned. Its overall sense of direction, flexibility and thrust would seem to have helped the country to set off industrial development. But one cannot be blind also to the confusion that has come in its trail. Licensing tools used by Government in pursuance of the resolution created enormous delays, encouraged wrong estimate and even corruption. The implementation of the public sector projects was largely within the control of the Government itself. The failure here reflected the inability to establish a viable or suitable machinery for public sector planning and execution. This also reflected a certain lack of coordination between various ministries and the Planning Commission, often resulting in administrative conflicts and sometimes horse trading. Persons with ideas of new projects were probably superfluous. But there was practically no machinery to ensure prompt and effective control over the implementation of projects or for efficient supervision on disbursement of funds, and no effective coordination either between the technical and the economic aspects of the schemes, in spite of the carefully worked out models and material balances of the Plans. Consequently, the rate of growth of industrial output has often fallen short of planned targets. We have also seen two phases of recession in a system that was intended to demonstrate to the world a stimulating trend rate of growth.

The Industrial Policy Resolution with all its ambivalence had made it clear that there would be no overlapping as between the public and private sectors, but that there would be "a great deal of dovetailing". In practice the private sector was considered the residual element and excluded from the mainstream of planning and allocation of resources. Target setting here was essentially an arithmetical exercise, useful but not always meaningful. The licensing system, more particularly in the earlier years, suffered from a variety of deficiencies and was probably the most important factor retarding growth. If plan target had any relationship with licensing, licensing did not strictly adhere to plan targets. This explains why in certain industries more licences had been issued than justified by the targets and in some others licensing lagged way behind targets. Indeed the major drawback of the licensing system was that the administrative machinery was not really geared to operational tasks of industrial programming or to review the programmes in accordance with the changing economic situation. As soon as the targets were announced, there was a rush of applications for industrial licences. This was especially so during the Second and Third Plan period. As against 1580 licences issued in the First Plan period, nearly 5,430 licences were issued in the Second Plan period. In the Third Plan almost 3,770 licences were issued. In the absence of a proper phasing of licences, there were sudden pressures on the financial institutions for rupee funds and foreign exchange resources. The successful entrepreneurs in the process pre-empted industrial capacities and encouraged concentration of economic power. All this created imbalances in the industrial structure with surplus capacities in certain industries and shortages in others, besides the incredible prosperity of non-essential industries.

In the light of experience, the Government proceeded step by step to liberalise the industrial licensing system. Several industries were freed from licensing and investment projects upto specified limits were delicensed. In the context of the Government's approach to the Fourth Plan, a "core sector" emerged: Industries of importance to the national economy, industries having direct linkage with such core industries and industries with long-term prospects for exports were all considered, as basic, critical and strategic for the growth of the economy. Larger houses were made eligible to participate in any of these listed industries provided the said industry was not reserved for public sector or for the small scale sector. Foreign branches and subsidiaries became eligible to participate in industries not included in the list. Industries other than those in the large category of houses were allowed free expansion. They could also set up new industries with investment upto Rs. 1 crore without licences. The impact of the new wind of liberalism was diluted somewhat by the Monopolies and Restrictive Trade Practices Act. The Monopolies Commission which came into being in 1970 sought to prevent concentration of economic power and to correct restrictive trade practices, both of which involved the control of allegedly anti-social behaviour by monopolistic undertaking. But the Commission has really not been effective in any of these fields. It is likely that the Commission is more of an irritant and less of deterrent. Table I and Table II show the comparative position of monopoly groups before and after the operation of the MRTP Act. It is clear from the table that of the 2,172 undertaking listed in the Licensing Policy Inquiry Report, only 849 had registered by October 1974. A majority escaped attention, and industrial houses continued to grow larger or undertaking multiplied with the Commission remaining a passive spectator.

TABLE I

Number of Undertakings, Registered under the M.R.T.P. Act from Large Groups and Other Categories (as on 31.10.1974).

A.   Registered Under M.R.T.P. Act in October 1974.

B.   No. of undertakings covered in Licensing Policy Inquiry Committee Report (1966).

C.   No. of undertakings covered in Licensing Policy Inquiry Committee Report but not Registered under M.R.T.P. Act column 4 minus column 3.

Sr. no.	Groups	A	B	C
(1)	(2)	(3)	(4)	(5)
1.	A and F Harvey	9	19	10
2.	A.C.C.	4	6	2
3.	Agarwala Ramkumar	–	40	40
4.	Amin	–	13	13
5.	Andrew Yule	16	43	27
6.	Ashok Leyland	2	1	(a)
7.	Bajaj	17	24	7
8.	Balmer Lawrie	–	10	10
9.	B.I.C	–	13	13
10.	B. N. Elias	–	5	5
11.	Bangur	32	93	61

(Table I continued)

(Table I continued)

Sr. no.	Groups	A	B	C
(1)	(2)	(3)	(4)	(5)
12.	Bhiwandiwala	2	1	(a)
13.	Bird Heilgers	12	76	64
14.	Birla	54	276	222
15.	Brooke Bond	9	1	(a)
16.	Caltex	2	1	(a)
17.	Chinai	–	18	18
18.	Chowgule	19	1	(a)
19.	Dalmia R. K.	–	11	11
20	Dalmia J.	–	18	18
21.	Dunlop	2	1	(a)
22.	Escorts	4	1	(a)
23.	G.E.C.	8	1	(a)
24.	Goenka	7	69	62
25.	G.K.W.	2	1	(a)
26.	Godrej	2	1	(a)
27.	Gillanders	–	33	33
28.	Hindustan Lever	2	1	(a)
29.	I.C.I.	7	6	(a)
30.	Indra Singh	–	12	12
31.	Indian Aluminium	1	1	–
32.	India Tobacco	5	1	(a)
33.	J. K. Singhania	33	51	18
34.	Jaipuria	2	18	16
35.	James Finlay	8	6	(a)
36.	Jatia G. D.	–	15	15
37.	Jardine Henderson	15	28	13
38.	J. P. Srivatswa	–	16	16
39.	Kamani	24	27	3
40.	Kapadia (Killick)	1	–	(a)
41.	Kasturbhai Lalbhai	20	36	16
42.	Kanoria R. K.	–	20	20
43.	Khatau	40	50	10

Sr. no.	Groups	A	B	C
(1)	(2)	(3)	(4)	(5)
44.	Killick	–	17	17
45.	Kilachand (Tulsidas)	2	24	22
46.	Kirloskar	13	22	9
47.	Kothari D. C.	–	20	20
48.	Larsen & Toubro	9	1	(a)
49.	Macneil Barry-Binny	26	49	23
50.	Mangaldas Parekh	–	18	18
51.	Mangaldas Jaisinghbai	–	15	15
52.	Martin Burn	–	24	24
53.	Mafatlal	20	34	14
54.	Mahindra & Mahindra	10	19	9
55.	Metal Box	2	1	(a)
56.	Modi	10	12	2
57.	Muthiah	–	11	11
58.	Murugappa Chettie	10	10	–
59.	Naidu G. V.	14	17	3
60.	Naidu V. R.	7	11	4
61.	Nowrosji Wadia	5	14	9
62.	Oberoi, M. S.	2	–	(a)
63.	Oil India-B.O.C	8	1	(a)
64.	Parry	7	11	4
65.	Philips	2	1	(a)
66.	Podar	–	20	20
67.	Prataplal Bhogilal	10	–	(a)
68.	Pierce Leslie	–	24	24
69.	Rallis	8	14	6
70.	Rula	11	24	13
71.	Salgaocar	1	–	(a)
72.	Sahu Jain	1	29	28
73.	Sarabhai	20	29	9
74.	Scindia	4	8	4
75.	Seshayee	1	13	12

(Table I continued)

225

(Table I continued)

Sr. no.	Groups	A	B	C
(1)	(2)	(3)	(4)	(5)
76.	Shapoorji J. Paloonji	–	29	29
77.	Shaw Wallace	–	26	26
78.	Shri Ambica (Harivallabhdas)	10	–	(a)
79.	Shri Ram	6	54	48
80.	Shriyans Prasad Jain	11	14	3
81.	Simpson	30	30	–
82.	Soorajmull Nagarmull	8	110	102
83.	Swedish Match	3	4	1
84.	Talukdar Law	–	13	13
85.	Turner Morrison	–	9	9
86.	T. V. S. Iyengar	15	22	7
87.	Tata	21	84	63
88.	Thackersey	1	29	28
89.	Thapar	28	63	35
90.	Thiagaraja	31	34	3
91.	United Breweries	13	–	(a)
92.	V. Ramakrishna	8	11	3
93.	Walchand	14	29	15
94.	V. S. Dampo	12	–	(a)
95.	Vissanji	–	10	10
	Total	775	2,129	1,470

	A	B	C
OTHER CATEGORIES:			
Nationalised Undertakings etc.	2	–	(a)
Single Large Undertakings	14	43	29
Dominant Undertakings:			
(a) Groups	15	–	–
(b) Single Undertakings	43	–	–
	74	43	29
Grand Total	849	2,172	1,499 (a)

(a) The excess in number of companies in column 3 due to new additions to groups is not accounted for in column 5.

TABLE II

Additions/Deletions of Monopoly Groups as per Registrations with M.R.T.P. Act.

	Additions of new groups		Deletions of old groups
1.	Ashok Leyland	1.	Agarwala, Ramkumar
2.	Bhiwandiwala	2.	Amin
3.	Brooke Bond	3.	B.I.C.
4.	Caltex	4.	B. N. Elias
5.	Chowgule	5.	Balmer Lawrie
6.	Dunlop	6.	Binny
7.	Escorts	7.	Chinai
8.	G.E.C.	8.	Dalmia R. K.
9.	Guest, Keen, Williams	9.	Dalmia (Jaydayal)
10.	Godrej	10.	Finlay
11.	Hindustan Lever	11.	Gillanders Arbuthnot
12.	Indian Aluminium	12.	Indra Singh
13.	India Tabacco	13.	J. P. Srivastava
14.	J. K. Singhania	14.	G. D. Jatia
15.	James Finlay	15.	Kanoria (Bhagirath)
16.	Larsen & Toubro	16.	Kanoria R. K.
17.	Metal Box	17.	Kothari G. D.
18.	Murugappa Chettier	18.	Mangaldas Jeysinghbhai
19.	Oberoi, M. S.	19.	Mangaldas Parekh
20	Philips	20	Martin Burn
21.	Prataplal Bhogilal	21.	Muthiah
22.	Salgaocar	22.	Pierce Leslie
23.	Shri Ambica (Harivallabhdas)	23.	Podar
24.	United Breweries	24.	Shapoorji Pallonji
25.	V. S. Dempo	25.	Shaw Wallace
26	Oil-India B.O.C.	26	Talukdar Law
		27.	Tube Investment
		28.	Turner Morrison
		29.	Vissanji
		30.	Wallace

227

There was a major difference in the definition of large industrial houses as adopted by the Industrial Licensing Policy Inquiry Committee and that given in the MRTP Act. While the former fixed an amount of Rs. 34 crores as the lower limit for a larger industrial house, the latter put the assets limit at Rs. 20 crores, but included the assets of inter-connected companies as well. The Commission's dismal record clearly shows a conceptual confusion both in the minds of those who framed the Act and those who manned the Commission. Frequently, the Commission and the Government appeared to be pulling in different directions and, when they were not doing so, the members of the Commission seemed to be drifting hither and thither. The lack of unanimity may not have been of much consequence if the objectives and activities of the Commission did not clash so badly with the basic government objective of speeding up industrialization and reducing unemployment. The Commission might have contributed something to the common task if it could have suggested constructive measures to further the economic and social objectives on the basis of its own finding and original research. The Government has also shown inadequate interest in the functioning of the Monopolies Commission. Indeed very little time and thinking have been devoted to the task of evolving the Commission and its procedures in the context of the Indian conditions. In the absence of research orientation and appropriate structure, the Commission has got bogged down in cumbersome legalities. The Commission remains poor in its administrative set up and hopelessly so in its investigative work. All this has resulted in persuading the Government to take less and less notice of the Commission. It is doubtful whether the Commission has made any impact on the structure of industrial policy, and its relationship to the licensing procedures remain vague.

In recent years the Commission has adopted a more pragmatic approach to matters referred to it. But this again reveals the fact that the Commission does not have a proper framework for decision making. This militates against industrial planning since the Commission does not also have research orientation. The enquiries and procedures, therefore, tend to be dilatory, irksome and frustrating. Every industrial house has to categories itself as a monopoly or dominant undertaking and to prove the requisite function to the Commission for purposes of registration. The Commission does not consider seeking and obtaining such date or relying on its own analysis and probes as a normal part of its function. The weak internal organization of the Commission and the conceptual confusion have prevented the Commission from setting out clearly the positive aspects of monopoly control for purpose of orderly industrial expansion.

The limitation of foreign investment to a minority of the equity in new projects is the declared policy of the Government. Exceptions are invoked here also. Two wholly foreign-owned and two foreign majority-owned ventures were licensed in 1956–57. In 1957–58, three foreign majorities were sanctioned, one with 83 per cent holding. Over the two years, 1958–60, no less than 18 ventures with foreign majorities were sanctioned, in some cases ranging up to 90 per cent and, at least in one case, 100 per cent. Multinationals are usually under fire in public debates and at least one report—the Hathi Committee Report (1974–75) has advocated strong action, including the takeover of drug companies. But administrative decisions are still guided by expediency, and foreign collaborations still find favour albeit for one reason or another. Foreign companies and multinationals make hay while the sun shines. They are operating not only in sophisticated areas of manufacture but also in such areas as soft drinks, biscuits, toothpaste, cosmetics, and a range of consumer products in which India has know-how to sell. During the last two decades more than 4,000 collaboration proposals had been approved of by the Government of which nearly 850 involved foreign investment. At present the inflow of private foreign capital and technology is being directed largely to priority sectors. If export of a major portion of production was guaranteed, foreign investment in industries would be considered even in the case of industries listed under Schedule (B). Yet the fact remains that even the selective liberalization planned in this field in the name of employing foreign savings in the process of industrial development cannot, after all is said and done, be easily squared up with policy pronouncements.

Table III gives an illustrative list of foreign companies operating in India with data on equity holding. The capital holding of foreign companies in Indian subsidiaries today probably averages

TABLE III

Pattern of Equity Holding in Selected Foreign Companies

Sr. no.	Name of indian subsidiary (Name & country of foreign holding company)	Industrial classification of subsidiary company	Paid-up capital of subsidiary company (Rs. in lakhs)	Assets of subsidiary company (Rs. in lakhs)	Amount of capital held by holding company in subsidiary company (Rs. in lakhs)	Foreign holding in the paid-up capital of subsidiary (percentage)
(1)	(2)	(3)	(4)	(5)	(6)	(7)
1.	Food Specialities Ltd. (Nestles holdings Ltd.) Bahamas Islands	Manufacture of food products	184.99	607.52	128.28	69.3
2.	Aluminium Production Co. of India Ltd. (Aluminium Ltd.) Canada	Commission	Rs. 600 only	–	Rs. 600 only	100.0
3.	Philips India Ltd. (N. V. Philips Gloeilampen Fabricken) Holland	Electrical and electronic goods	546.00	2,949.77	378.00	69.2
4.	Industrial & Chemicals Plants Pvt. Ltd. (Participazionten Estore) Italy	Manufacture of machinery	1.00	11.13	1.00	100.0
5.	Mingoa Pvt. Ltd. (Messrs. S. P. A.) Rome	Production and export of iron ore	55.00	282.56	55.00	100.0
6.	Sesa Goa Pvt. Ltd. (Messrs. S. P. A) Rome	Production and export of iron ore	100.50	357.93	100.49	100.0
7.	Indo Asahi Glass Co. (Asahi Glass Co. Ltd.) Japan	Glass & glassware (except optical lenses)	160.00	193.96	160.00	100.0

No.	Company	Nature of business				%
8.	Duchem Laboratories Ltd. (Pfizer Corporation) U.P.A. Panama	Dealing in medicinal products	0.10	0.34	0.10	100.0
9.	Pfizer Ltd. (Pfizer Corporation)	Drugs and pharmaceuticals	398.64	1,375.48	300.00	75.3
10.	Asea Electric (India) Pvt. Ltd. (Allamanna Svenska Electriskar Aktiebolagel) Sweden	Electrical goods	5.00	753.02	5.00	100.0
11.	Atlas Capco (India) Pvt. Ltd. (Atlas Capco Aktiebolag) Sweden	Pneumatic equipment	19.36	259.79	19.36	100.0
12.	S.K.F. Ball Bearing Co. Pvt. Ltd. (Aktiebolaget Svenska Kullajerfabriken Gotenberg and its nominees) Sweden	Importers/Exporters	0.40	326.48	0.40	100.0
13.	Bata Shoe Co. Ltd. (Messrs. Leader A.G.) Switzerland	Foot-wear	250.00	2,823.20	248.75	99.5
14.	Favre-Leuba & Co. Ltd. (Valic Holdings A) Switzerland	Sale and repair of watches	4.50	22.25	3.05	67.8
15.	General Superintendence Co. (India) Pvt. Ltd. (Societe Generale) Switzerland	Cargo supervisors	2.00	9.43	2.00	100.0

(Table III continued)

(Table III continued)

Sr. no.	Name of Indian subsidiary (Name & country of foreign holding company)	Industrial classification of subsidiary company	Paid-up capital of subsidiary company (Rs. in lakhs)	Assets of subsidiary company (Rs. in lakhs)	Amount of capital held by holding company in subsidiary company (Rs. in lakhs)	Foreign holding in the paid-up capital of subsidiary (percentage)
(1)	(2)	(3)	(4)	(5)	(6)	(7)
16.	Roche Products Ltd. (F. Hoffmann-La-Roche & Co. Ltd.) Switzerland	Drugs and pharmaceuticals	100.0	491.53	89.00	89.0
17.	Rolex Watch Co. Pvt. Ltd. (Rolex Holding) Switzerland	Sale and repair of watches	2.00	4.36	1.97	98.5
18.	Alfred Herbert (India) Pvt. Ltd. (Alfred Herbert Ltd.) United Kingdom	Machine tools, industrial machinery	15.00	208.61	15.00	100.0
19.	All India Tobacco Co. Pvt. Ltd. (Exchange Tobacco Co. Ltd.) U.K.	Tobacco products other than cigarettes	0.03	0.15	0.03	100.0
20.	Aluminium Hindustan Pvt. Ltd. (British Aluminium Co. Ltd.) U.K.	Dealing in Aluminium & aluminium products	10.00	21.69	10.00	100.0
21.	Avery India Ltd. (Averys Limited) U.K.	Weighing, counting and testing machines	141.96	402.47	101.40	71.4
22.	Bank Line (India) Pvt. Ltd. (Andrew Weir & Co. Ltd.) U.K.	–	1.00	8.49	1.00	100.0

23.	Beecham (India) Pvt. Ltd. (Beecham Group Ltd.)	Tooth paste and cosmetics	6.00	65.47	6.00	100.0
24.	Bhularbararee Coal Co. Ltd. (East India Coal Co. Ltd.) U.K.	Coal	14.30	67.15	13.49	94.3
25.	Birds Eye Foods (India) Pvt. Ltd. (Unilever Ltd.) U.K.	Foods	Rs. 30 only	Rs. 50 only	Rs. 30 only	100.0
26.	Black Wood Hodge (India) Pvt. Ltd. (John Blackwood Hodge Co. Ltd.) U.K.	Trade	3.50	61.09	3.50	100.0
27.	Bombay Company Pvt. Ltd. (Wallace Bros. Co. Ltd.) U.K.	Trade	30.00	7.40	30.00	100.0
28.	Boots Co. (India) Ltd. (Boots Pure Drug Co. Ltd.) U.K.	Drugs and pharmaceuticals	75.00	273.30	45.00	60.0
29.	British India Steam Navigation Co. (India) Pvt. Ltd. (British India Steam Navigation Ltd.) U.K.	–	Rs. 30 only	–	Rs. 30 only	100.0
30.	British Metal Corpn. (India) Pvt. Ltd. (British Metal Corporation Ltd.) U.K.	Metal products and paints	7.00	10.58	7.00	100.0

(Table III continued)

(Table III continued)

Sr. no.	Name of Indian subsidiary (Name & country of foreign holding company)	Industrial classification of subsidiary company	Paid-up capital of subsidiary company (Rs. in lakhs)	Assets of subsidiary company (Rs. in lakhs)	Amount of capital held by holding company in subsidiary company (Rs. in lakhs)	Foreign holding in the paid-up capital of subsidiary (percentage)
(1)	(2)	(3)	(4)	(5)	(6)	(7)
31.	British Steel Piling Co. (India) Pvt. Ltd. (British Steel Piling Co. Ltd.) U.K.	Metal products	0.10	Negligible	0.10	100.0
32.	Brooke Bond India Ltd. (Brooke Bond Liebig Ltd.) U.K.	Tea plantations	670.00	2,992.2	502.50	75.0
33.	Burroughs Wellcome & Co. (India) Pvt. Ltd. (Burroughs Wellcome International Ltd.) U.K.	Drugs and pharmaceuticals	50.00	208.30	50.00	100.0
34.	Cadburry Fry (India) Pvt. Ltd. (Cadbury Schweppes Overseas Ltd.) U.K.	Bakeries and confectioneries	12.96	364.11	12.96	100.0
35.	Candy Filters (India) Ltd. (Ganon Dunkerbay & Co., U.K.)	Sanitary works	10.00	40.23	10.00	100.0
36.	C. B. Fulford (India) Pvt. Ltd. (C. B. Fulford Ltd. U.K.)	Drugs and pharmaceuticals	5.00	18.55	5.00	100.0
37.	Clevland Construction Co. (Pvt.) Ltd. (Clevland Bride & Engg. Co. Ltd., U.K.)	Trade	0.10	3.40	0.10	100.0

No.	Company	Business			%
38.	Coats of India Ltd. (Coates Bros. & Co. Ltd.) U.K.	Paints and varnishes	36.10	71.29	24.06	66.6
39.	Columbia Gramophone Co. of India (Pvt.) Ltd. (Columbia Gramophone Co. Ltd.) U.K.	Music magazines	0.20	0.14	0.20	100.0
40.	Courtaulds (India) Pvt. Ltd. (Courtaulds Ltd.) U.K.	Silk reeling, spinning and weaving	0.01	2.39	0.01	100.0
41.	Cycle & Automobile Components Pvt. Ltd. (G. Atherton & Co. (Eastern) Ltd.) U.K.	Automobile and cycle parts	0.50	1.43	0.50	100.0
42.	Dobson & Barlow (Rayon Plants) Pvt. Ltd. (Platt International Ltd.) U.K.	Indenting Agents	3.00	0.13	3.00	100.0
43.	E. Hill & Co. Pvt. Ltd. (Oriental Carpet Mfr. Ltd.) U.K.	Carpets and rugs	8.00	85.85	8.00	100.0
44.	Ennore Foundries Ltd. (Leyland Motors Ltd.) U.K.	Smelting & founding of non-ferrous metals	174.00	325.73	130.50	75.0
45.	F. L. Smidth & Co. (Bombay) Pvt. Ltd. (F. L. Smidth & Co.) U.K.	Consulting engineers	6.00	10.87	6.00	100.0
46.	General Electric Co. of India Ltd. (General Electric Co. Ltd.) U.K.	Electrical equipment	177.50	3,513.56	125.00	70.4

(Table III continued)

(Table III continued)

Sr. No.	Name of Indian subsidiary (Name & country of foreign holding company)	Industrial classification of subsidiary company	Paid-up capital of subsidiary company (Rs. in lakhs)	Assets of subsidiary company (Rs. in lakhs)	Amount of capital held by holding company in subsidiary company (Rs. in lakhs)	Foreign holding in the paid-up capital of subsidiary (percentage)
(1)	(2)	(3)	(4)	(5)	(6)	(7)
47.	Gestetner Duplicators Pvt. Ltd. (Gestetner Ltd.) U.K.	Duplicating machines	13.00	338.98	13.00	100.0
48.	Glaxo Laboratories (India) (Glaxo Group Ltd.) U.K.	Drugs and pharmaceuticals	799.68	1,448.91	620.00	77.5
49.	Goodlass Nerolac Paints Ltd. (Goodlass Wall & Lead Industries Ltd.) U.K.	Paints and varnishes	90.00	406.46	72.00	80.0
50.	Gordon Woodroffe & Co. (Madras) Pvt. Ltd. (Gordon Woodroffe & Co. Ltd.) U.K.	Finished leather goods	11.81	271.74	9.10	77.1
51.	Gordon Woodroffe (Belting) Pvt. Ltd. (Gordon Woodroffe & Co. Ltd.) U.K.	Leather belting and leather sundries	4.25	10.25	4.25	100.0
52.	Hindustan Ferodo Ltd. (Asbestos, Magnesia & Friction-materials Ltd.) U.K.	Motor parts	248.30	567.35	198.33	79.9

The name and country of foreign holding are indicated below each entry.
Data relate mostly to 1971–72. Some dilution might have taken place in the intervening period.

about 68.8 per cent. Looking at the structure of equity holdings of foreign companies in 217 Indian subsidiaries operating in India, about 43 per cent (93 companies) seemed to have 100 per cent holdings, 14 companies had equity capital participation ranging between 80 per cent and 100 per cent. Another 25 companies had 70 to 80 per cent participation, and an equal number had equity participation ranging between 60 per cent and 70 per cent. There were four companies with equity participation of less than 50 per cent. In recent years some of the companies have gone in for dilution of foreign capital holding.

The guidelines issued in 1973 explicitly declared Government's objectives of ensuring dilution of equity capital held by foreign companies. They were required to raise for all expansion equity capital from Indian investors through the open market. Yet there was no reference in the policy guidelines to any reduction in the holding of shares by foreign investors. This meant that dilution could take place only in relation to the enlarged capital base and that too in terms of percentage and not in absolute terms. Whatever the contribution of foreign companies, India has had to pay dearly for it. Many Indian companies in simpler areas of manufacture are driven to the wall or forced to fall back upon Government subsidies and other forms of protection undesirable on a long-term basis. New Indian enterprise is often stifled and the development of indigenous know-how discouraged. Worse still, the operations of these companies have caused a drain on Indian's slender foreign exchange reserves. Collaboration ventures accounting for over Rs. 2,000 crores worth of output result in an outflow of more than Rs. 90–100 crores from our exchange reserves every year in the form of payment for technical know-how, royalties, profits and dividends. Besides, wholly owned subsidiaries of foreign companies operating in India remitted Rs. 211.4 crores between 1968 and 1971 by way of profits, dividends and technical fees—Rs. 105.14 crores by way of dividends, Rs. 38.80 crores as profits, Rs. 51.61 crores as technical fees and Rs. 15.81 crores as royalties. The Finance Ministry recently informed the Lok Sabha that dividend remittances by these companies had increased since 1971 by nearly Rs. 12 crores per annum. There was also a rise in other remittances.

Another aspect of industrial policy which has sparked off a controversy in the business circles—is the decision of the

Government to insert a clause in all financial agreements providing for convertibility of institutional loans into equity in accordance with the guidelines issued in 1971. The decision to seek convertibility had been widely interpreted as a backdoor move to take over companies. This has been stolidly denied by the Government and the spares use of the convertibility clause has confirmed the impression that the Government's approach is pragmatic and that convertibility is intended to control the flow of finance and perhaps yield reasonable profits to the Government institutions. The convertibility preference also reflects the Government's concern at the excessive reliance of companies on loans from the Government's financial institutions. By 1975 this convertibility clause had been introduced in agreements with 142 companies by the Industrial Development Bank of India (IDBI), 140 companies by the Industrial Finance Corporation of India (IFCI), 100 companies by the Industrial Credit and Investment Corporation of India (ICICI) and 63 companies by the Life Insurance Corporation of India (LIC). Business circles have been apprehensive about conversion of loan into equity also because of its impact on the structure of capital ownership. The Government is certainly in a commanding position in the financial world and can shape the financial structure of companies besides acquiring ownership rights over a large area.

Yet the convertibility clause has been invoked in only a few cases. For example, by mid-1975, the IDBI had invoked the clause in the case of four companies involving Rs. 43.04 lakhs against a total of Rs. 151.28 lakhs; the ICICI had sought conversion in the case of five companies involving a sum of Rs. 29.31 lakhs out of loans of Rs. 149.75. The LIC had exercised the right of conversion in three cases involving Rs. 33.10 lakhs and the Unit Trust of India in the case of two companies involving Rs. 17.80 lakhs. These figures must be read with caution because in a number of companies the loans are granted jointly by two or three institutions at the same time. Some of the companies which have attracted the conversion also fall in the category of sick companies. In the case of new projects conversion is made applicable to 20 per cent of the rupee loan and the range varies between 10 and 20 per cent in the case of all expansion and modernization.

Some ministerial utterances recently stirred speculation about a possible amendment to the Industrial Policy Resolution. However, the Prime Minister scotched all such report saying there was no question of any amendment to the Resolution and so the framework still holds goods. Its sense of direction is perhaps valid even today. But certainly the Government should think seriously of setting a target date for the full implementation of the Resolution. This is necessary to spur a more rapid rate of expansion of the public sector. The industrial policy also needs to be integrated with India's industrial planning. And industrial planning has got to be more comprehensive so that all available resources and skills are effectively put to use for the betterment of the society. Investment of the kind that creates permanent employment and prosperity will only revive when our present system of partial industrial planning gave way to fuller industrial planning and an integrated approach is adopted to the economic roots of industrial problems and policies. There is, therefore, a strong case for an objective review of industrial matters, perhaps by an independent industrial commission.

Some of the controls have been in operation for two decades or more. There has been no comprehensive and inter-related evaluation of the structure of controls ranging from industrial licensing to controls on foreign exchange, trade, pricing, distribution, raw materials and capital issues. Most of the studies and reviews in this category have been limited to certain aspects of industrial licensing such as size-wise implications, procedures and behaviour of large firms. The social and economic forces that induce or encourage the growth of industrial enterprises are strong in India as elsewhere. And this problem has attracted considerable political attention. But the negative aspects of crushing monopoly must not dilute the more positive aspects of policy such as the objective of realizing the productive and innovative skills of large enterprises without the abuse of monopoly position and to maximize output and employment. An objective study of the inter-related policy problems might throw interesting light on an area of development which often arouses more emotion and less of empiricism, something which produces distortions and tends to make decisions counter-productive. In the case of large industries, for example, resale price maintenance, price setting agreements, restrictive distribution arrangements, and at times attempts to pressurise the Government for blanket protection or to prevent the entry of rivals in the public or private sectors would seem to be nearly as serious and as relevant to our stage of industrialization as product concentration or branch monopoly or multifirm holdings. Similarly, the question of effective barriers to entry in certain areas of manufacturing because of high capital costs relative to size does not seem to have been studied in depth. There are several other issues concerning the minimum optimal plants, cost curves, capacity utilization, inventory holdings etc., which merit an independent study in order to guide policy and decisions. The tendency to license industries merely because domestic or foreign financing is available must be done away with in favour of an economic evaluation in terms of clearly set guidelines. Even if the Government wanted to break a cartel to encourage new competition in any branch today it would come up against data block in the absence of a comprehensive examination of industrial problems.

The difficulties of controlling large industrial enterprises must be recognised. It may be difficult to eliminate licensing, and one must consider whether it is not possible progressively to move towards a more effective way of channelising investment. After all, licensing is a negative instrument capable of denying or discouraging. The present system of licensing or other controls cannot ensure that investment is directed and industries develop in accordance with priorities. A much better weapon for the purpose is the tax system. A more effective tax on the consumption of luxury goods would be far more effective than prohibition of production through licensing. For one thing such a tax brings in revenue; secondly, it induces redistribution of income from the rich to the poor; and thirdly, production of luxury goods for export may get a new stimulus in the right perspective. Profit today is directly linked to the degree of protection when good profit should emerge from producing efficiently and economically. A case could be made out for promoting industry with fiscal reliefs rather than by excessive protection. And if protection is unavoidable then it should be conferred by tariffs rather than by quantitative import control and subsidies. Indeed the aim should be to use policy tools to encourage a pattern of production and prices which would better reflect the social costs and benefits and encourage socially oriented production.

Note

The complete bibliographic information for this article is as follows:
D. K. Rangnekar, 'Industrial Policy', *The Economic Times*, Annual, 1975.

Conclusion and Afterword

Reading through the essays collected here one cannot escape a strong sense of *déjà vu*. We are struck by the foresight and keen perception of the Late Dr D. K. Rangnekar. *Plus ca change, plus c'est la meme chose.* Not only has so much remained the same, despite so much change, but so much of the commentary on change remains relevant today as it was when Rangnekar wrote these essays.

Contained in this volume are essays that cover almost the first half century of India's development. For today's students, researchers in economics, as well as for our policymakers, these essays show how enduring some of our developmental challenges are, and how stale so many of our contemporary debates are.

For my generation of students in the 1970s, Rangnekar was a torchbearer. Through his columns and editorials in *The Economic Times* and *The Business Standard* he showed us the way forward in thinking about economic policy issues. An earlier generation, in the 1960s, read him in the pages of the *Economic (and Political) Weekly*.

Rangnekar was a true patriot. A nationalist and a liberal. His deep commitment to India's development and to change comes through these essays. He was a modernist. He wanted to see India industrialised, developed, urbanised. He wanted to improve the quality of life of the peasantry and the rural folk. Even as he edited a newspaper for the businessman and the stock market investor, he never lost sight of the larger developmental challenges India

242

faced and the need to resolve these in order to ensure India's industrial development.

His essay on 'Nehruism and the Second Phase' (July 1964), written shortly after Panditji's death, shows a deep understanding of Nehru's contribution to economic policy and planning in India and steers clear of conventional views on planning and economic development in India. Neither the doctrinaire 'Left' nor the 'Right' have ever understood or interpreted correctly Nehru's vision of development. Indeed, many in the Congress party too fell victim to standard 'Left' or 'Right' critics of Nehru. Rangnekar adopts a balanced and realistic approach. A 'vital gap' in Nehru's approach to development, says Rangnekar, is that the 'institutional aspect of change was neglected. If adequate attention had been paid to institutional reform, conditions today would have been much more favourable for a take-off into self-sustained growth and structural change.'

This neglect of 'institutions' lies at the core of so many of the challenges we face today. Many ideas about economic and administrative reform that we still discuss today find elaboration in Rangnekar's columns.

In a 1971 column in *The Illustrated Weekly of India* Rangnekar writes,

> In a country where political propaganda and electoral campaigns have stirred the underprivileged masses and beckoned them to a new economic and social order, the budget becomes much more than a catalyst; budgeting itself becomes a social and managerial process of modernization and social change.

The budget day television cacophony in our times has helped to further enhance the political salience of this policy instrument.

It is not just his views on economics and economic policy that ring true even today. Consider his essay on non-alignment and India's relations with the Soviet Union, written as long back as in 1965 in *Seminar*. Rangnekar offers a balanced perspective on Nehru's vision of non-alignment, pooh-poohing both Western critics and Left-wing supporters. Nehru's only objective was India's economic development. If remaining non-aligned was the best way to make use of a divided world in furthering India's developmental interests, so be it. 'Nehru actually took a pragmatic view of Soviet aid' says Rangnekar,

> He had no illusions about the ideological clash in the world, and the rival quest for political supremacy, but he did not regard the Soviet Union as the menace that it was held to be by the western political strategists.... The availability of a new source of trade, aid and technology (*i.e. the Soviet Union*) provided a new and unforeseen balancing factor in the international economy.

While acknowledging this 'potential' role of USSR, Rangnekar went on to examine its actual role as a trade partner and found the Soviets wanting. Says Rangnekar, 'What is even more discouraging is that in the Soviet Union's growing volume of foreign trade, India's share has been dwindling, something which is lost in the sea of wishful thinking in Delhi.' But he recognised the supportive role that Soviet help played in helping India to widen its developmental options. Rangnekar's fact-based analysis of Indian foreign economic policy offers us a window to view contemporary debates on Indian foreign policy. India's priority then, as now, is its own economic development and the eradication of centuries-old poverty, ignorance and disease. Any country that is willing to help us realise our developmental objectives is a friend.

Rangnekar was a realist and a pragmatist. His prescriptions on policy were based on his analysis of facts. He had no time for ideological predilections, or empty theorising.

He was deeply concerned about mass poverty. As the editor of a business daily he had reasons to be. The home market for manufactured goods in India would not expand unless the spending power of the people was enhanced. A poor country cannot produce a vibrant business class. Poverty eradication was important in itself, but also as a means to widen the market for goods and services. This fuelled the engines of development. So, Rangnekar did not fall prey to the 'growth vs distribution' debate. He saw growth as essential to improved distribution and vice versa. Contemporary ideas of 'inclusive growth' can, therefore, be traced back to his essays on poverty and development.

'Modernisation of one-fifth of mankind is not the easiest task in the world' begins an essay on 'India: The Emerging Industrial Power' published in the *TIME* magazine in November 1978. Offering an upbeat view of India's development and prospects to an American audience, Rangnekar drew attention to the new sense of confidence in the post-Green Revolution India. 'In the wake of these developments the entire face of the country is changing, slowly perhaps, but surely. Industry and business are emerging as an important element in the nation's social system.' I would strongly recommend this essay to every student of Indian economic development today. Apart from showing Rangnekar's brilliance and foresight, this essay brings out the elements of continuity and change in our economic policy framework.

In his later years Rangnekar became more critical of the Government and our policy making system. In a column written in *Business Standard* in August 1981, he complained,

Desperation is not the word to describe New Delhi's atmosphere today. A charitable view of New Delhi's apparently neutral stance on crucial matters of economic and social policy would be to say that all Congressmen are praying to God to save the economy and the system. The immediate task of economic management has become the most outstanding casualty of dithering.

Rangnekar became increasingly critical of our incompetencies as he saw Asia to our east march ahead and India getting left behind. Our Nehruvian foundations were good, but the post-Nehruvian edifice was inadequate. Institution building had weakened. Systems of governance and administration were failing. The middle class was only then beginning to make its presence felt, and the business class was not yet doing enough. In 1981 India was on the cusp. Between the three decades of slow growth, at 3.5% per annum, and the coming two decades of accelerating growth.

Today's Rangnekar would have been less pessimistic about India's economic prospects, though he would have been even harsher in his criticism of administration and governance. India's business and middle classes have delivered higher rates of economic growth, but a creaking governmental system is as yet unable to deliver better public services, especially basic infrastructure, education and health.

Writing in 1971 in the Annual Number of the *Economic and Political Weekly* Rangnekar had said, 'Unless we give serious thought to our political institutions and their functions, we may get deeper and deeper into a crisis which might extend beyond an inadequate rate of economic growth.' Four decades later we can say that we have less reasons to worry about the prospects for growth, but even more reasons to worry about political institutions and governance.

Rangnekar would have worried more about corruption, lack of accountability and the monumental inefficiency of our public services today than he would have four decades ago. Even in the nation's capital clean drinking water is not available on tap even in the poshest of areas. Twenty-four-hour electricity is a luxury for most urban Indians, not to mention rural folk.

India's strength is its democracy. The fact that we have many Rangnekars today who can give voice to the voiceless and contribute to a sensible national discourse on development is what makes India tick. I certainly hope these essays inspire the journalists of today to invest more of their time in the gathering of facts and its analysis before news is purveyed. If there is a remarkable freshness to Rangnekar's essays even today it is because they ring so true. He brought to his labours a deep commitment to facts and their uncovering. Journalism is not just about what is happening, it is also about why it is happening. It is in explaining the 'why' while analysing the 'what' that Rangnekar informed and educated my generation. This book will help educate several more.

Dr Sanjaya Baru
Editor, *Business Standard*
Director for Geo-economics and Strategy
The International Institute for Strategic Studies
Former Official Spokesman and Media Advisor to PM of India

INDEX

agriculture contribution, 38
policy-makers, in New Delhi,
107
economy, world, 78–79
Electronic Export Processing
Zone, 189
Emergency, political, 16
equity holding pattern, in foreign
companies, 230–237
Eurocurrency market, 86
European Monetary system, 86
exchange rate
fixation of, 212
fluctuations in, 86
liquidity problem impact on,
xxii
export growth rate, annual, 122
external debt, 9, 211

famine, in 1972–73, peasants slow
march to death, 51–52
fertiliser policy, of Indian
government
capital expenditure, 110–112
controversy over, 108
foreign capital, 112–117
no control, over distribution
and pricing, 109–110
Food Corporation of India, 53
foodgrain markets, world
surplus availability in 1973, 51
food grains, 52–53, 57
net availability of, 57
record production in 1970–71,
50
food imported
discontinuation of concessional
terms after 1971, 61
quantity during 1972 and 1973,
60
food management, in India, 51
food policy, xxiv

food procurement, failure of,
53–55
foreign assistance, 104
foreign capital, xx, 112–117
foreign exchange reserves, 52,
124–125, 237
foreign trade, share in India, 120

Gandhi, Indira, 15, 59, 99, 105, 133
addressed rally at Parliament
house, after Nasik revolt,
18
visit to United States, xx
Garibi Hatao slogan, 15
General Agreement on Trade and
Tariff (GATT), 86
Generalized System of Preferences
(GSPs), 89
government receipts and
expenditure, trends in,
160
green revolution, 12, 42, 51, 81
failure of, 57–59, 192
feature of, 30
gross domestic product (GDP),
classification of sectors in,
37–38
gross fixed investment, in public
sector, 6
Group of 77, 94–96. *See also* OPEC;
Third World countries

Harijan, 23. *See also* Mahatma
Gandhi
Hathi Committee Report
(1974–75), 229
household, Indian
average spending of income
by, 52
humanist economics, as public
reason, xviii–xxvi
HYV wheat, 59

Nasik farmers agitation, xxvi. *See also* Joshi, Sharad
aspects of, 28–29
demands of farmers, 33–34
in mid-1980 of onion and sugarcane, 17–18, 28
national income volume, 176
national integration, 143
National Seed Corporation, 55. *See also* Adulteration, of seeds
NATO, 84
New International Economic Order (NIEO), 88–89
radical transformation, in poor countries economies, 91
non-alignment movement, 72, 92, 96, 121–122
non-development expenditure, of Centre, 168
non-oil producing Third World countries, 90
trade deficit of, 125
non-plan budgetary commitments, 167
non-trade receipts, 186
North–South divide, xxii
no tax campaign of Naidu, in Tamil Nadu, 29
NRI investment, 5
nutritional deficiency, 11

OPEC, 80, 93–94, 211. *See also* Group of 77

parallel economy, India, 140, 171–172, 212
Patel, H. M., 137
Patwardhan, Achyut, 21
peaceful adjustments, 14
peasant revolt, 17
per capita income, 6

Petroleum Conservation Action Group, 210
Planning Commission, 216, 221
planning, Indian
isolated half, 149–151
political framework of, 155–156
real issues in, 147–149
from underwriter to undertaker, 154–155
PL 480 revolution, 208. *See also* Mehta, Ashoka
20-point programme, 16. *See also* Emergency, political
political leaders, 20, 25
political pricing, of products, 72
political structure, 14
political uncertainty, 9
politicians, obsessed with success, 4
politics, Indian, 3
poor, transformation of, 30
population, below poverty line, 8
poverty, 12. *See also* Inequality
consumption expenditure, 194
estimation of, 194
price rise, impact on Indian ministers, 159
private sector investment, during Third plan, 220
production sector, 37
Protectionism
affect on rate of growth of world trade, 87
tide in developed countries, 89
protectionist measures, 86
public debt
outstanding in 1980–81, 211
share in total liabilities, 8–9
public distribution system, 60, 212
public investment
deficiency of, 7
impact of, 6

ABOUT THE AUTHOR

D. K. Rangnekar (1931–84), an economist, author and futurologist, was a student of the Bombay University later proceeding to Cambridge University for his Tripos and then the London School of Economics for his PhD in Economics as a Tata Fellow. Though trained as an economist, he soon moved into journalism with an initial stint at *Ceylon Daily News* in Colombo and later in 1963 as Resident Editor of *The Economic Times*. He swiftly took over as the Editor of the paper and steered it till January 1979. He then proceeded to be the Editor of *Business Standard* till his early demise in 1984. While most of his writings are in these two economic dailies, he did write widely. This includes magazines and journals like *Seminar, Economic and Political Weekly, Mainstream* and the *Illustrated Weekly of India* and international magazines, like *TIME*. Separately he also authored a couple of books, such as *Poverty and Capital Development in India* (Royal Institute of International Affairs), *India Britain and ECM* and pamphlets, such as *Bokaro: A Story of Bungling* (self-published, 1963).

In his time he served on a number of government-appointed committees like the National Council for Science and Technology's Futurology Panel and the Export Strategy Committee (the Tandon Committee), among others. Not bound by doctrinaire ideology or party-politics, his contributions to these committees were known for their critical independence, which in some instances took the form of a 'Note of Dissent'. His prescient observations can be gauged by the fact that it was in the 1970s and early 1980s that he wrote about India's need to de-license to create competitiveness and to exploit the opportunities of a knowledge economy hub, in addition to a number of other relevant observations.

His scholarship and leadership on such issues led to wider recognition, including a nomination amongst TIME magazines' 500 global leaders in the late 1970s. His broad spectrum of interests and activities also included films (he actively participated in the National Film Development Corporation) and music (he was an early member of the first Jazz Yatra). Preoccupation and interests like these, among others, led to his unique stamp on the shape and coverage of the two economic dailies he edited where cultural and political issues got adequate space.